OCR
Critical Thinking

Roy van den Brink-Budgen

Jacquie Thwaites

HODDER
EDUCATION

OCR

Hodder Education, an Hachette UK company, 338 Euston Road, London NW1 3BH

Orders

Bookpoint Ltd, 130 Milton Park, Abingdon, Oxfordshire OX14 4SB

tel: 01235 827827

fax: 01235 400401

e-mail: education@bookpoint.co.uk

Lines are open 9.00 a.m.–5.00 p.m., Monday to Saturday, with a 24-hour message answering service. You can also order through the Hodder Education website: www.hoddereducation.co.uk

© Roy van den Brink-Budgen, Jacquie Thwaites 2012

ISBN 978-1-4441-7754-1

First printed 2012

Impression number 5 4 3 2

Year 2016 2015 2014 2013

Typeset by DC Graphic Design Limited, Swanley Village, Kent.
Printed in Dubai
OCR examination questions used with permission of OCR.

P01984

Contents

Unit 2   Assessing and developing argument

Section C Analysis of argument

Introduction

About this book

This book looks at the precise skills that are required for the OCR AS examination in critical thinking. It covers Unit 1: Introduction to critical thinking and Unit 2: Assessing and developing argument.

The book has been endorsed as a textbook by OCR, which means that it has been accepted by the exam board as matching the:

➤ OCR specification (the skills that you are expected to learn)
➤ OCR assessment (the types of questions that you will be expected to answer)
➤ OCR terms and expressions (the key terms you will be expected to use)

It therefore focuses closely on what you need to know for good performance in the examination.

Features to help you succeed

Learning objectives
➤ Each chapter begins by telling you which skills it aims to develop. These skills are explained with clear examples to help you to understand what is being said.

Activities

The activities are designed to introduce you to the skills used in critical thinking and will help you to practise them in an interactive way.

Key terms
➤ Clear, concise definitions of the essential key terms are provided on the page where they appear.

Exam tips

Throughout the book, there are tips on how to apply the particular skills in the exam to help you boost your final grade.

Exercises

Use the exercises to test out your skills and check your understanding.

Summaries

> A summary is included at the end of each chapter to remind you of the key points — use them in your revision.

Past paper practice

Exam questions change over time, but they are a useful tool for focused practice. Use the past OCR examination questions referred to in the book to practise each particular skill.

Practice exam-style questions

Practice exam-style questions are provided for each section of the exam. Use them to consolidate your revision and practise your exam skills.

Answers

Where appropriate, suggested answers are provided in the text or at the end of each unit for the Activities, Exercises, Past paper practice and Practice exam-style questions. The past OCR examination papers referred to in the text can be found at:

www.ocr.org.uk/qualifications/type/gce/hss/critical_thinking/documents/

About critical thinking

Critical thinking is a set of skills that help you to reflect about reasoning. Here 'critical' means looking for both the strengths and weaknesses in reasoning, rather than the everyday meaning of finding fault. It looks at how conclusions are drawn from claims to make arguments.

Critical thinking skills are transferable and so should help you in your other A-level subjects, in undergraduate studies and in life in general. With these skills you will be able to pick out the lines of reasoning in arguments, assess how effective they are and construct your own persuasive arguments.

We use these skills everyday and like other skills they can be improved by reflection and practice. For most people running is a natural skill, but with some reflection on technique, training and hours of practice, the skill of running can be dramatically improved upon. Similarly, if you practise the skills of thinking critically, you have the chance of becoming better at the process of reasoning.

Unit 1

Introduction to critical thinking

Unit 1

The Unit 1 examination

Unit 1 (F501) is one of four units — two at AS level and two at A2. It represents 50% of the AS marks and 25% of the full A-level marks

The Unit 1 examination can be taken in January or May/June and it is assessed by a written paper of 1 hour 30 minutes, which is divided into two sections:
- **Section A:** The language of reasoning (35 marks)
- **Section B:** Credibility (40 marks)

There is no coursework or controlled assessment.

Unit 1 examines the three key reasoning skills:
- analysing argument (deconstructing argument into its component parts)
- evaluating argument (identifying strengths and weakness)
- developing argument (constructing your own reasoning)

In the specification, these three skills are expressed as three Assessment Objectives:
- **AO1:** 'Analyse critically the different kinds of reasoning in a wide range of contexts'.
- **AO2:** 'Evaluate critically the use of different kinds of reasoning in a wide range of contexts'.
- **AO3:** 'Develop and communicate relevant and coherent arguments clearly and accurately in a concise and logical manner'.

In Unit 1, these three skills attract an almost equal number of marks, although the skill of analysis is examined more in Section A, while Section B deals with evaluation and making a reasoned case to support judgements.

Track your progress

As its title implies, Unit 1 introduces you to a range of skills that are examined at a basic level. The skills required are very specific and are closely matched by this book. Use the charts below to keep track of your progress and to note down your levels of confidence in each particular skill. That way, you will have a record of the areas that may need further attention.

As you work through the skills required for Unit 1, use the traffic light system to record your confidence levels:

■ I feel confident with this skill

□ I need a little more practice

■ I need more guidance and practice

Re-visit those skills which you have identified in red as needing further practice. Read the relevant examples in this book to see if you can gain a firmer grasp of these skills. The third column shows the chapter you can go to for explanation, exercises and guidance.

Section A topic	Skills required	Chapter	Confidence level		
Argument elements	• Identify argument • Identify argument elements (conclusion, reason, hypothetical reasoning, evidence, example, counter-assertion, counter-argument)	1, 2, 3, 4			
Argument indicator words	• Identify argument indicator words • Group and link argument indicator words to argument elements • Use argument indicator words	1			
Definitions of argument elements	• Define argument elements	1, Glossary			
Assumptions	• Identify assumptions • Apply the negative test	5			
Evidence and example	• Identify evidence and example • Assess evidence and example • Consider sample size, apply relevance, representativeness, ambiguity, alternative explanation	4, 6			
Link between the reasoning and conclusion	• Assess the link between reasoning and conclusion • Apply relevance, and look for assumptions	7			
Reason to support a conclusion	• Give a relevant reason without other argument elements attached	8			

Section B topic	Skills required	Chapter	Confidence level		
Credibility of documents	• Assess credibility of claims • Apply credibility criteria — RAVEN	11, 12			
Credibility of claims	• Assess credibility of documents • Apply credibility criteria — RAVEN • Identify what else you would need to know	11, 12, 13			
Corroboration, consistency, conflict	• Identify corroboration • Identify consistency • Identify conflict	14			
Plausibility	• Assess reasonableness • Assess likelihood	15			

Chapter 1

Analysis: the building blocks of arguments

Learning objectives

By the end of this chapter you will be able to:

➢ identify an argument

➢ begin to link argument indicator words to particular argument elements

➢ begin to define argument elements

Identifying an argument

The OCR specification for Unit 1 begins: 'The unit is designed to give candidates an understanding of how arguments are constructed and how they differ from other types of written material.'

What is not an argument?

To gain an understanding of what is not an argument (in critical thinking terms), try the following activity.

Activity 1

The Monty Python sketch 'Argument Clinic' (approximately 6 minutes in length) explores the concept of an argument. You can watch this on YouTube or download a transcript from the internet. Make a note of what is not considered to be an argument.

In the Monty Python sketch the man is trying to have an argument; however he is confronted with several examples of non-argument. You will have probably noticed that these included **abuse**, **contradiction** and **complaint**.

Here is another example of abuse:

> You're so stupid to get a tattoo done.
>
> I'm not stupid. You're the stupid, pathetic one.

It is not an argument because no reason is given to support the assertion that person is not stupid.

Consider this example of contradiction:

> You're so stupid to get a tattoo done.
>
> No, I'm not stupid.
>
> Yes, you are
>
> No, I'm not.
>
> Yes, you are.

Again no reason is given to support the claim that the person is not stupid.

Another form of non-argument is an **assertion**. Here are five examples:

> 1 in 4 of the present generation of the UK's 16-year-olds will reach their hundredth birthday.
>
> Barcelona is the best club football team in the world.
>
> Paris is the capital city of France.
>
> An electron has a negative charge.
>
> We should give generously to charities that try to reduce animal suffering.

At one level, assertions such as these have no significance. They are what we might call 'raw'. It's only when someone takes an assertion and does something with it that assertions take on a further meaning. Think of assertions like ingredients in a recipe. Until someone takes the ingredients and does something with them, they remain merely separate ingredients. When someone starts doing things with the ingredients, then things move on: we get something happening. It's the same with assertions.

As you can see, the five assertions just sit there. Any significance they might have is something that needs to be added to (or drawn from) them.

What is an argument?

When someone does something with an assertion (rather than just tries to explain it), then we often move away from assertions on their own to what, in critical thinking, are called **arguments**.

Key terms

➢ **assertion:** where one claim, or several claims, are made and nothing further is drawn from them.

➢ **argument:** a written or spoken attempt to convince or persuade, using reasons to support a conclusion.

Now let's look at one of the assertions above.

1 in 4 of the present generation of the UK's 16-year-olds will reach their hundredth birthday.

What can be done with this? Here's one thing:

Reason   1 in 4 of the present generation of the UK's 16-year-olds will get to their hundredth birthday.

Conclusion So the present generation of young people should expect to have a retirement age of at least 80.

What should the retirement age be in the future?

As you can see, the assertion now becomes a **reason** which seeks to persuade you of what the author thinks it means for the retirement age. In other words, the assertion (now a reason) has been used to support a **conclusion** that the retirement age needs to be much higher than the present low figure. This is now an argument.

But the assertion could be used as a reason to support a different conclusion:

Reason   1 in 4 of the present generation of the UK's 16-year-olds will reach their hundredth birthday.

Conclusion So young people of today will need to choose their partners with great care.

This is also an argument, but with a different point of persuasion. In this argument, the author uses the assertion in a different way, as a reason to seek to persuade you about the choice of partner, as a result of the predicted long life that would be spent with him or her.

Does an argument have to involve a disagreement?

The term 'argument' runs through everything you'll do in this subject.

> **Key terms**
> ➢ **reason:** a claim that is used to support a conclusion.
>
> ➢ **conclusion:** what the author wants to persuade you to accept based on their reasons.

You might think that there's nothing special about the word 'argument'. After all, you know what an argument is. You might have had quite a few (with friends and family members, and so on). You'll also have seen others engaged in argument (such as politicians in Parliament, people in the street, in shops, on the radio). The essence of argument in these situations is *disagreement*, but it can be as stark as the following:

> I think Istanbul is the best city in the world.
>
> I disagree. I think New York is.

This is not an argument even though two opposing assertions are being given, because neither of these is used as a reason with a conclusion.

However, one thing to note about the use of arguments in critical thinking is that, although they can involve disagreements, they don't have to. So what's going on in them? Let's take another look at the previous argument:

> 1 in 4 of the present generation of the UK's 16-year-olds will reach their hundredth birthday. So the present generation of young people should expect to have a retirement age of at least 80.

When we say 'arguing', we mean that the author is *putting a case* for young people having to work until they're at least 80. Putting a case for something is a useful way of capturing what we mean by 'argument' in this subject.

In our example, although we have said that the author was arguing that young people should expect not to retire until they're at least 80, there was nobody giving the other side:

> No, they shouldn't. Given that only 1 in 4 of the UK's 16-year-olds will reach their hundredth birthday, we can't have a retirement age based on what only a quarter of the population will experience.

This lack of a disagreement (or, if you like, the lack of someone presenting the other side) makes no difference to whether the author had given an argument.

You have seen then that an argument in critical thinking terms can be a very simple presentation of a case for (or against) something, without there being any necessary disagreement.

At its most basic, an argument consists of just a reason and a conclusion:

> **Reason**   Sending e-mails is becoming less and less popular with the under-25s.
>
> *so*
>
> **Conclusion**   E-mails will cease to be used for anything but business purposes in future years.

The author is using the reason to *argue for* (or put the case for) the conclusion. This relationship between the two can be emphasised by reversing their order:

> **Conclusion**   E-mails will cease to be used for anything but business purposes in future years.
>
> *because*
>
> **Reason**   Sending e-mails is becoming less and less popular with the under-25s.

Exercise 1

Look at the following dialogues. In each case, decide whether there is at least one argument in the dialogue. It could be that just one character is using an argument, both are, or neither is. If you think that there is an argument, identify the character(s) A or B using it.

Dialogue 1

A It doesn't matter where Topshop gets its T-shirts made. They're really cheap and good quality.

B I disagree with you on this.

Dialogue 2

A People should get a lot of their clothes from Topshop.

B Why?

A They're good quality and not too expensive.

B I don't buy many clothes. But I buy ones that are much more expensive than those in Topshop.

Topshop — good for T-shirts?

Dialogue 3

A We're planning to go to the zoo tomorrow.

B I really wish you wouldn't go. Zoos keep animals in artificial environments that are often far too limiting for the animals' needs. This means that zoos cause animal suffering.

A But some species of animals might not survive without zoos – like tigers and rhinos. This must mean that zoos aren't a bad thing.

Check your answers against those on page 158.

Past paper practice 1

OCR Unit F501, January 2009

Look at Document 1, paragraph 1 in the Resource Booklet. Identify the argument that is presented in this paragraph. (In the examination paper this was an argument given against the main argument.)

Check your answer with that given on page 158.

Beginning to link argument indicator words to particular argument elements

You can see, then, that putting forward an argument involves thinking in terms of 'because' and 'so'. At the very least, an argument links two claims in this way.

What are called **argument indicators** often help to distinguish these two components or elements. For example, words like 'therefore' or 'because' often show that reasoning is taking place.

There are many other argument indicator words which we use without thinking in our everyday reasoning. You may recognise some of them as 'connectives'. Try making an argument using a few of them in the next activity.

> **Key term**
>
> ➤ **argument indicators:** words which show that reasoning is going on; they signpost argument elements such as reasons and conclusions.

Activity 2

Make an argument using the following argument indicator words:

'because', 'for example', 'additionally', 'however', 'as', 'but', 'so'

You may want to try this as a class activity with each person taking one of the words to continue the argument. You will need to think of a claim to start the argument. Here is an example:

'We should start shopping early for Christmas.'

It might continue something like this:

because	shops soon run out of the most popular presents
for example	last year some Wii products sold out in November
additionally	the shops become very overcrowded in December
however	there are many attractive reductions and special offers just before Christmas
as	shops want to clear their Christmas stock
but	these goods may not be what you would want to buy
so	it may be better after all to shop for the presents you really want earlier than in December

Now try making an argument of your own with the same indicator words using a different claim.

The chapters that follow will introduce you to a larger range of argument indicator words and link them to the particular argument elements that they signpost. You might like to use the table in Activity 3 to keep track of them as they appear. By the end of Chapter 8, you would then have a comprehensive list at hand to help you to analyse arguments.

Activity 3

The following table contains a list of argument elements that you may be asked to identify in the Unit 1 examination. Add the argument indicator words that can be used to signpost each argument element as you come across them. An example has been given for each one to start you off.

Argument element	Indicator words (add in other examples)
Conclusion	*therefore*
Reason	*because*
Hypothetical reasoning, including: hypothetical assertion hypothetical reason hypothetical conclusion	*if...then*
Evidence (types of information)	*data*
Example	*for instance*
Counter-assertion	*despite*
Counter-argument, including: counter-conclusion counter-reason	*despite*

Beginning to define argument elements

Throughout this book you will be given definitions in the key terms boxes, for easy reference. In this chapter, for example, the definition of 'argument' was set out for you. You can use some of these definitions directly in your answers in the Unit 1 examination where a question may quote part of a text and then ask you to:

> identify which argument element this is

> explain your answer (which you can do using a definition)

Exam tip

In the exam, you can use the definitions of the argument elements to help you explain why you have identified them as such in your answer. You do not need to refer to the text quoted in the question in your explanation.

A list of these argument elements was given in the table in Activity 3. You could extend the table and keep a record of their definitions as you come across them, as shown in Activity 4.

Activity 4

Enter the definitions as well as the argument indicator words for each argument element. This can act as a useful revision tool.

Argument element	Definition	Indicator words
Conclusion		therefore
Reason		because
Hypothetical reasoning, including: hypothetical assertion hypothetical reason hypothetical conclusion		if...then
Evidence (types of information)		data
Example		for instance
Counter-assertion		despite
Counter-argument, including: counter-conclusion counter-reason		despite

Exam tip

This is the list of argument elements in the OCR specification that you might be asked to identify and from which you might be asked to explain your choice. For such questions in Unit 1, you do not need to look beyond this list.

Summary

➢ An argument is an attempt to persuade the reader or listener to accept a conclusion by giving at least one reason. It doesn't have to be a disagreement, i.e. two-sided.

➢ A reason is a claim that is used to support a conclusion.

➢ A conclusion is what the author wants to persuade you to accept based on their reasons.

➢ Where argument indicator words appear, they signpost the argument elements. Spotting them therefore can be helpful when analysing reasoning.

Chapter 2

Analysis: reasons and conclusions

Learning objectives

By the end of this chapter, you will be able to:

➤ identify reasons and conclusions in an argument

➤ use four tests to help you do this

➤ identify counter-arguments and counter-assertions/claims

In Chapters 2 to 5 we will be looking at the analysis of argument. This is a skill that requires deconstructing the argument into its component parts. Although this might sound daunting, it is simply a case of splitting up the argument and naming the function of each part, such as conclusion, reason, example and evidence.

Identifying reasons and conclusions in arguments

In the previous chapter, you have seen that arguments consist of at least a reason and a conclusion each of which has a specific function in that argument.

Look again at an argument we used earlier:

Reason   Sending e-mails is becoming less and less popular with the under-25s.

so

Conclusion   E-mails will cease to be used for anything but business purposes in future years.

We can describe what's going on in two different ways.

The reason is used to *support* the conclusion.

The conclusion is *drawn from* the reason.

You can see this as a process, with the two different ways of looking at it. Think of it like this:

Conclusion

Reason

The reason supports or holds up the conclusion; the conclusion is supported or held up by the reason.

Put another way, the **reason** is why the author makes the conclusion.

Let's get this point fixed clearly:

➢ A reason supports a conclusion.

➢ A reason is when a word like 'so' could usefully follow it to link it with a conclusion.

Conclusion

↑   (could be seen as 'so' or 'it follows that' or 'therefore' or 'thus', and so on)

Reason

Now that we know what reasons are, what about a conclusion? In everyday language the word 'conclusion' means 'the end' or 'the final section'. In critical thinking a **conclusion** is what comes at the end of a sequence of reasoning (in that it follows from the reason). However, as you have seen, the writer may choose to put it first. So, when trying to find a conclusion in a piece of writing you will need to search for it throughout the text.

Applying four tests for finding reasons and conclusions

Here are four tests to help you to distinguish between reasons and conclusions. The first two use argument indicator words to help you.

The therefore test

You have seen that the word 'therefore' gives you a good indication that a conclusion is being used. Conclusions can also be introduced by words such as 'so', 'thus', 'it follows that', 'consequently', 'as a result' and 'we can conclude that'. You need to remember, however, that the word 'so' does not automatically indicate that a conclusion is being drawn. Look at the next example:

Can the northern white rhino survive?

> There are only eight specimens of the northern white rhino left alive in the world, and all of these are in captivity. So that something of the species can survive, it might be that they have to breed with the southern whites. This needs to be looked at.

Although the second sentence begins with 'so', you will have seen that it isn't the conclusion. This is the last sentence. The 'so' in the second sentence has the meaning of 'in order', as in the following example:

> **A**   Why did you choose to apply to that university?
>
> **B**   So that I could still live at home.

The because test

You have seen that the word 'because' gives you a good indication that a reason is being used. So, if you are asked to find what are called **reason indicators** in an argument, 'because' is a prime candidate. But you could also look for words like 'since', 'given that…', 'as a result of…' and, of course, 'the reason is…'.

The persuasive language test

A conclusion is a claim that is presenting something that has been argued for. As a result, an author is likely to use language, or **conclusion indicators**, that show this. Look again at the conclusion of the argument about the northern white rhino:

> There are only eight specimens of the northern white rhino left alive in the world, and all of these are in captivity. So that something of the species can survive, it might be that they have to breed with the southern whites. This needs to be looked at.

The words 'needs to be' fit with this point about something having been argued for. The author has given reasoning to show why 'this *needs to be* looked at'.

Here's another example:

> Parents need to limit the time young children use electronic media. When young children are using mobile phones and computers for communicating, they're not interacting with anyone face to face.

There are many other words (or, more generally, types of language) that often indicate that a conclusion has been drawn.

Key terms

➢ **argument indicators:** words that signal the various argument elements, e.g. reasons, conclusions, examples.

➢ **reason indicators:** words such as 'because', 'since', 'given that', 'as a result of' that show that a claim is being used to support another.

➢ **conclusion indicators:** words such as 'so', 'thus', 'therefore', 'in consequence', 'it follows that', that often show that a claim is being drawn from at least one other claim. Conclusion indicator words may also include words such as 'should', 'must', 'ought', and their negative forms.

> Iceland has the highest male life expectancy in the world; Japan has the highest female life expectancy. The UK should learn from Iceland and Japan in order to improve its life expectancy.

The word to spot in this conclusion is 'should'. It fits again with the point that a conclusion is what the author has argued for. You can see that the words 'needs to' could be substituted for 'should' without changing the meaning of the conclusion.

Other words that often indicate a conclusion are 'ought to' and 'must'. In addition, there are the negative versions of any of these: 'should not', 'ought not to', and 'must not'.

Here are two examples:

> Afghanistan has the lowest male and female life expectancy in the world. The UK should not look at this country in order to improve its own life expectancy.

> Parents ought not to let their young children have unlimited time using electronic media. When young children are using mobile phones and computers for communicating, they're not interacting with anyone face to face.

However, just as you saw with the word 'so', the presence of words like 'should' does not always indicate the conclusion of an argument. Look at the next example:

> Whether or not rich countries should give more aid to developing ones is a question that's difficult to answer. There is not necessarily good evidence to show that increased aid achieves much in terms of improved education, health and living conditions in developing countries. It is a good idea to look for more evidence before spending more on aid.

The word 'should' appears in the first sentence. But the conclusion is the last sentence. The first sentence presents the problem that the last sentence seeks to answer.

The recommendation test

You may also have noticed that the conclusion of the above argument does not contain any of the word clues we've been looking at. So, looking for words like 'so' and 'should' does not always help to find a conclusion. But, if we combine the language test with another one, we get closer to finding conclusions.

This further test makes use of the point that conclusions are very often recommendations. Look again at the conclusion of the last argument:

> *It is a good idea* to look for more evidence before spending more on aid.

This certainly fits with being a recommendation, as do these.

> The UK should learn from Iceland and Japan in order to improve its life expectancy.
>
> Parents need to limit the time young children use electronic media.
>
> Young people of today will need to choose their partners with great care.

As with the language tests, however, the recommendation test is only a rule of thumb. It often works, but not always:

> The price of oil rose sharply in 2008, then fell again. The present high price will also fall.

In this argument, the conclusion is a **prediction**. It is drawn from a claim about the past. Neither the recommendation nor the language test would highlight this as the conclusion. In the end, in looking for conclusions, you also have to work out what the author is arguing for. What do they want us to accept or believe or do?

Trying out the first two tests

We'll try the first two tests out on the following simple argument already seen above:

> When young children are using mobile phones and computers for communicating, they're not interacting with anyone face to face. Parents need to limit the time young children use electronic media.

So which is the reason and which is the conclusion?

Try the therefore test first: put the word 'therefore' between the two sentences, connecting them in either order:

> When young children are using mobile phones and computers for communicating, they're not interacting with anyone face to face. *Therefore* parents need to limit the time young children use electronic media.

> Parents need to limit the time young children use electronic media. *Therefore* when young children are using mobile phones and computers for communicating, they're not interacting with anyone face to face.

Is parental supervision needed?

Which version fits better with the sense of what's being argued?

In the first version, young children not interacting face to face is used to support parents needing to limit the time children spend using electronic media.

In the second version, parents needing to limit their children is used as a reason for children not interacting face to face.

It's clear that the first version fits well with the sequence of the reasoning. It's also clear that the second doesn't work. The claim that parents need to limit their children's use of mobile phones and computers doesn't work well as a reason for children not interacting face to face when using electronic media.

Now try the because test:

> When young children are using mobile phones and computers for communicating, they're not interacting with anyone face to face, *because* parents need to limit the time young children use electronic media.
>
> Parents need to limit the time young children use electronic media, *because* when young children are using mobile phones and computers for communicating, they're not interacting with anyone face to face.

You can see that the because test gives us the same answer. The second version shows us that children not interacting face to face is a reason for parents to limit time. The first version highlights that parents limiting time is not a reason for children not interacting face to face.

You can see, then, that either test will work. This is because each test is doing the same thing but from the opposite direction.

We said above that although the conclusion marks the end of a sequence of reasoning, it doesn't have to come literally at the end of passage which is an argument:

> Parents need to limit the time young children use electronic media. When young children are using mobile phones and computers for communicating, they're not interacting with anyone face to face.

In this version, the conclusion comes before the reason. This is perfectly acceptable and often found. The author states what they want to persuade you about and then supports it. If you put this argument in dialogue form, you can see how it works:

A Parents need to limit the time young children use electronic media.

B Why?

A When young children are using mobile phones and computers for communicating, they're not interacting with anyone face to face.

Because the conclusion doesn't have to come last in an argument, we need to use either the therefore or the because test (or both) when trying to find the conclusion.

Exercise 2

With each of the following arguments, work out which sentence is the reason and which is the conclusion.

1 There should be a ban on hair extensions. Hair extensions can damage the scalp and hair follicles.
2 Thinking deeply about sweets can reduce your wish to eat lots of them. People with a craving for sweets should think deeply about them.

3 About two-thirds of the population are at risk of mental and physical health problems due to poor sleeping. It is important that doctors pay more attention to how much their patients sleep.

4 Over time, tattoos go fuzzy and fade, with fine details in them being lost. People who choose to have them done need to choose designs with simple shapes and large bold lines rather than ones with intricate details.

Will this tattoo stand the test of time?

Check your answers against those on page 159.

Finding reasons and conclusions in less simple arguments

The simplest of arguments have one reason leading to one conclusion. Although you'll find these simple arguments often enough, you'll also need to work with less simple ones. One of the ways that arguments can be less simple is for them to have more than one reason. In fact, there is no limit to the number of reasons an argument can have.

Here is an example of an argument with more than one reason:

> It has been shown that boys have a higher risk of peanut allergy than girls do. It's also been shown that children from better-off homes have a higher risk of this allergy than those from poorer homes. We need to do more research to explain why boys and better-off children have these higher risks of peanut allergy.

You can see that, in this example, the conclusion fits with both the language test ('need to') and the recommendation test. It is drawn from two reasons, each of which supports the conclusion.

Here's another example:

> Feeding children lots of processed food (such as sausages, burgers and sugary snacks) at a young age has been shown to lower their future intelligence. Giving them a diet rich in vitamins (including fruit, vegetables, rice and pasta) can make children more intelligent. Parents should be strongly encouraged to limit their children's consumption of processed food and to increase their consumption of vitamin-rich foods.

As before, the conclusion fits with the language test ('should') and the recommendation test ('strongly encouraged to…'). The two reasons both lend support to this conclusion.

As you will have seen, finding more than one reason isn't that difficult. So try the next exercise.

Exercise 3

Identify the reasons and the conclusion in each of the following arguments.

1 People need to see the eating of eggs differently from how they used to. People used to think that eating more than a few eggs a week was bad for their health. Eggs these days have low levels of cholesterol. They have also been shown to have high levels of vitamins.

2 Many parents are using allergy-testing kits on their children (bought online or on the high street) which simply don't work. These unauthorised allergy-testing kits must be banned. When the kits show a positive result for an allergy, children are often put on an unnecessarily restricted diet, which makes it more difficult for doctors to diagnose any possible allergies.

3 Happily-married couples eat more healthily than other groups. They also have more friends than others. In addition, they take better care of each other than people who live unhappily with others. It is important that schools tell young people about the benefits of a happy marriage.

In doing this exercise, you will have seen that you were using the same skills as you used in looking at arguments with just one reason. You were working out what the author was arguing for (the conclusion) and how this conclusion was supported.

Check your answers against those on page 159.

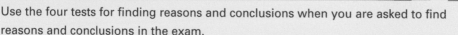

Exam tip

Use the four tests for finding reasons and conclusions when you are asked to find reasons and conclusions in the exam.

When you're asked to *state* the reasons and conclusions, it is important that you give the exact words used by the author. This means that you shouldn't paraphrase the reasons and conclusions, because you will have failed to 'state' them. In addition, by paraphrasing, you run the risk of being inaccurate.

Signposting further reasons

We'll meet this point again later, but it's worth noting here that an argument can reveal something of its structure by the use of 'signposting' words. We've already met some of these with words that might indicate a conclusion ('so', 'thus', and so on). But you'll have seen words that might indicate further reasons in the arguments you've just looked at. These were 'also' and 'in addition'. These are often used to show further reasons.

Identifying counter-arguments and counter-assertions

Arguments, as we have seen, provide at least one reason to support the conclusion. They also contain other features, as we will see later, but here we will note one particular aspect of what you often find when you're looking at arguments.

Arguments don't always just sit there surrounded by nothing. Although the ones we've considered have looked like this, with nothing around them, sometimes they might be part of a bigger passage. At other times, they sit with what are called **counter-assertions** and **counter-arguments**.

In OCR Critical Thinking, the counter-argument is taken to be the argument that is argued against, i.e. it supports the opposite position to that argued for by the author. The author often introduces it as a target which they wish to knock down or to dismiss. (Note that this differs from the more usual use where, if you argue against something, you are said to be 'countering' it.)

Look at the next example:

Key terms

➢ **counter-assertion:** a statement that supports the opposite position to that argued for by the author.

➢ **counter-argument:** an argument that supports the opposite position to that argued for by the author. A counter-argument will contain at least one counter-reason and at least one counter-conclusion.

It is often argued that people should walk or cycle to work or school rather than use a car. This is because, it is claimed, using a car contributes much more to global warming. However, the production of food requires so much energy that far more carbon is emitted in providing a person with enough calories to walk than would be emitted by using a car. Thus the climate would benefit if we exercised less and drove more.

Is cycling necessarily good for global warming?

You will have seen that the author presents opposing positions: 'people should walk or cycle to work or school rather than use a car' and 'the climate would benefit if we exercised less and drove more'. But only one of these is the position he or she is arguing for — the second one.

The author presents the first in order to argue against it. The crucial shift in the passage occurs with the word 'however'. This could have been 'but' or 'alternatively' or 'on the other hand'. It signifies that the author is about to disagree with what's been presented so far.

> **Exam tip**
>
> Watch out for words like 'however' and 'but'. They can often indicate that a counter-assertion has been given, with the author about to argue against it.

You will have seen that the first two sentences consist of a reason and a conclusion. In other words, the first two sentences provide an argument. Because this is a counter-argument, it has what are called a 'counter-reason' and a 'counter-conclusion'.

Counter-conclusion	It is often argued that people should walk or cycle to work or school rather than use a car.
Counter-reason	This is because, it is claimed, using a car contributes much more to global warming.

More clearly:

Counter-reason	Using a car contributes much more to global warming than walking or cycling.
Counter-conclusion	Thus people should walk or cycle to work or school rather than use a car.

> **Exam tip**
>
> Being asked to find the counter-reason and the counter-conclusion in a counter-argument is just the same as being asked to find reasons and conclusions in any argument.
>
> When asked to *state* counter-assertions, counter-reasons and counter-conclusions, you need to remember to use the exact words of the author. Paraphrasing is a recipe for losing marks. You should also not use ellipses ('...'), as only the words that you give on your paper can be counted as the answer.

Look now at the next version:

> It is often argued that people should care about the environment by walking or cycling to work or school rather than using a car. However, the production of food requires so much energy that far more carbon is emitted in providing a person with enough calories to walk than would be emitted by using a car. Thus the climate would benefit if we exercised less and drove more.

In this version, although the author refers to an argument ('It is often argued that...'), it is not presented in the form of one. In this example, then, the counter-position is given in the form of a single assertion. This assertion goes against the author's argument so it is a counter-assertion.

Why do authors include a reference to the opposing position?

There could be two reasons:

➤ One could be in order to knock it down. By stating the other side's position (or, at least, an account of it), authors can deal with any objection to their position by fitting their argument to this (as you can see with the example about walking and cycling).

➤ Another could be to provide some context for the argument, indicating there is an alternative position to theirs. But, of course, the main point of showing context in this way is to demonstrate that their own argument is the better one.

You need to remember that, by putting in some version of the counter-position, the author should not be seen as being contradictory. (The exception to this would be where the author argues for both positions.)

Exercise 4

In each of the following passages, identify either a counter-assertion or a counter-argument. If you think there is a counter-argument, identify what is the counter-reason and what is the counter-conclusion.

A new way of reading?

1 Parents and teachers worry that video games and digital phones will greatly cut into the time that children spend reading. They shouldn't worry so much. Digital devices such as computers and e-readers are an increasingly popular means of reading for children.

2 It's often said that young people should go to university for economic reasons. This is because there is evidence that salaries of graduates are higher than the average. Unfortunately, it depends what country is being considered. Although British graduates aged 25–34 earn on average £34,826, which puts them well above the average wage, Swedish graduates earn only an average of £22,855 (which does not).

3 Planets similar to the Earth are probably orbiting one in four stars that are like the Sun. It follows that well-developed life forms will be found on thousands (or millions) of planets in our galaxy (let alone all the other millions of galaxies in the universe). It is claimed by some that the Earth is unique in having well-developed life forms. They will need to change their position.

Check your answers against those on page 159.

Past paper practice 2

OCR Unit F501, January 2010

You can use this past paper to test out the skills of analysis introduced in this chapter. Look at Document 1, paragraphs 1 and 3 in the Resource Booklet. See if you can answer these examination questions that were asked in this paper:

1 State the main conclusion of the argument.

2 State three argument indicator words used.

3 State the conclusion of the counter-argument.

4 State one reason given in the counter-argument

Check your answers with those given on page 159.

There is one other feature of arguments that we should note. This is that sometimes arguments are introduced by (or simply include) material that is not strictly part of the argument.

Here is an example:

There's been a huge growth in dating websites. These are websites where people looking for partners register and can then connect with what they take to be suitable ones. Although, overall, men are more likely to make 'moves' towards women on these websites, this varies from country to country. In Spain, women are more likely than men to make the first move. They made on average 1.33 contacts per month, almost double that for British women (only 0.78 contacts a month). British women should be more like Spanish ones if they want to get the most out of these dating websites.

You can see that the first two sentences play no part in the argument itself. They simply introduce the subject of dating websites. If these sentences were not there, the argument would be untouched.

Exam tip

Watch out for material that is not strictly part of the argument, and see that it plays no part in either the argument or any counter-position.

The argument indicator word is technically not part of an argument element, so you do not need to include it, although you won't be penalised for doing so.

Summary

➤ Argument indicator words can help you to find reasons, additional reasons, conclusions, counter-assertions, counter-reasons and counter-conclusions.

➤ Additionally looking for persuasive language and recommendations can also help you to find a conclusion.

➤ A counter-argument is the same as an argument, except that it supports the opposite position.

➤ When asked to identify argument elements in the examination, you should use the exact words of the author — no paraphrase, no omissions, no additions and no ellipses ('...').

➤ You should identify only the argument element required and no other argument elements preceding it, within it or following it.

Chapter 3

Analysis: hypothetical reasoning

Learning objectives

By the end of this chapter, you will be able to:

➢ use argument indicator words to help you to identify hypothetical reasoning

➢ identify hypothetical conclusions, hypothetical reasons and hypothetical arguments

➢ check to see how hypothetical words are used in an argument

Applying argument indicator words to help to identify hypothetical reasoning

At the end of Chapter 2, you looked at the following argument:

There's been a huge growth in dating websites. These are websites where people looking for partners register and can then connect with what they take to be suitable ones. Although, overall, men are more likely to make 'moves' towards women on these websites, this varies from country to country. In Spain, women are more likely than men to make the first move. They made on average 1.33 contacts per month, almost double that for British women (only 0.78 contacts a month). British women should be more like Spanish ones if they want to get the most out of these dating websites.

Do British women get the most out of dating websites?

ALAMY

The conclusion of the argument is the last sentence (the word 'should' is a useful indicator word here), but when you look at it closely, something about the conclusion needs attention.

What if British women don't 'want to get the most out of these dating websites'? Then the conclusion has no useful significance. This is because the conclusion (like the question we've just asked) is a **hypothetical** one:

> *If* they want to get the most out of these dating websites, (*then*) British women should be more like Spanish ones.

As you can see, we've emphasised its hypothetical nature. What exactly do we mean by this?

The term 'hypothetical' has a number of different meanings. It can be used to mean 'a possible explanation for something until more evidence suggests otherwise' (as in 'that's an interesting hypothesis') or, more generally,

> **Key term**
>
> ➤ **hypothetical reasoning (reason or conclusion):** one in which a condition is given for a consequence to follow; for example: 'If this...then that...'

'something that isn't definite' (as in 'I'm speaking only hypothetically'). Someone raising a hypothesis is likely to be saying 'this is possibly the case but, whether or not it is depends on certain things being done/happening/etc.' ('Arsenal will win every trophy next season if they spend lots of money on new players.') This sort of hypothesis is always in the form of *if...then* or a near equivalent such as *suppose/were this to be the case...then*.

A hypothetical claim of whatever form in an argument has two parts: the condition and the consequence:

> *If* they want to get the most out of these dating websites [the condition], (*then*) British women should be more like Spanish ones [the consequence].

In this example, if British women don't want to get the most out of these dating sites, then the condition does not apply. Given that the condition doesn't apply, neither therefore does the consequence.

Identifying hypothetical conclusions, hypothetical reasons and hypothetical arguments

Hypothetical forms are found in three different versions:
➤ hypothetical conclusions
➤ hypothetical reasons
➤ hypothetical arguments

Identifying hypothetical conclusions

We have already seen an example of a hypothetical conclusion. In this example, the author could have given one that was not hypothetical and could have concluded something much more definite:

> In using dating websites, British women should be more like Spanish ones.

Here there is no condition, so there is no consequence, just a baldly stated conclusion.
Look at another example:

> According to the Green Party representative Chris Goodall, driving a typical car for 3 miles adds about 0.9 kg of carbon dioxide to the atmosphere. On the other hand, walking 3 miles will typically use about 180 calories. To replace these calories would require about 100 g of beef. Given that the production of beef requires so much energy, 100 g of beef results in 3.6 kg of emissions (four times the amount for taking the car). Therefore, if people reduced their levels of exercise and if as a result ate less, then global warming would be reduced.

In this example, the conclusion is again hypothetical. You can see that the consequence ('global warming would be reduced') requires the condition ('if people reduced their levels of exercise and thus ate less') to be satisfied.

But you might have noticed something else in this hypothetical conclusion. Look again at the condition:

> ...if people reduced their levels of exercise and if as a result ate less...

Here there is a condition within the condition:

> ...if people reduced their levels of exercise and if, as result, they ate less...

What the author is really saying is: here is a condition (reducing exercise) that would give us this consequence (eating less), which is a condition for the consequence of reducing global warming.

In later chapters, we look at the big topic of judging whether arguments are weak or strong. Unpacking an argument like this makes it easier to make these judgements, because we are clearer about what is going on in it.

Identifying hypothetical reasons

Read the next example:

> The consequences of junk food can be seen everywhere in the US: overweight and unhealthy children who become even more overweight and unhealthy adults. If the present trends continue, according to the US Center for Disease Control and Prevention, one in three American adults will have diabetes by 2050. Action must be taken by US health agencies to prevent this from happening.

In this example, the conclusion (indicated by the word 'must') is the last sentence. It clearly is not a hypothetical one. However, you will have spotted the hypothetical element in the previous sentence. No doubt you'll have identified this sentence as a reason. So we've found a hypothetical reason.

The same point about a consequence requiring a condition is there: 'one in three American adults will have diabetes by 2050' (consequence); 'if the present trends continue' (condition).

If the conclusion *is* accepted (and action is taken), then the present trends would not continue, so the consequence will not happen.

Read the next example:

> According to Professor Edzard Ernst, an expert in what's called 'alternative medicine' (homeopathy, 'quantum healing', reiki and so on), 95% of the products of the alternative medicine industry do not do what they claim to do. Advertising of these products should be very strictly controlled. If the product works, then it's a medicine, needing regulation like other medicines. If it doesn't work, then it shouldn't be allowed to make claims suggesting it is.

This argument has two hypothetical reasons supporting the conclusion. Each one provides a condition (product works/product doesn't work) followed by a consequence (it's a medicine needing regulation/it shouldn't be allowed to claim it is). From the evidence reported in the first sentence, and these two hypothetical reasons, the author draws the conclusion in the second sentence. (Note that the conclusion in this example sits in the middle of the argument.)

Sometimes hypothetical reasons are not packaged in an *if…then* form:

> It is important for people to realise what effects they will have on the environment if they eat beef and other meat. People should worry much more about this than whether or not their television is off standby and what sort of light bulbs they're using. A public education campaign should be created which brings home to people what they're doing when they next tuck into a beefburger.

In this example, the conclusion is drawn from the previous reasoning about the effects on the environment of meat-eating. But is there hypothetical reasoning going on? Does the 'if' indicate a hypothetical?

Look at the relevant sentence carefully:

> It is important for people to realise what effects they will have on the environment if they eat beef and other meat.

In the following example the hypothetical is still there but the order has been reversed. What's going on here is this:

> It is important for people to realise that, if they eat beef and other meat, (then) there will be effects on the environment as a result.

This provides us with the structure: here is a consequence that will follow if this condition is satisfied. It makes no difference to the meaning (or significance) of the hypothetical reason if it is reversed.

Identifying hypothetical arguments

Read the next argument:

> There is evidence from studies with rodents and baby monkeys that giving anaesthetics can cause brain cell death. One of the researchers in these studies is Dr Randall Flick. As he has explained, 'You don't have to be a rocket scientist to say, "If this is true that it happens in monkeys, then there's a high probability that something like this occurs in humans."' In consequence, if a very young child needs an anaesthetic for a surgical procedure, doctors should think very carefully about the need to use this procedure.

Here you will probably have seen that there were two hypothetical forms in the argument.

There's a hypothetical reason ('if this is true that it happens in monkeys...humans') supporting a hypothetical conclusion ('if a very young child...use this procedure'.) This gives us, then, two conditions and two consequences.

In this example the whole argument is based on hypothetical forms, with a hypothetical reason supporting a hypothetical conclusion. As a result, if it could be shown that the effect of anaesthetics on brain cells seen in baby monkeys is not actually shown in human children, then the conclusion cannot be drawn. But, in addition, the recommendation to doctors obviously does not apply if a surgical procedure could be carried out without anaesthetic.

Checking to see how hypothetical words are used in arguments

Although the words *if...then* and their equivalents normally indicate that an argument is going on, we need to be careful.

Read the next example:

> We'll never know what precisely would have happened to all the species on Earth if humans had never evolved. However, we have significant evidence, based on fossil-fuel records, that the rate of extinction of species increased up to 1,000 times after the arrival of the various human species (including the Neanderthals). As a result, it can be seen that the evolution of humans was (and very much still is) bad news for many other species on Earth.

You will have seen that the first sentence has a hypothetical look to it, but it's an incomplete hypothetical: there's no 'then' in it:

If humans had never evolved, then…?

You might say that the argument itself provides the 'then':

If humans had never evolved, then the rate of extinction of species would have been much lower.

You are right to say this. However, the argument is not presented in hypothetical form. The author starts with an unsolvable problem (especially with the word 'precisely') but provides something of a general answer to a more general question.

Watch out for examples like this.

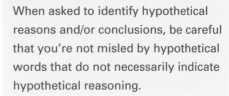

Exam tip

When asked to identify hypothetical reasons and/or conclusions, be careful that you're not misled by hypothetical words that do not necessarily indicate hypothetical reasoning.

Exercise 5

Read the following arguments. If you think that there is hypothetical reasoning in an argument, identify where you think this reasoning occurs.

1 The future for UK summers is likely to be one in which the temperatures would routinely be in the high 30s. In addition, increases of up to 40 cm in sea levels mean that coastal areas will be at severe risk of flooding. The UK is simply not planning effectively for these scenarios. It is clear that, if the UK waits rather than acts, it will be too late. Action must now be taken to prepare us for the future.

Is the UK prepared for rising sea levels?

2 Research has shown that drinking more than four cups of coffee a day can cut the chances of a woman getting pregnant by about a quarter. So, if a woman wants to get pregnant, she should cut down significantly on coffee (and other highly caffeinated drinks).

3 When species die out, history has shown that other species fill the gap left by their disappearance (such as the mammals after the extinction of the dinosaurs). There is no reason why this process should not continue in the future. Richard

Dawkins has argued that, if humanity were to be wiped out by a nuclear war, rodents would come to dominate the Earth. As he explains, 'Rodents would emerge as the ultimate post-human scavengers. Within 5 million years, a whole new range of new species could replace the ones we know. Herds of giant grazing rats are stalked by sabre-toothed predatory rats' (*The Ancestor's Tale*, 2004). With nuclear war always a possibility, we should stop thinking of ourselves as the permanently top species on the planet, and look at rats as our successors.

Check your answers against those on page 160.

Past paper practice 3

OCR Unit F501, January 2010

Look at Document 1, paragraphs 1 and 3 in the Resource Booklet. State the hypothetical reason given in this text. Check your answer with that given on page 160.

Exam tip

When identifying hypothetical reasoning, you need to make sure that you include both parts of the reasoning — the condition and the consequence.

Summary

➤ Hypothetical reasoning usually takes the 'if…then' format.

➤ It poses a condition and gives the consequence.

➤ However the consequence is often given before the condition.

➤ Assertions, reasons, conclusions and arguments can all be hypothetical.

➤ When asked to identify the hypothetical reasoning in the examination, it is important to state both the condition and the consequence.

➤ It is important to check and discount any reasoning that simply has an 'if' clause by itself without a following consequence.

Chapter 4

Analysis: evidence and examples

Learning objectives

By the end of this chapter, you will be able to:

➤ identify evidence

➤ identify examples

Identifying evidence

You have already met the use of **evidence** in arguments. Here are some arguments based on evidence, some of which you saw in earlier chapters. The evidence is shown in bold:

Iceland has the highest male life expectancy in the world; Japan has the highest female life expectancy. The UK should learn from Iceland and Japan in order to improve its life expectancy.

The price of oil rose sharply in 2008, then fell again. The present high price will also fall.

It has been shown that boys have a higher risk of peanut allergy than girls do. It's also been shown that children from better-off homes have a higher risk of this allergy than those from poorer homes. We need to do more research to explain why boys and better-off children have these higher risks of peanut allergy.

As you can see, the term 'evidence' is used to mean 'information'. It can include:

➤ information from surveys (such as on public opinion and people's behaviour)

Key term

➤ **evidence:** information that can be used to support a reason, or it may stand alone as an assertion or counter-assertion.

> information from findings of research studies (such as the effects of certain policies, the effects of medical drugs and experiments)
> information from history (such as written sources like diaries and official documents)
> information from organisations and individuals (such as what happened in a particular case or in similar cases)

The first three also fit with another term that is widely used: 'data'. We often see terms such as 'survey data', 'experimental data' or 'historical data'.

Evidence in arguments

The information that comes under the heading of evidence can be used in a number of ways. It can be used:

> as a reason
> to support a reason
> as a counter-assertion
> as information that is not strictly part of the argument

It is entirely possible for arguments to be based only on evidence for their reasons:

> Life expectancy in rich countries is always relatively high. However, life expectancy in poor countries is always relatively low. Therefore, giving money to charities to help people in poor countries is of little value, unless it deals with this problem.

It is also entirely possible for arguments to include no evidence of any sort:

> Animals deserve respect in the same way that humans are entitled to respect. This respect includes the right not to suffer unnecessary pain and suffering. Therefore no animals should be used in medical research that would involve pain and suffering.

It is perhaps most common to find evidence that supports a reason:

> Women can increase their chances of giving birth to daughters rather than sons by changing their diet. In a study of 172 couples, 80% of mothers gave birth to girls after eating foods rich in calcium and magnesium (from fruit, vegetables and rice) and avoiding potatoes (with their boy-encouraging potassium). Thus women who want to have a child of a particular gender should pay careful attention to their diet before they intend to conceive.

Boy or girl? Is it down to diet?

In this example, the specific evidence on the link between the gender of a child and the food eaten by its mother before its conception is used to support the reason in the first sentence. You can see its supporting role by seeing what happens when it is removed from the argument:

> Women can increase their chances of giving birth to daughters rather than sons by changing their diet. Thus women who want to have a child of a particular gender should pay careful attention to their diet before they intend to conceive.

The argument still works. It has the same structure as before.

When we say that evidence can be used to support a reason, we mean that the evidence increases the power of the argument: evidence gives us some grounds for believing a claim to be true. However, the degree to which it does that is something we need to look at (and we'll do that in the next chapter).

In the example just considered, you can see that the evidence supported the reason by showing that, in 80% of cases, changing diet increased the chance of a woman having a female child. But the evidence also provided detail not specifically mentioned in the reason. In this way, evidence can not only support a reason, but clarify an aspect of it.

In the next example, we find evidence being used as a counter-assertion:

> 50% of women graduate in science subjects, showing that women are well-equipped for careers in science. However, only 9% of science professors in Britain are women. It's clear that women have a long way to go before they can achieve very high levels of success in science in Britain.

You can see that the thrust of the argument is shown in the conclusion. This is supported by some evidence, which is used as a reason ('only 9%...women'). The evidence in the first sentence provides a contrast, leading one to think that the argument was going the other way.

In the next example, we find evidence not being part of the argument itself, a point first introduced in Chapter 2:

> There is considerable debate about whether badgers are responsible for cattle developing what is called 'bovine TB' (bTB). Between 1998 and 2006, there was a study to see what effects killing badgers had on the spread of bTB. Eleven thousand badgers were killed across England. The results of this study showed that killing badgers could actually increase the amount of bTB. It's clear that any further plans to kill badgers should be dropped.

In this example, the argument consists of only the last two sentences. What comes before is information that is relevant to but not strictly part of the argument (with much of it necessary to explain what the argument is about). It provides useful detail about the study, and it also provides some support for the conclusion by providing detail on the size of the study.

Identifying examples

If evidence can be seen as information, what are **examples**? Quite simply, they are also information. So is there a difference between the two?

We can explain the relationship in this way: evidence includes examples. But the relationship between the two can be unpacked further. Although both evidence and examples provide support for reasons, examples give specific instances and provide illustrations to aid understanding.

Read the following argument:

> There is a debate as to whether the way girls and boys play as children is determined either by their genes ('nature') or by their upbringing ('nurture') (or, of course, both). One way of trying to answer this question is to look at other primates. A 14-year study of chimpanzees has produced important findings. Young female chimpanzees often treated sticks they played with as mother chimpanzees treated their young (such as by putting them into their nest, or even building a separate nest for them). Young males, on the other hand, were much more likely than the young females to use sticks for aggressive games. Given how genetically close humans are to chimpanzees, it's clear that young human children's play can be explained (at least in large part) by genes.

In this argument, the author uses evidence from the study of chimpanzees to draw the conclusion in the last sentence. The evidence on the different behaviour of male and female chimpanzees when playing with sticks is used to provide two reasons for this conclusion.

But you might also have noticed two examples. These appear in the evidence on young females: the author gives us two illustrations of the distinctively female play with sticks ('*such as* putting them in a nest, or even building a separate nest for them'). The words 'such as' have been emphasised here to show the nature of an example. It is likely that other examples of this type of play have been seen. (Indeed they have. Young females sometimes play the 'airplane game' with their sticks, lying on their backs balancing them across their upraised hands.) The role of these examples was to provide illustrations or instances. They showed in more detail how the behaviour of the young female chimpanzees was distinctive. Technically, they were not necessary for the author's argument, but they did aid understanding through the detail.

Read the next argument:

> The breaking of sporting records is often seen in terms of very small improvements — say 0.01 of a second. But Usain Bolt's performance in the 100 metres at the 2008 Olympics when he broke the record with a stunning 9.69 seconds and his 9.58 performance at the 2009 World Championships show that bigger improvements will continue. We should be careful of predicting that sporting records are likely to last for some time.

Olympic record breaker, Usain Bolt

In this argument, the author draws a conclusion on the strength of just one example — Usain Bolt. (Technically there are two examples, but both of them are of Bolt's performances.) In this argument we have an example that is used as evidence.

To turn the example into one that illustrates evidence, we would have to have something like this:

> The continued breaking of sporting records is inevitable. Evidence from many sports, such as golf, athletics and weightlifting shows continued improvement in training methods and equipment. Usain Bolt's performance in the 100 metres at the 2008 Olympics when he broke the record with a stunning 9.69 seconds and his 9.58 performance at the 2009 World Championships show that big improvements will continue.

In this argument, the evidence is illustrated by reference to the examples of three sports — 'golf, athletics and weightlifting'. In addition, Usain Bolt is given as an example of an instance of improvements in athletics.

In this argument, then, we had an example of an example...

Sometimes you'll find examples within reasons and conclusions. The next example shows the same argument but with an example put into the conclusion:

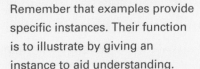

Exam tip

Remember that examples provide specific instances. Their function is to illustrate by giving an instance to aid understanding.

> The breaking of sporting records is often seen in terms of very small improvements – say 0.01 of a second. But Usain Bolt's performance in the 100 metres at the 2008 Olympics when he broke the record with a stunning 9.69 seconds and his 9.58 performance at the 2009 World Championships show that bigger improvements will continue. We should be careful of predicting that sporting records, like those in athletics, are likely to last for some time.

Although the conclusion now includes the words 'like those in athletics', you are not expected to include these if asked to state the conclusion. The conclusion is the general point and the example merely clarifies it.

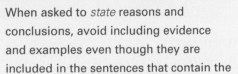

Exam tip

When asked to *state* reasons and conclusions, avoid including evidence and examples even though they are included in the sentences that contain the reasons and conclusions.

Exercise 6

For each of the following arguments, work out whether the author provides evidence, examples or both.

1 Men who think that being physically attractive is enough to be successful with women should think again. In a study, women were asked by psychologists to rate

the characteristics of potential mates. Although physical characteristics were on the list, acting unselfishly (which included donating blood) was much higher. Acting unselfishly is probably a good predictor for being a good, long-term parent.

2 Love is as effective as medical drugs in blocking pain. Tests were carried out on students who said that they were in the passionate early stage of a relationship. Researchers showed the students photos of their loved ones while giving them electric shocks to their palm. They also administered electric shocks to them without showing them the photos. When looking at the photos, the students rated pain up to 45% lower than when the photos were absent.

Does love block out pain?

3 In 2010, goods worth £4.8 billion were stolen from British shops. The most common target was clothes. The consumer is the biggest loser from these high levels of shoplifting. Shops pass on the cost of lost sales from shoplifting to the consumer by increasing prices. Therefore it is in everybody's interests to report shoplifting whenever it's seen or suspected.

4 Scientists at the European Food Safety Authority examined more than 800 claims made by food companies that probiotic drinks and yoghurts could strengthen the body's defences and reduce digestive problems. They concluded that none of these claims could be proved. It's clear that people should not be taken in by the claims made about these probiotic products.

5 The colour of the clothes we wear can significantly affect how other people see us. In a study carried out at a university in New York, a photo of a 'moderately attractive' woman in a red top was shown to one group of male students, and a photo of the same woman in a blue top was shown to a different group. When asked what they would talk to the woman about, the students shown the photo with the red top asked much more flirtatious questions than the students shown the blue top photo.

Check your answers against those on page 160.

Past paper practice 4

OCR Unit F501, January 2011

Read the last three sentences in Document 1, paragraph 5 in the Resource Booklet. State the examples that are given to support the reasoning in this extract. Check your answers with those given on page 160.

Exam tip

When you are looking for examples, make sure that they are given as instances, rather than a list of all the cases.

Summary

➤ Evidence is information which may take the form of numerical data.

➤ Evidence can have many functions in an argument. In many cases it gives support to a reason or another argument element, but it can also stand alone as an assertion or as a counter-assertion.

➤ An example is a specific instance that is often given as an illustration to aid understanding.

➤ Not all lists are examples. They may be lists of the only cases or every case involved.

➤ When asked to state other argument elements in the examination, make sure that you don't include the evidence or example, as these are additional argument elements on their own.

Chapter 5

Analysis: assumptions

Learning objectives

By the end of this chapter you will be able to:

➢ identify assumptions as gaps in the reasoning

➢ apply the negative test to check that an assumption has been found

Identifying assumptions as gaps in the reasoning

What is an assumption?

We have seen that arguments have reasons and conclusions. We have also seen that sometimes they have counter-assertions and counter-arguments. They also have something else: **assumptions**. The problem with assumptions is that we can't see them. This is because the author of the argument has not, for whatever reason, stated them.

Everyday meanings of 'assumption'

We should note that the everyday use of the word 'assumption' does not apply here. People tend to use the word 'assumption' to mean something like 'believe without proving, or giving evidence'. Thus, if you were to say that 'cats make better pets than dogs for old people', someone might respond 'you're just

assuming that, because you're not giving any evidence to back that up'. In our use of the word 'assumption', you were not assuming it at all, having just clearly stated it.

OCR AS Critical Thinking

This is what we mean by assumption in critical thinking:

➢ An assumption is a reason that is necessary for the conclusion to be drawn.

➢ An assumption is a reason that the author has *not* stated.

Finding assumptions

We'll use a simple argument to find some assumptions:

> Scientists have shown that Omega-3 (found in fish oil, walnuts and soya among other things) can improve both children's ability to concentrate and their behaviour. It would be a good thing if Omega-3 supplements were given to children in schools.

Omega-3 supplements—good for children?

Before we find some assumptions in this argument, it will be helpful for you to find the conclusion. There are only two claims, so this shouldn't be too difficult.

The conclusion is, of course, the second sentence. You will have seen that it's a recommendation, which would have clearly indicated it as the conclusion.

At one level, it's a simple argument.

But, when we think more about this argument, we can see that there's much more to it than a simple R → C.

This is because, in order to draw the conclusion from the reason, other unstated reasons are necessary. To see this, we need to ask the following question: 'What else is necessary to draw this conclusion from this reason?'

Here's something:

> Children are not already given Omega-3 supplements.

If children *are* already being given these supplements, then it's an odd thing to conclude that schools should also give them. It isn't stated, but it must be a further reason being used in the argument.

Here are some further assumptions:

> Children's concentration is not already as good as it can be.

> Children's behaviour is not already as good as it can be.

Having looked at some of the assumptions (and there are more), you might think that some of them are so glaringly obvious that it is not worth looking for them. The last two possibly fall into this category. You might say that nobody will believe the opposite. Although this is probably true, it's still worth noting that in this argument they are necessary in order to draw the conclusion.

A useful way of remembering that assumptions are both necessary and unstated reasons is to think of what we see when we look at an X-ray photograph.

Such a photograph shows that what we see on the outside is only a part of the whole thing. Without a skeleton, a body could not function. Similarly, an argument is (normally) more than what we see given to us. It has an unseen structure of statements that connect the parts that we can see. With this image in mind, you will never make the mistake of giving a *stated* reason as an assumption. But the image also reinforces the point that assumptions are necessary parts of an argument, even though they are hidden.

Quality of arguments

There's something else that we need to note. Finding assumptions is not in itself a way of saying whether an argument is strong or weak. It's difficult to think of arguments (of the everyday type that we look at in doing this subject) in which the author has not made some assumptions (often lots of them). So *finding* assumptions does not mean that we can say anything about the quality of the argument, unless these are false assumptions.

Expressing an assumption

You might, however, be tempted to challenge an assumption instead of expressing it. For example, you might want to say to the author of the Omega-3 argument:

> But children might already be having Omega-3 supplements.

As you can see, this challenges the author's assumption that 'children are not already having Omega-3 supplements'. As such, you have not found an assumption but you've done some useful thinking towards finding one. Be careful, then, that you don't waste this thinking by simply expressing an assumption as a challenge. Quite simply, stating an assumption is *never* giving a challenge.

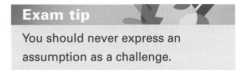

Exam tip

You should never express an assumption as a challenge.

Exercise 7

With all this in mind, see if you can find any more assumptions in the argument we looked at earlier about Omega-3 supplements (page 41). See if you can find at least two more. (Answers on page 160.)

Applying the negative test to check that an assumption has been found

The negative test comes from a feature of assumptions identified earlier.

An assumption is a reason that is necessary for the conclusion to be drawn.

The **negative test** works by taking what we think might be an assumption and putting it into its negative form, to see what then happens to the argument. Take one of the assumptions identified earlier in the Omega-3 example.

If we apply the negative test to 'Children aren't already given Omega-3 supplements', then we need to turn the reason into its negative form:

Children are already given Omega-3 supplements.

In this form, the claim simply wouldn't work in the argument. If we were to put this version into the argument, it would make nonsense of the conclusion. If children are already having the supplements, then why would it be a good thing if schools also gave them? So we know we are likely to have found an assumption here.

> **Exam tip**
>
> In order to check whether you've found an assumption in the exam, always use the negative test.

Be careful when applying the negative test that what you are stating is actually relevant, as turning irrelevant statements into the negative form and putting this into the argument can also seem like nonsense. For example, you don't have to assume:

Parents would agree to their children being given the supplements.

as this would be irrelevant to whether it was 'a good thing'. It might make it easier, but not good. However, if you used the negative test, it also seems nonsense:

Parents wouldn't agree to their children being given the supplements.

So you need to use the negative test together with relevance when deciding whether a statement is an assumption.

Exercise 8

Look again at your answers to Exercise 7 on finding assumptions. To check them, use the negative test. (Answers on page 161.)

Claims that are not assumptions

In looking for assumptions we need to remember that there are some claims that are not necessary for the conclusion to be drawn. Look at the next example:

Omega-3 supplements have a pleasant taste.

When we apply the negative test to this, we find this:

Omega-3 supplements have an unpleasant taste.

We can see that the negative version doesn't prevent the conclusion from being drawn. This is an important point. Finding assumptions is not just finding claims the author has not stated. There will be countless things that aren't stated. Finding assumptions is finding claims that, although not stated, *have to be stated* because the conclusion requires them in order for it to be drawn.

Here's another example:

> The scientists who studied the effects of Omega-3 supplements on children have studied many other things that might affect behaviour and concentration.

You might think that this is highly likely to have happened. But the argument does not require it.

Being careful with words when stating assumptions

You have to be very careful that you state an assumption in an accurate way.

Look again at one of the assumptions we found in the Omega-3 argument:

> Children's concentration isn't already as good as it can be.

In this form, it's a correct version of what the author must believe. But look at the next version:

> Children's concentration isn't already good.

This is too weak for the argument. It could still be good, but could be better. This version, quite simply, is not required for the conclusion to be drawn.

The negative test will help you here:

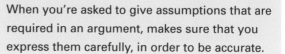

Exam tip

When you're asked to give assumptions that are required in an argument, makes sure that you express them carefully, in order to be accurate.

> Children's concentration is already good.

This again shows that the claim is not specific enough as it doesn't prevent the conclusion from being drawn, so we know that we haven't found an assumption.

Exercise 9

Find at least five assumptions that the author of this argument must make.

Cuba has the lowest rate of population per doctor in the world. The number is only 156 people per doctor. (Tanzania has the highest rate, with 125,000 people per doctor.) Therefore Cuba provides the best healthcare of any country in the world.

Check your answers against on those on page 161.

Exercise 10

Read the passage and then select which *one* of the given claims A–D is an assumption of the argument.

A recent study has shown that only 39% of us sleep well. This means that the majority of the population is putting itself at risk of physical and mental health problems. So doctors should do more to deal with people's sleep problems.

A People with sleep problems don't report these problems to their doctor.
B Poor health can cause sleep problems.
C Sleep problems can be treated by doctors.
D People who sleep well have no health problems.

Check your answers against on those on page 161.

In the next exercise, you're going to select which of the given claims is *not* an assumption. You need to be warned here. This is a more difficult exercise, because you're used to looking *for* the assumption rather than for what is *not* an assumption. However, as you might see, importantly it's the same exercise. When you're looking for what's an assumption, you rule out what is not.

Exercise 11

Read the passage and then select which *one* of the given claims A–D is NOT an assumption of the argument.

Evidence from the US has shown that fake smiling at work worsens a person's mood and can reduce their efficiency. However, staff whose smiles are the result of positive thoughts and so express genuine happiness were more efficient than others. Employers should therefore employ people who smile a lot.

All smiles at work?

A People who smile a lot are not faking their smiles.
B People who are inefficient at work are unhappy.
C Employers want to employ people with high levels of efficiency.
D People who are happy smile a lot.

Check your answers against on those on page 162.

Past paper practice 5

OCR Unit F501, January 2009

Look at the image at the beginning of Document 1 in the Resource Booklet. State the assumption that is needed to support the reasoning about ecotown houses in the caption under the image. Check your answer with that given on page 162.

Summary

- ➢ An assumption is a missing reason in an argument, which is necessary for the conclusion to be drawn.
- ➢ An assumption is therefore never stated in the text.
- ➢ So, when identifying an assumption, you should not quote anything from the text, or paraphrase anything from the text.
- ➢ You should express an assumption as a reason and not as a challenge.
- ➢ You can use the negative test to check whether an assumption has been found. If the conclusion cannot still be drawn, then you are likely to have found an assumption. You must also use the relevance test.
- ➢ When stating an assumption, be sure to be accurate and state it precisely.
- ➢ Finding an assumption does not mean that the argument is weak, unless it is a false assumption.

Chapter 6

Evaluation: evidence

Learning objectives

By the end of this chapter, you will be able to:

➢ assess the impact of sample size

➢ assess the representative nature of the sample or example

➢ assess the relevance of the sample

➢ assess findings in terms of ambiguity

➢ suggest alternative interpretations of statistics

Chapters 6 and 7 will now move from analysis of argument to dealing with evaluation. Evaluation looks at assessing both the strengths and weakness in the reasoning. This chapter concentrates on assessing evidence, while the following chapter looks at the structure of the argument and tries to determine how far the conclusion is supported by the reasoning.

The OCR specification has selected five key areas to consider when looking at the strengths and weakness in evidence and these are our learning objectives above.

Assessing the impact of sample size

How many people were surveyed is something that we might need to take into account in judging statistical evidence. But it isn't necessarily as simple as 'the bigger the better'. We can have unreliable evidence from 2,000 people and reliable evidence from 1,000 or fewer. We need to consider:

➢ how the evidence was collected, rather than the numbers involved

➢ what proportion of the number in the whole group was surveyed; if we're looking at a small group (such as people who've sailed single-handed round the world), then a survey of only a small number of people could well be adequate

Assessing the representative nature of the sample or example

A central issue in the evaluation of evidence is that of **representativeness**. We need to consider whether the evidence is representative (or typical) of the wider picture. This could be as simple as any of the following (in which the word 'typical' could also be the word 'representative').

➤ Is today typical of the other days of this week?

➤ Are you typical of others in your class?

➤ Is your class typical of other classes?

➤ Is your school or college typical of other schools or colleges?

➤ Is the UK typical of other countries in western Europe?

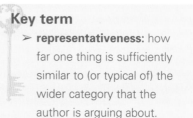

Key term

➤ **representativeness:** how far one thing is sufficiently similar to (or typical of) the wider category that the author is arguing about.

> **Exam tip**
>
> When asked about representativeness, this can relate to similarities and differences. Be aware of exactly what the question is asking. 'How far' would mean that either similarities and differences can be used or both. A weakness would mean looking for differences.

In answering these questions, you are looking for both similarities and differences. It might well be, for example, that you are representative (typical) of others in your class in terms of your previous educational qualifications and what you're going to do after school or college. But it might be that you're not typical (unrepresentative) in terms of specific features, such as sporting abilities, that you don't drink or smoke and so on.

In evaluating the significance of evidence for representativeness, you need to consider whether we can move from this evidence to the wider group. This is where you need to look at shared characteristics.

The European School Survey Project on Alcohol and Other Drugs

There's a big study carried out called 'The European School Survey Project on Alcohol and Other Drugs'. As the title indicates, this surveys young people in many European countries. It does this by asking students in schools at different age stages to complete questionnaires. As the title further indicates, the questionnaires are concerned with young people's use of alcohol, tobacco and various (illegal) drugs.

The survey is carried out some time in the months of March and April, avoiding a recent holiday period (which might distort the results). The study gathers information on the behaviour of the population of 15–16- and 17–18-year-olds in each country. It does this in the following way:

➤ It aims to get 2,400 students in each country.

➢ The sample is spread normally very evenly between males and females.

➢ It uses young people in schools.

➢ Within schools, it gets whole classes to complete the questionnaires.

In the most recent study, this translated into the following:

➢ Between 83% and 95% of selected young people completed the questionnaires (with absence due to sickness being the main reason for non-involvement).

➢ Some countries had many more than 2,400 students involved. (Italy was the highest with 5,130.)

➢ Some countries had many fewer than 2,400 students involved. (Latvia was the lowest with 1,640.)

Among the findings, we have the following:

➢ A majority of the students in all countries have smoked cigarettes at least once.

➢ About half of the students in the majority of the countries have been smoking during the past 30 days.

➢ More than 90% of the students have been drinking alcohol, and in some countries almost all (98% in Greece, Latvia and the Slovak Republic) have done so at least 1–2 times in their lives.

A majority of students have tried smoking

To assess whether or not these students are representative of young people generally in Europe, you would have to ask if the latter share these characteristics.

Exam tip

When asked about representativeness, make sure that you identify the characteristic in the evidence or example and then assess whether this is typical of others.

Exercise 12

Based on the information given above, how representative do you think the findings of the European School Survey Project on Alcohol and Other Drugs will be? (Answers on page 163.)

With very large groups, there are more problems. For example, the editor of the girls' magazine *Bliss* said that a survey it did in 2005 on teenage sexual behaviour involved '2,000 girls spread across the UK, which we thought was a pretty representative sample'. It might be that the 2,000 were indeed representative, but we would need to know (rather than 'think'). In other words, we'd need to look at whether the 2,000 as far as possible mirrored girls generally in terms of education, occupation, regions, income levels, racial groups, religious groups and so on.

This is something that a good survey organisation is likely to get right. And, by getting it right, it doesn't necessarily need to survey 2,000 people. So, although you might be told that size matters, it's more quality that matters: quality of the sample surveyed in terms of known representativeness.

Exercise 13

Read each of the following passages. With each one, consider whether the evidence presented is sufficient for the conclusion that's drawn from it. In each case, you are looking at the issue of representativeness.

1 Experts at the University of Cambridge have concluded that brain-training games such as those sold by Nintendo are a waste of time and money. They studied 11,430 healthy people between the ages of 18 and 60. After doing a series of tests, these people completed a 6-week brain-training programme. At the end of this time, they did the tests again. It was found that there was no significant difference in their performance from the first to the second test.

Brain-training games — a waste of money?

2 Facebook has caused the big increase in syphilis in the UK. In the north-east (in places such as Sunderland, Durham and Teesside), there has been a fourfold increase in the number of young women with the disease, and several of them admitted they had met partners on social networking sites such as Facebook. Young people in the north-east were 25% more likely to log on to social networking sites than those in the rest of the country.

3 Parents should stop over-praising their children. All this 'that's brilliant darling' (when it isn't) and 'you're so clever' (when you're not) has the opposite effect to that intended. In one study of 400 nine-year-olds in New York, telling them the six words 'you are so smart at this' before a test reduced their scores by 20%. Given that this is just one short sentence, the effect of all the constant over-blown praising from effusive parents must have an even greater effect.

4 For the first time since records of this were kept in 2002, there are now more single men than single women in every age group except the over-75s in the UK. Given that the average age of first marriage is now 32 for men and 30 for women, this means that single women in the UK can afford to wait until Mr Right comes along.

5 In an 18-month study of juries in courts, a number of important findings have emerged. The study included 69,000 jury verdicts, nearly 800 jurors and 551,669

charges. One of the findings was that female jurors are more likely than male jurors to change their mind when the jury members discuss the case. Another was that some courts are more likely to commit than others. Teesside and Harrow have the highest conviction rates; Swansea and Preston have the lowest. This shows that the chances of a defendant being convicted can vary from place to place and from jury to jury.

Check your answers against on those on page 163.

Assessing the relevance of the sample

Here's some evidence being used to support an argument:

> Young women don't seem to have been influenced by campaigns to discourage them from sexual activity below the age of consent. In 1999, 25% of teenage girls had experienced underage sex. However, a 2006 poll carried out by Radio 1 found that, of the 16- to 24-year-olds surveyed, 30% had had underage sex.

What can we say about this statistical evidence?
➢ It is certainly **relevant** to the content of the conclusion (first sentence).
➢ Although we know something about the 2006 poll (it was carried out by Radio 1), we don't know anything about the 1999 one.
➢ However, with regard to the Radio 1 poll, we don't know how it was carried out and how many people were asked.
➢ There is a crossover period between the two polls that might or might not be relevant. Thus, some of those surveyed in 2006 might also have been included in the 1999 survey.

Key term
> **relevance:** how closely things relate to the same topic.

Does it matter that we don't know anything about the 1999 poll? Yes, it does. In order to evaluate the significance of statistical evidence, we need to know how the information was obtained (including the way in which the questions were asked and how many people were asked). For example, if the study was one in which young women filled in a questionnaire in a magazine, we could make at least two points. (1) It could be that the magazine's readership wasn't very typical of young women in general. In this way, distortion of the 'real' picture is probable. (2) It may be that those young women who actually responded to the questionnaire were not typical of the wider readership.

Exam tip

Relevance can be used to assess strength. Lack of relevance would indicate weakness, which may be only one of degree. Note that this is not the same as irrelevance, where there is absolutely no connection between the two things.

Although we know something about the 2006 poll, we still need to ask questions about how the evidence was collected:

➤ Was it a phone-in poll?
➤ Was it a text/e-mail poll?
➤ How many young women responded?
➤ Are those young women who listen to Radio 1 typical of all young women?
➤ More generally, are people who respond to radio polls more or less typical of the group from which they're drawn?

Another thing we can do is to look at the conclusion in relation to the evidence. The author sees the evidence as not only relevant to the conclusion, but also sufficient for it. We've already looked at why the evidence might have problems, but has the conclusion also got a problem?

> Young women don't seem to have been influenced by campaigns to discourage them from sexual activity below the age of consent.

Do the statistical data support the conclusion?

This conclusion needs specific statistical evidence, not necessarily given in the rest of the argument. Perhaps the best would be a well-constructed survey on the particular issue of the conclusion: evidence showing whether young women were or were not influenced by these campaigns. Without this, the author infers from the change from 25% to 30% of young women having underage sex, that the campaigns are not working. But, of course, we could look for alternative explanations here:

➤ Perhaps the campaigns are working with some young women in that, had there been no campaigns, the percentage would have been even higher than 30%.
➤ Perhaps the 1999 survey was inaccurate and the real figure was actually higher than 25% (perhaps even higher than 30%).
➤ Perhaps the 2006 survey was inaccurate and the real figure was actually lower than 30% (perhaps the same as or even lower than the 1999 survey).

(You might have seen that we're back into assumptions here, with the author having to assume that none of the above is actually true. Try the negative test on them to see.)

Assessing findings in terms of ambiguity

Look at the next two passages. The first is from the *Daily Mail* in 2007:

> Binge drinking is getting out of control in Britain. One in four adults in Britain are binge drinkers and the UK recently topped a poll as Europe's heaviest alcohol consumers.

The second is from someone called Colin from Newark who commented on the story on the newspaper's online comments forum:

> I see no harm in the occasional binge-drinking session. I do it about once a month and it's done me no harm.

Though both the *Daily Mail* and Colin from Newark talk about 'binge drinking', is it at all clear what it means?

How is the term used above?

➤ It's getting out of control in Britain.
➤ One in four British adults is a binge drinker.
➤ Colin from Newark goes binge drinking once a month and it does him no harm.

> **Key term**
> ➤ **ambiguity:** the problem of a word or findings having two or more possible interpretations, and it is not clear which is intended.

So what is getting out of control and what does Colin from Newark get up to once a month?

Exercise 14

Below is a list of ten possible definitions of binge drinking. Select those that you think have been used (there's more than one) in reports of the problem.

1   Drinking at least double the recommended safe limit for consumption.
2   Drinking that results in the drinker feeling at least partially drunk.
3   Heavy drinking over an evening or similar time span.
4   Drinking in order to get drunk.
5   Drinking such that the drinker feels very drunk at least once a month.
6   Continual drinking over a period of days by someone who is alcohol-dependent.
7   Drinking that results in the drinker vomiting.
8   Drinking over a period of time such that usual activities and obligations can't be carried out.
9   Five or more drinks in one session.
10 Ten or more drinks in one session.

Check your answers against on those on page 164.

As you will have seen in looking at the possible definitions of binge drinking in Exercise 14, we are going to have a problem in being able to deal with any arguments on the subject. Quite simply, unless an author makes it clear what they mean by the term, we don't know whether the argument works or not.

One approach would be to look for evidence that could help in clarifying or creating a definition:

➤ You will remember that the *Daily Mail* gave us this information:

> One in four adults in Britain are binge drinkers and the UK recently topped a poll as Europe's heaviest alcohol consumers.

It would appear that the second part of the evidence might be being used to support the previous claim about binge drinking. There could be problems with doing this. Even if the UK population is the heaviest consumer of alcohol, this does not translate into very high levels of binge drinking except, of course, if this provides the definition of binge drinking. People in the UK could drink the most in Europe but perhaps in ways that do not involve binge drinking.

➤ In October 2007, the *Liverpool Daily Post* called the city 'England's "capital of the binge culture"'. Why might it have given Liverpool that (presumably undesirable) title? Well, earlier in the month, evidence from the NHS showed that in 2005–06, Liverpool had the highest number of alcohol-related emergency hospital admissions of any English council (just ahead of Manchester).

➤ In 2007, the *Sun* carried the headline: 'Brit girls are binge drinking' over a photograph of a girl slumped on her back along a street bench. Then we're told:

> A girl lies limp on a bench, her fingers trailing the ground, empty bottles of alcopop by her feet. Yet nobody bats an eyelid as they walk past — it's a routine sight in town centres across the UK every weekend.

The evidence for binge drinking here is that it's 'routine' to find girls in this state every weekend. Binge drinking here has an assumed definition of something like 'drinking to a state of unconsciousness'.

➤ A report by the British Medical Association (BMA) on binge drinking is a good example of where the definition is built into the evidence:

> Recent data…show that, in younger age groups, women may now be binge drinking more often than men. Among 15 and 16 years olds in the UK, 26% of boys and 29% of girls reported having five or more drinks in a row at least three times during the last 30 days.

How is binge drinking defined?

In the evidence from the BMA we have now a better definition of binge drinking. (Although, as you will have spotted, we're back to the familiar problem of honesty. Might the boys and girls have been under-reporting, over-reporting, or indeed telling the truth?)

But, even with the clearer definition of the BMA, we still have a possible problem. What is meant by 'drinks'? (Cider, vodka, singles, doubles...?)

This is the problem of **ambiguity**. Trying to nail down a definition of 'binge drinking' turns out to be a big problem, with the term being used in various ways (especially regarding quantity and frequency). Sometimes (as you saw with binge drinking) the ambiguity can come from the difficulty of nailing down the meaning of a word or phrase, given that there could be two or more meanings.

Here's another example.

> It is argued that those people who object to big chains being allowed to open their stores in town centres are opposed to progress. But it's the exact opposite. Progress isn't about turning every town centre into a clone of every other. So, for the sake of real progress, opposition to allowing these big-name stores on to high streets should continue.

It's pretty clear that the word 'progress' is being used in reference to the counter-position and in the argument itself. The content of the term is, however, unclear.

Sometimes the ambiguity comes from the wording of a sentence itself, as in the following.

> Bill needs more difficult homework.
>
> Sue isn't working until six o'clock.
>
> They stopped the prisoners from escaping with the handcuffs.

Sometimes there is ambiguity in the way in which evidence is presented.

> Our research shows that in tests up to 84% of dogs tested preferred our new dog food.

This claim (a real one) tells us remarkably little. Just think why this is so.

Suggesting alternative interpretations of statistics

Authors often present evidence to support their conclusions. However, there is a weakness if statistics can be interpreted differently. Often you will be looking for a different cause. Take the following example:

> A US survey found that 23% of teenagers drinking one can of fizzy drinks carried a weapon and that rose to 43% when they consumed at least 14 of these drinks a week. A headline 'Fizzy drinks "boost gun crime risk"' appeared in relation to these statistics.

Is it possible that an alternative interpretation can be made of these statistics? The British Soft Drinks Association certainly thought so. They claimed that this, 'does not take into account family income and parenting practices, and so what it can tell us about the behaviour of teenagers is of limited value'. This in itself is a challenge rather than an alternative interpretation, but it does head us in the right direction. We could say that the type of teenager who exists on fizzy drinks as a large part of their diet might be more prone to gun crime if they lacked overall parental guidance. So, the fizzy drinks would be a symptom accompanying gun crime, the cause of both being lack of parental guidance.

> ### Exam tip
>
> When asked to evaluate statistical evidence, always consider questions about how the evidence was collected, and what different interpretations could be put on the evidence. You could put this in a hypothetical way by, for example, making the point that 'if the questions could result in misunderstanding, then…' and 'if the sample of respondents wasn't representative, then…'

Past paper practice 6

> ### OCR Unit F501, June 2010
>
> Look at Document 3, paragraph 2 in the Resource Booklet. Explain two ways in which this example might or might not be representative. Check your answers with those given on page 164.

Summary

> ➤ Assessing evidence can require looking at both strengths and weaknesses.
>
> ➤ However, you should look carefully at what the question is asking you to do. You may be asked for two weaknesses or two strengths, or one of each, or only one point of either. 'How far' means that you could use either or both strength and weakness.
>
> ➤ Sample size is not in itself an indication of strength or weakness, unless it was so small that it could not be representative.
>
> ➤ Representativeness involves identifying a characteristic in the evidence and asking whether this is shared by a related group.
>
> ➤ When discussing relevance, claiming that something is irrelevant often goes too far. A measured response would be to point out that lack of precise relevance weakens the reasoning.
>
> ➤ An alternative interpretation of statistics often involves looking for a different cause for an effect.

Chapter 7

Evaluation: the link between the reasoning and the conclusion

Learning objectives

By the end of this chapter, you will be able to:

➢ assess how far the reasoning is relevant

➢ assess how far the reasoning is adequate

➢ assess how far the conclusion is overdrawn

You need to remember that, in the sorts of arguments you will be dealing with, there is *always* an issue of whether the conclusion might need some other supporting reasoning. At most, you'll be able to say that the conclusion very probably follows from the reason (rather than it *must* follow).

So how should you judge whether reasons support conclusions?

> **Exam tip**
>
> You need to refer to the precise wording in the reasoning and the conclusion.
> It may be sufficient to refer only to one word in each. For example, reasoning about rising crime in 'urban' areas is not sufficient to draw the conclusion that we should 'all' be 'fearful of walking alone at night'.

Assessing how far the reasoning is relevant

A claim that is irrelevant to a conclusion will not add any strength to the argument:

> Plastic is an organic compound that can be used to create many different objects. We should support strategies designed to reduce our use of plastic shopping bags.

In this example, information on the nature and use of plastic does nothing in relation to the conclusion. The first claim is, in this way, irrelevant to the conclusion.

What about the following claim?

> In Ireland, a tax of 15 cents (about 13p) was put on all supermarket plastic bags, which led to a decrease of 90% in their use.

On its own, does this add anything? It is certainly relevant to the issue of strategies designed to reduce the use of plastic bags, in that it provides an example of a strategy that had some success. But it doesn't give a reason why we should support such strategies. Just because something can be done doesn't mean that it should be done. (For example, I could work out a strategy for banning people from noisily eating crisps in public, but that doesn't mean that crisp-eating should be banned.)

Thus, although the example of Ireland could play a part in dealing with a possible counter-argument that strategies don't work, putting this claim on its own as a reason for the conclusion is a problem:

> In Ireland, a tax of 15 cents (about 13p) was put on all supermarket plastic bags, which led to a decrease of 90% in their use. We should support strategies designed to reduce our use of plastic shopping bags.

So, one of the most effective ways that we can judge the power of reasons is to look for relevance. We need to focus very much on what the conclusion is about. In this case, it's about plastic bags but, essentially, it's about the need to *reduce* our use of them. That's the core point. So claims have to be relevant to that core point if they are to serve as good or strong reasons.

We can illustrate the importance of focusing on the specific wording of the conclusion by seeing how the example of Ireland supports a different conclusion:

> Ten billion plastic bags are handed out every year to UK shoppers (which is equivalent to 290 per person). Plastic bags are used in the UK for an average of 12 minutes (but take 500 years to degrade). We should support strategies designed to reduce our use of plastic shopping bags. In Ireland, a tax of 15 cents (about 13p) was put on all supermarket plastic bags, which led to a decrease of 90% in their use. Therefore the Government should tax plastic bags in order to help reduce their use.

This is impressive. The evidence of Ireland now works well as a reason for a new conclusion. It's focused on the two essential points of 'tax' and 'reduce'.

So when you're asked to evaluate the reasons used in an argument, one of the central things to look for is relevance in terms of the essential point of the conclusion. Relevant reasons contribute to the strength of the conclusion being drawn.

Assessing how far the reasoning is adequate

It might be useful to work backwards, starting with a conclusion and considering what reasons (including evidence) could support it. Here's the conclusion:

> We should support strategies designed to reduce our use of plastic shopping bags.

Now we'll look at some potential reasons for this conclusion. Here's the first:

> It used to be said that there weren't any options to plastic bags, but now there are plenty.

This both refers to and responds to a possible counter-position. In that sense, it might be seen as providing some strength to the conclusion. The weakness is that it doesn't explain why plastic bags are a problem. In other words, just because there are alternatives to plastic bags doesn't mean that we should use them. You can see that at least two assumptions are needed here to connect this as a reason with the conclusion:

➤ Plastic bags create problems.
➤ The alternatives to plastic bags do not have problems greater than those associated with plastic bags.

You can see that this first assumption will always be required if there is no reason given that details these problems.

We'll now look at a second possible reason:

> Ten billion plastic bags are handed out every year to UK shoppers (which is equivalent to 290 per person).

This has the same problem as the first statement. Alarming (and bizarre) though these statistics are, they're relevant only if, as before, plastic bags create problems. We could go with the simplest of the possible problems, that of waste (which must be a likely consequence of 10 billion bags).

In this connection, here's a third possible reason:

> Plastic bags are used in the UK for an average of 12 minutes (but take 500 years to degrade).

This has some strength as a reason in two ways. It picks up on the implied problem of waste in the second reason by giving us some possibly relevant detail (only 12 minutes of average use). It also gives us information that can be used directly to support the conclusion. This is that plastic bags 'take 500 years to degrade', which is a reason not to use them. (The weakness is that we don't know about the time needed for the alternatives to degrade. This would have to bring in the assumption that the alternatives do not take as long, or longer.)

Now we can see how claims can give strength to each other. If we put the second and third claim together, we can see how they can usefully act to support the conclusion:

> Ten billion plastic bags are handed out every year to UK shoppers (which is equivalent to 290 per person). Plastic bags are used in the UK for an average of 12 minutes (but take 500 years to degrade). We should support strategies designed to reduce our use of plastic shopping bags.

How should we reduce our use of plastic shopping bags?

Putting the two claims together as two reasons shows us the increased power of the two together.

Perhaps we could even add in the first claim we considered, now that we've provided the necessary reasoning to give it significance:

> Ten billion plastic bags are handed out every year to UK shoppers (which is equivalent to 290 per person). Plastic bags are used in the UK for an average of 12 minutes (but take 500 years to degrade). It used to be said that there weren't any options to plastic bags, but now there are plenty. We should support strategies designed to reduce our use of plastic shopping bags.

This claim about options other than plastic bags now works usefully with the conclusion. Because we have reasons not to use plastic bags, the existence of alternatives now more usefully supports the conclusion.

We have been looking at the issue of **adequacy** in judging reasons in an argument. You have seen that the claims can act as stronger reasons when used in conjunction with other claims. On their own, they were inadequate; together with additional reasoning, their adequacy increases.

It is useful to remind ourselves what we're doing when we're using the term 'adequacy'. Reasoning that is *entirely* adequate is not the sort you'll find when you're doing AS critical thinking.

An example would be the following:

Key term

> **adequacy:** the degree to which a reason provides support for a conclusion.

> All dogs have a much better sense of smell than humans do.
>
> Basset hounds are a type of dog.
>
> Therefore basset hounds have a much better sense of smell than humans do.

In this example, the two reasons are entirely adequate for the conclusion. If each reason is true, then the conclusion must be drawn from them (and no other reason is needed).

However, in the sorts of arguments that you'll be dealing with, the most you'll be looking at or for is increasing the adequacy of the reasoning.

Assessing how far the conclusion is overdrawn

You are familiar with the term 'drawing a conclusion'. Clearly, any conclusion can be drawn from any claim, even if it straightforwardly shouldn't be:

> Teachers get longer holidays than any other occupation. Therefore teachers will be the least stressed people in the country.

Are teachers the least stressed people in the country?

Even if the first claim is true (which it is), the conclusion doesn't usefully follow. The reason might well be relevant to a conclusion about stressful (or unstressful) occupations but it is not adequate. It is what we call an **overdrawn conclusion**.

The term 'overdrawn' is used to mean that more has been taken out of a bank account than was in there to be spent. In the same way, an overdrawn conclusion is one that has taken more out of the reason(s) than was available to be drawn from.

The more adequate and relevant the reasons, the more there is to be drawn from, just as the more money there is in a bank account, the more that can be spent. Again, as with bank accounts, there are degrees of being overdrawn. A conclusion can be very overdrawn if it goes much further than is available to be drawn from in the reasoning. Similarly, adding a further reason can reduce how far a conclusion can be overdrawn, just as adding money into a bank account will reduce the overdraft:

> Teachers get longer holidays than any other occupation. They are never more than six weeks away from their next holiday. Therefore teachers will be the least stressed people in the country.

Exam tip

When you're asked to assess how strongly reasons support a conclusion, you need to see this assessment in terms of how adequate and relevant the reasons are. Do the reasons support a different conclusion? What more is needed to better link the reasons to the conclusion?

You should not assess whether the claims are true or false, as the question is asking about the adequacy and relevance of what is given. You need to assess this on the basis that what you have been told is true.

Exercise 15

In this exercise, you are given a conclusion and possible reasoning to support it.

You need to consider each point of reasoning and work out whether it supports the conclusion.

The conclusion is concerned with the issue that, every October, the clocks are put back by 1 hour in the UK, with the effect that it gets darker an hour earlier. This practice was introduced in 1916.

Conclusion

We should no longer put back the clocks by 1 hour every October in the UK.

Forwards or backwards?

FOTOLIA

Reasoning

1 Many years ago most people used to get up at dawn to work on the fields.
2 Darker late afternoons in the winter in the UK have higher numbers of road accidents than the afternoons in the weeks before the change in the clocks.
3 People don't exercise so much in winter.
4 By changing the clocks in October, the UK has a different time to the rest of Europe.
5 Some people like getting up early ('larks') and some people like staying up late ('owls').
6 A much higher proportion of criminal offences that are committed in semi-darkness occur at dusk rather than at dawn.
7 Children come home from school in darkness or semi-darkness during the winter.

Check your answers against on those on page 165.

Past paper practice 7

OCR Unit F501, June 2011

Look at Document 1, paragraph 6 in the Resource Booklet. Assess how strongly the reasoning gives support to the conclusion 'allotment-grown food is the best way to eat locally'. You should make two developed points that refer directly to the links between the reasoning and the conclusion.

Check your answer with that given on page 165.

Summary

➢ You should assess the link between the reasoning and the conclusion and not the reasoning in isolation.

➢ You should make reference to specific words in the reasoning and the conclusion that form the link.

➢ Overdrawn conclusions with related lack of relevance and adequacy are likely to help you identify points as are finding assumptions.

➢ This task should not involve assessing whether the reasoning is true or false.

Chapter 8

Developing reasoning: giving reasons to support a conclusion

Learning objectives

By the end of this chapter, you will be able to:

➤ give a relevant reason of your own to support a given conclusion

➤ do this without adding any extra argument elements

Giving a reason of your own to support a given conclusion

You need to consider what reason(s) would support a given conclusion which has not already been argued for.

A useful approach to this is to try to come up with relevant points and then turn these into reasons.

Here's an example.

Given conclusion People who put graffiti on public property should be punished severely.

What sort of points would be relevant to this conclusion?

➤ the cost of removing the graffiti
➤ graffiti can be offensive
➤ the need to stop people from putting graffiti on public property
➤ the effect of graffiti on neighbourhoods

These points can then be developed into reasons.

➤ The cost of removing graffiti is very high.
➤ Graffiti often offends lots of people.
➤ People who spray graffiti on public property need to be deterred from doing so.
➤ Graffiti on public property can make an area look run-down.

As you can see, each of these reasons can support the conclusion. The third one specifically addresses the words 'should be punished severely' with the others giving reasons why the punishment of people who spray graffiti on public property is justified.

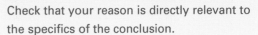
What is the effect of graffiti on neighbourhoods?

Exam tip

Check that your reason is directly relevant to the specifics of the conclusion.

So if you need to think of reasons to support an already given claim that will act as a conclusion, it's helpful to start by just thinking of points that would be relevant. Then you can focus these points into reasons.

Giving a reason without adding any extra argument elements

This is a technical question, which examines whether you can give a relevant reason without any extra argument elements. Here is a possible question:

Give an additional reason to support the possible claim that, 'the rise in undergraduate tuition fees will discourage potential students from applying to university'.

See if you can spot the mistakes in the following answers:

1 Students cannot afford to pay higher tuition fees, because their loans are not also being increased in line with this.
2 Students cannot afford to pay back increased debts, which are brought about by higher tuition fees.
3 Students cannot afford to pay back higher tuition fees, such as the £9,000 now being charged by most universities.

You probably spotted that the first answer is an argument. The 'because' gives this away. It contains a conclusion followed by a reason. The second tacks an explanation onto the reason, while the third includes an example, signposted by the argument indicator words, 'such as'. In this question, you need to stop at the end of the reason, even though it may be tempting to make it sound better by adding other argument elements. An answer, 'Students with limited funds will not be able to afford the increased debt,' would gain full marks.

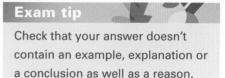

Exam tip

Check that your answer doesn't contain an example, explanation or a conclusion as well as a reason.

Past paper practice 8

OCR Unit F501, June 2011

Suggest one reason of your own to support a possible claim:

It is more difficult to grow your own food in an allotment, than in your own garden.

You must only give a reason and not add other argument elements.

Check your answer with that given on page 166.

Summary

➢ When thinking of a reason, make sure that it relates directly to the specifics of the conclusion that you are given.

➢ If the conclusion given includes a comparison, make sure that your reason includes a comparator word, for example 'more', 'greater', 'less'.

➢ Make sure that you stop at the end of the reason and don't go on to add further argument elements, such as examples.

Chapter 9

Putting your skills together: Unit 1, Section A

You are now half way through the skills required for Unit 1. Here is a chance to consolidate your learning, before you go on to develop the skills required for Section B: Credibility. You can test out your skills by answering the practice exam-style questions below for Section A.

However, just before you attempt these questions:

➤ Look back at the tracking sheet for Section A on page 3 and re-visit those skills which you identified in red as needing further practice. Read the relevant examples in this book to see if you can gain a firmer grasp of these skills.

➤ Then look back at the table on page 12 and see if you can remember the definitions and group the indicator words to the argument elements.

Test your skills with practice exam-style questions

Now see if you can answer the practice exam-style questions. When you have completed them, look at the answers on page 166 and to use the guidance to hone up your skills.

This should give you a good foundation in targeting the skills required, after which you could attempt to answer past examination papers from OCR. You can download these and the mark schemes free from the exam board website at:

www.ocr.org.uk/qualifications/type/gce/hss/critical_thinking/documents/

Practice exam-style questions

Unit 1, Section A

Analysing argument

Read the following paragraph then answer questions 1 to 5.

You shouldn't drive any vehicle, including cars and lorries, while using a mobile phone, as your full attention can't be given to both phoning and driving at the same time. Despite the fact that many people think it's safe, as they do it every day without any problems, it's actually against the law and it's the cause of many accidents. Disturbingly, AA reports show that they are called out to a growing number of mobile-phone-related accidents on a weekly basis, among which are those caused by drivers phoning business clients.

1 State the main conclusion of the argument in the passage.

2 State **two** argument indicator words that are used in the passage.

3 State the reason given in the counter-argument.

4 State the evidence given in the passage.

5 'those (accidents) caused by drivers phoning business clients'
  (a) Name the argument element used.
  (b) Explain your answer.

Identifying assumptions

State one assumption that is needed to support the following argument:

We should close up the greenhouse tonight, as there was a definite frost early this morning.

Assessing evidence

'Staybright toothpaste will make your teeth look cleaner for longer.'

In a recent trial, 90% of students taking part claimed that their mouths felt fresher for a greater part of the day. The trial involved over 5,000 British students studying in five different major universities.

Explain **two** ways in which the evidence might give **weak support** to the claim 'Staybright toothpaste will make your teeth look cleaner for longer'. You should use two of the following criteria to help you to evaluate the evidence.
  ➤ Representativeness
  ➤ Relevance
  ➤ Alternative interpretation of statistics

Assessing the link between reasoning and conclusion

Consider the argument presented in the following passages. Assess how strongly the reasoning supports the main conclusion. You should give one strength and one weakness for each argument.

1 If employees want to eat healthy food they should buy their meals from the canteen, as it now offers low-fat options. There are also more tables to accommodate the larger workforce and the menus are very competitively priced.

2 Sleep trials have shown very clearly that teenagers need 8 hours' sleep a night in order for their brains to function at their best. So, students clearly need to restrict having late nights out to the weekend.

(Adapted from OCR materials, 2010)

Check your answers against those on page 166.

Chapter 10

Introduction to credibility

Learning objectives

By the end of this chapter, you will be able to:

➤ define credibility

➤ identify how it is assessed in Section B

The title for Section B of OCR's Unit 1 Critical Thinking is 'Credibility'. Credibility is the focus of the whole of Section B, so it is very important that you are clear about what this involves.

Defining credibility

Credibility simply means 'believability'.

When assessing a claim in an argument, or a source such as a document or a person or organisation, one of the central questions to ask (and answer) is 'how believable is this?'

This is particularly important when trying to decide who to believe:

➤ in a dispute such as some divorce or criminal proceedings

➤ when people have different interpretations of what happened in an event, such as war reports or accounts of natural disasters

➤ when people are putting forward different recommendations, such as how to make savings in public services or how to address a problem

The issue of credibility very much affects the possible importance of claims and sources. If a claim is made by a credible source, then its credibility increases (and so too does its possible importance). On the other hand, if a claim is made by a source that is not believable, then its credibility decreases (and so too does its possible importance).

However, being 'credible' or 'not credible' does not mean that a statement is 'true' or 'false'. A statement can be credible/believable but false, or not credible/unbelievable but actually true. All that we are being asked to do, when assessing credibility in Section B, is to determine whether or not a statement is believable by looking at its source.

The following activity is designed to help you to explore the skills required when assessing credibility. It looks at an incident where people have different interpretations of what happened.

Activity 5

As a group activity, read the document on the next page relating to a traffic accident. Use the questions below to guide your discussions. The *'and why'* in each of the questions is important as this will justify your assessment. See if others in the group used the same justifications.

Questions

Looking at the document itself
1 How far would you believe what this document/the author claims, and why?

Looking at the claims within the document
2 Whose evidence would you believe and why?
3 Whose evidence might you doubt and why?
4 Are there any claims that conflict (both can't be true at the same time)?

Making an overall judgement
5 Who do you think was most likely to blame for the accident and why?

Check your answers with the guidance on page 168.

Was the Renault driver or the van driver at fault?

Yet another accident on the new link road

Yesterday the accident, involving a Renault and a Ford transit van on the new roundabout linking the Cornish market town of Littlebrook with the by-pass, marked the 20th such incident since the link road opened a year ago. Although a minor incident, it should make planners re-visit the road layout, as the situation can only get worse with increasing traffic.

Who was responsible was not immediately clear.

The driver of the Renault claimed, 'It was 8.55am and I was already pressed for time because of the amount of traffic. The driver of the van in front of me in the queue approaching the roundabout reversed into me with such sudden force that he split my number plate. He didn't even acknowledge what had happened. He just drove away, but I was quick enough to write down his registration number.'

However, the company van driver claimed, 'The Renault drove into the back of me when I stopped pulling onto the roundabout, as some silly fool sped out of the blind junction to my right. You could see that the Renault had had a previous history of bad driving from all its dents and scrapes. It was annoying, but it was only a bump. Not what you would call an accident.'

A witness in the queue added, 'The queue had been stopping and starting for several minutes. I was a couple of cars behind the Renault and saw its driver get out and wave their arms angrily, but the van driver just drove away. The van driver must have been at fault. When the Renault pulled to the side and I drove past, I realised that its driver had been a colleague of mine. He was top of his profession and was known not to take unnecessary risks.'

When we phoned the company employing the van driver the manager stated, 'The company is not aware of any accident and there is no damage to the company van. The driver has been with us for many years and has never had an accident, so I find it very hard to believe that he caused an accident and didn't stop. Driving carefully is part of his job, as he transports very fragile goods.'

(littlebrook.campaignforsaferroads.co.uk)

Assessing credibility

Your discussions will have involved you in some of the following skills, each of which we will develop in the chapters that follow.

Assessing credibility using criteria

When you were making your judgements about credibility, how did you decide who to believe? You might have found that some individuals were more believable because they could see what happened more clearly than others, or that some had more of a motive to misrepresent what happened than others. Chapter 11 will help you to firm up the standards by which you assess credibility. These are called **credibility criteria**. You can use these to assess the credibility of documents (developed in Chapter 12) and the credibility of claims (developed in Chapter 13).

Weighing up the credibility of individual sources

When you were discussing the claims of different individuals, you might have found that they had points that weakened their credibility and points that strengthened their credibility. For example, one person might clearly have had the opportunity to see what happened which strengthened the credibility of their claim, but at the same time had a strong motive to misrepresent what happened, which weakened the credibility of their claim. Chapter 13 will help you to develop the skill of weighing up the credibility of a source.

Weighing up the relative credibility of the two sides

You might have tried to consider the bigger picture by looking at all the sources that supported each side in the dispute. In doing this you would have been assessing collective credibility. Chapter 16 will help you to develop these skills.

Identifying corroboration, consistency and inconsistency

You might have noticed that some claims supported each other while others could not both be held to be true at the same time. Chapter 14 will help you to spot such claims.

Judging plausibility

When you asked questions about what was the most likely thing to have happened in this accident, you would have been considering **plausibility**. Chapter 15 will explain this further and Chapter 16 will help you to judge the relative plausibility of two possible outcomes or interpretations.

As an introduction to these skills, look at some preliminary observations on page 168 to check these against those you made about the traffic incident.

Identifying the skills required in Section B

Whereas the Section A questions concentrate on analysis and evaluation of argument, the Section B questions deal with issues of credibility. There are fewer questions in this section and the questions involve longer answers that require you to assess credibility and come to judgements based on this.

The skills assessed on the exam paper match those identified above when considering the traffic accident.

In Section B, credibility is assessed by asking questions about:
➤ the believability of documents
➤ the believability of claims
➤ the wider picture, so that you can also identify corroboration, consistency and inconsistency
➤ the likely outcome, by making an overall judgement based on the credibility of each side and the plausibility of alternative outcomes

Past paper practice 9

OCR Unit F501, January 2012

Look at this exam paper on micro-chipping dogs and use it to identify where the above credibility skills are tested. Look carefully at the wording of the questions in Section B to work out what skills you need to answer each question.

Check your findings against those given on page 169. Use the chapters that follow to help you to develop those skills.

Summary

➤ Credibility means believability.

➤ There are criteria to help assess credibility.

➤ These can be used to assess the credibility of sources and their claims.

➤ Section B involves longer questions intended to gradually build up your assessment of the credibility of the sources and their claims, so that you can make a judgement about the overall issue.

Chapter 11

Credibility criteria

Learning objectives

By the end of this chapter, you will be able to:

➤ select and apply relevant credibility criteria

➤ assess motive using bias, vested interest, reputation and neutrality

➤ assess perception using an ability to perceive, and expertise and experience

Selecting and applying relevant credibility criteria

In the previous chapter we saw that a **credibility criterion** is a standard by which the believability of sources and their claims can be assessed. There are two important questions that need to be answered here:

➤ Does the source have any possible motive to misrepresent the situation?

➤ Does the source have the ability to perceive and interpret the situation correctly?

The credibility criteria that can help you to assess each of these are explained below.

> **Key term**
> ➤ **credibility criterion:** a standard that can be used to judge the believability of a source and their claims (plural *credibility criteria*).

> **Exam tip**
>
> You need to make sure that you know the credibility criteria by name and can use them explicitly and appropriately in your answers in Section B. You can use the mnemonic RAVEN to help you to remember them:
>
> **R**eputation
>
> **A**bility to perceive (see, hear etc.)
>
> **V**ested interest
>
> **E**xpertise/experience
>
> **N**eutrality (lack of bias or vested interest/bias (lack of neutrality)

Assessing possible motive

In this section we look at how a source's claims may be influenced by motive, resulting in possible distortions, omissions and even lies! These would weaken the credibility of the claims, whereas the absence of a motive to misrepresent the situation would strengthen the credibility.

The credibility criteria associated with motive are:

➤ bias
➤ vested interest
➤ reputation
➤ neutrality (lack of motive whether bias or vested interest)

Assessing possible motive: bias

The criterion of **bias** can be used to identify the tendency to favour:

> **Key term**
> ➤ **bias:** the tendency of a source (individual or organisation) to present or interpret claims selectively because of a position that they favour.

A person, e.g. a friend

Looking back at the traffic accident described on page 72, did you spot anyone who might be biased? The witness in the queue might have been biased in favour of his colleague because of the view that he had of him, as a person who was not known to take a risk. This might have led him to believe that the Renault car driver waving his arms was doing this because he was innocent.

A position taken, e.g. for or against animal experimentation

See the examples below — the positions taken by the Huntingdon Life Sciences (HLS) organisation and the pressure group Stop Huntingdon Animal Cruelty (SHAC).

The bias will be the *reason* for being selective in what is said or not said.

Bias in favour of a particular position

People, whether they are speaking as an individual or as an organisation, have beliefs, values and preferences which lead them to be in favour of some things rather than others. This may be a deliberate choice or a subconscious preference. This is particularly obvious when we look at pressure groups and organisations with a particular aim. We would expect, for example, that:

➤ HLS, which carries out research using experiments on animals, would always favour the argument that animal experiments are necessary for medical science. It is straightforwardly biased in that direction.
➤ Similarly, SHAC would be straightforwardly biased in the opposite direction — that is, against using experiments on animals.

Exam tip

If you use the criterion of bias, you need to explain why a particular source is biased. It is not enough to say that it is.

Bias as being selective

The consequence of favouring one side is that they will probably be selective about the information they present. This can sometimes be called 'cherry-picking', where individuals or organisations choose only the most favourable parts of a case in order to argue for their position. They leave out important information that would weaken their case. This might be a simple subconscious preference relating to the way that they view things.

Exam tip

In explaining how a source has shown that it is biased, you need to point out what has been selected and what has been left out.

Both HLS and SHAC will make claims ('cherry-pick') based on selective evidence, *because* they come to the debate from a particular position. Each of these two organisations holds particular views about animal experimentation.

HLS says about itself:

It is our job to ensure that these tests are **performed to strict scientific criteria**, provide reliable results that can be reproduced, and with **leading standards of animal care and welfare**. This places an important burden of responsibility upon us, one which we do not take lightly. We have to **respect the needs of the animals** and be fully aware of the welfare issues involved. We are committed to providing the **highest levels of animal husbandry and welfare.**

www.huntingdon.com

However, SHAC says about HLS:

Huntingdon Life Sciences (HLS) are the largest contract testing laboratory in Europe. They have about 70,000 animals on site, including rabbits, cats, hamsters, dogs, guinea-pigs, birds and monkeys. **These animals are destined to suffer and die in cruel, useless experiments.**

HLS will test anything for anybody. They carry out **experiments which involve poisoning animals** with household products, pesticides, drugs, herbicides, food colourings and additives, sweeteners and genetically modified organisms. **Every three minutes an animal dies** inside Huntingdon totalling 500 innocent lives every single day.

www.shac.net

Both sides agree that animals are used in the work carried out by HLS, but their claims about how this is carried out are very different. HLS omits to mention the scale of deaths and SHAC does not deal with scientific practice.

Summing up, bias can help us assess selective accounts in which the selectivity is as *a result of* being predisposed to a particular position.

SHAC are against using experiments on animals

Activity 6

In groups, use the internet to find an organisation or a pressure group (a group that works to benefit some individuals or to bring about — or stop — certain policies). Present a selection of their materials to the rest of the class. Without naming the organisation, get the class to identify what position is being favoured and to work out how the organisation might have been selective in what it has put forward.

Assessing possible motives: vested interest

How is **vested interest** different from the criterion of bias?

The key difference is that someone may have a vested interest when there is something to be gained, or a loss to be prevented. Bias, on the other hand, relates to situations where any selectivity does not relate to personal gain or loss involved. In the traffic incident (page 72), the witness had nothing to gain by defending his former colleague.

Key term

➤ **vested interest:** *either* a motive to misrepresent the situation for personal gain or to prevent a loss, *or* a motive to represent the situation accurately, again for personal gain or to prevent a loss.

Exam tip

If the motive is to prevent loss or for gain, the appropriate credibility criterion to choose is vested interest, not bias.

Vested interest to lie weakens credibility

In this case the vested interest leads to making distorted claims. The motive could be for financial gain such as an insurance claim that exaggerates damage and losses. Alternatively the motive could be to prevent a loss, such as a report distorting what happened in a car accident to avoid losing a no-claims discount.

In the traffic accident you probably identified that the credibility of both the evidence of the Renault car driver and that of the van driver would be weak if they were the guilty party. If guilty, they would have a motive to misrepresent the situation in order to avoid being held responsible for the damage caused. As the van driver was driving a company van, there might also have been a motive to avoid possible negative consequences with their employer.

We saw that HLS was likely to be biased in the way that it dealt with claims about animal experimentation. However, this selectivity could also be motivated by vested interest as it has a financial interest in its position being presented and accepted, because it earns its money this way. If a source can be assessed with both the criteria of bias and vested interest, it is important that you use these correctly. If the motive is connected with gain or preventing loss, you need to use the criterion of vested interest.

An interesting example of vested interest is a court case in the United States in 2005:

> The trial was of Timothy Wilkins who was accused of acting as a drug mule (someone who carries drugs for others).
>
> The psychologist appointed by the defence reported to the court that Mr Wilkins had an IQ of 58 and so, because he did not understand the court proceedings, should not stand trial.
>
> However, the psychologist appointed by the prosecution reported to the court that Mr Wilkins had an IQ of 88 and so, because he understood the proceedings, should stand trial.
>
> The judge ruled out both reports because, as he put it, they 'cancelled each other out'.
> Mr Wilkins' lawyer agreed. 'One's biased for the defence. The other's biased for the state.
> I think it's who's signing their pay check.'

Here the motive is vested interest, as the psychologists are interpreting the data in order to gain the effect either that the accused should or should not stand trial.

Vested interest to tell the truth strengthens credibility

Alternatively, the motive may be to tell the truth, because of a particular benefit. We can think of plenty of examples in which vested interest will lead someone to tell the truth. There may be a vested interest to tell the truth because the consequences of being found to be lying would be negative, such as loss of professionalism.

It is important to refer to this as a vested interest to tell the truth to prevent loss of 'professionalism' and not 'reputation', as we often do not know the reputation of individuals or organisations (unless of course this is specifically stated in the text). 'Professionalism' refers to the general qualities or typical features of a career or occupation. Honesty, accuracy and impartiality might be some of the common general characteristics expected to be held. Thus without knowledge of a specific reputation it might be reasonably claimed that professionals would not wish to misrepresent a situation for fear of making their line of work look disreputable.

This might be the case with police officers and people in high places. However, it is by no means certain which groups might be regarded as having a positive professionalism. Presumably medical doctors might be seen as having this (despite examples such as Andrew Wakefield, the doctor who caused the worry over the MMR vaccine, and the serial killer Harold Shipman). What about the police? Presumably here there is a mixture of both positive and negative professionalism. What about nurses? Generally we hope for positive professionalism, although some scandals about the treatment of vulnerable people have emerged. Social workers? (Baby P etc? Not such good press about some social workers.) MPs? (A bit of a mixture there.) Teachers?

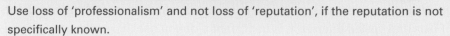

Exam tip

Use loss of 'professionalism' and not loss of 'reputation', if the reputation is not specifically known.

Summing up:

➢ A person or organisation with a good reputation might have a vested interest to tell the truth, in order not to damage that reputation and risk loss of public confidence. Established organisations in the public eye might fall into this category.

➢ Somebody with a strong belief in the need to always tell the truth would feel very upset by having to lie.

➢ An organisation might have a vested interest to tell the truth because the truth is beneficial to that organisation (and/or damaging to a rival organisation).

Exam tip

Vested interest can both strengthen and weaken a claim because there could be a vested interest to tell the truth as well as a vested interest to lie.

Exercise 16

Consider the following case that illustrates both bias and vested interest. As you read through it, see if you can identify where each might occur.

Derek Bentley

In this famous case, Derek Bentley was hanged at the age of 19 for a murder carried out by his younger accomplice, Christopher Craig. Although both Craig and Bentley were found guilty of murder, Craig was too young to be executed.

Derek Bentley

The bare details of the case are that on the night of 2 November 1952, when Craig and Bentley were seen trying to break into a warehouse, the police were called and quickly captured Bentley. While being held by the police, he was supposed to have shouted 'Let him have it, Chris'. You can, as so many have, consider the possible ambiguity of the words — did he mean 'Shoot him, Chris' or 'Let him have the gun, Chris'. However, at the trial, there was a dispute that the words were said at all.

At the end of the trial, Lord Chief Justice Goddard, the trial judge, gave this summing-up to the jury:

'The police officers that night, and those three officers in particular, showed the highest gallantry and resolution; they were conspicuously brave. Are you going to say they are conspicuous liars? Because if their evidence is untrue that Bentley called out "Let him have it, Chris" those three officers are doing their best to swear away the life of that boy.

'If it is true, it is, of course, the most deadly piece of evidence against him. Do you believe that those three officers have come into the box and sworn what is deliberately untrue; those three officers who on that night showed such a devotion to duty for which they are entitled to the thanks of the community?'

Summarising Bentley's defence and denial of those words, the trial judge said:

'Against that denial, which of course is the denial of a man in grievous peril, you will consider the evidence of the three police officers who have sworn to you positively that those words were said.'

Now check your answers against those on page 169.

Exam tip

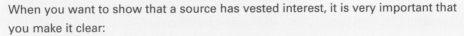

When you want to show that a source has vested interest, it is very important that you make it clear:

➢ **Why it has** vested interest. It is not enough just to claim that '*x* has vested interest'. You need to explain what the benefit will be.

➢ **What this vested interest leads to**, e.g. misrepresenting the situation or reporting it accurately.

Assessing possible motive: reputation

The credibility criterion of **reputation** is unusual in that:

➢ it is based on another's judgement of the source

➢ it is used on the basis of past performance.

Both of these need careful consideration.

Key term

➢ **reputation:** the judgement made by others of the trustworthiness or reliability of a source. In some cases, the judgement of reputation (especially a good one) might be self-acclaimed, i.e. made by the individual or organisation itself, stressing their own reputation for such things as fairness, honesty or expert service.

Where did the reputation come from?

In the first instance, we need to consider where the reputation came from.

Someone else

Can we trust the judgement of this further source? This begins to be a double credibility exercise. The credibility of the source becomes dependent upon the credibility of the person giving the reputation. In the traffic incident the company manager gave the company van driver a reputation:

> 'The driver has been with us for many years and has never had an accident, so I find it very hard to believe that he caused an accident and didn't stop. Driving carefully is part of his job, as he transports very fragile goods.'

We might want to ask whether the company manager had a vested interest to say this in order to persuade others that the van driver was innocent. The motive would be so that the company would not have to pay out on their insurance for the accident, if the van driver was to blame. Using 'reputation' as a credibility criterion can, then, be a tricky business, where someone else's testimony is involved.

The source themselves

There is also a problem if the reputation is self-acclaimed. This is where the source gives information about themselves. We often see this in the 'About us' section on websites. Should we question a self-acclaimed reputation, if this is not supported by an independent source? The answer is inevitably 'yes', as the source will have a vested interest to make the most of what they have done in order to make people trust them. The credibility becomes circular, as we are asked to believe the credibility of the source because of things which they claim about themselves.

Past paper practice 10

OCR Unit F501, January 2009

Look at Document 2 from this exam paper: 'Ecotowns: Helping to deliver a change in the quality and availability of homes for the people of England'. It comes from the Town and Country Planning Association. If you read the note below the text, you will find what they say about themselves:

'We are an independent charity that inspires government, industry and campaigners to take a fresh perspective on major issues, including climate change and regeneration.'

How would you assess this in terms of reputation? When you have written down an answer, compare it with that given on page 170.

Does past performance indicate that we should believe that this will continue?

Second, we need to consider that when the criterion of reputation is used, we're saying that what happened in the past affects our judgement of the present credibility of a source.

We might say, 'The BBC has a good reputation for being fair in its reporting of the Middle East as seen in its refusal to broadcast an appeal for a Palestinian fund'. (This was in January 2009. The BBC and Sky refused to broadcast an appeal for aid for the Palestinian area of Gaza. Both the BBC and Sky argued that it was important to be seen as impartial in Israel's conflict with the Palestinians.) In this example, the *previous* behaviour of the BBC is being used as evidence for a *present* judgement of them being unbiased. To make this assessment we would need to be certain that BBC policies had not changed.

Past paper practice 11

OCR Unit F501, January 2010

Consider the provenance (information written about the organisation making the claims) of Document 2 in this exam paper. This extract from AA.com gives the following information about itself:

'Looking after the interests of its members as motorists has been at the heart of the AA since it was founded in 1905. With such a long pedigree in motoring affairs, it's no surprise that the AA is looked to by government, decision makers and politicians to help guide policy.'

Can you spot the two problems if you were to use reputation as a credibility criterion here? What would you have to add to your assessments to make them sound convincing? You may find it helpful to use hypothetical reasoning: 'If... then...'.

Compare your answers with those given on page 170.

Summing up, using 'reputation' as a credibility criterion can be a problem in that you are likely to have to justify why you think that a source has a good or a bad reputation. You can justify this in terms of how the source is seen (by the public, fellow experts, and so on) and/or how its past performance has contributed to the reputation (good or bad).

Exam tip

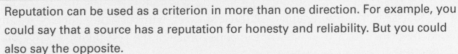

Reputation can be used as a criterion in more than one direction. For example, you could say that a source has a reputation for honesty and reliability. But you could also say the opposite.

Exam tip

Reputation could be linked to vested interest either as a known reputation or as 'professionalism', in wanting to maintain this by telling the truth.

Assessing possible motive: neutrality

This is a lack of motive either to be selective in what is said or to distort the claims in order to benefit from them. In many ways it is the opposite of both bias and vested interest. Someone or some organisation that is not biased will be seen as **neutral**. An account of something that is not selective will also be seen as neutral.

> **Key term**
> ➢ **neutrality:** being impartial, such that a neutral source has no reason to favour either side in a dispute.

Roles that involve neutrality

➢ An obvious example of what is meant by being neutral is a referee or umpire in sport, or a judge of events such as gymnastics, tennis and rugby. The role of a referee or umpire is to implement the rules of the game and to make an independent (unbiased) judgement of how those rules apply to specific cases in a game. For example, whether or not a player is 'time-wasting', and whether or not a player deliberately fouled another, are both examples in which an unbiased judgement is required. The importance of neutrality for judges of sporting events when they have to give a score was highlighted in the 2002 Winter Olympics. It was discovered that the French judge in the figure-skating event had been 'pressured' by the Russian judge to vote highly for a Russian competitor. This lack of neutrality undermines the whole process of judging.

The blindfold symbolises the supposed neutrality of the law

➢ Another example of neutrality is a driving-test examiner. The role of the examiner is to assess the driving ability of the test-taker, without being affected by any other factors (such as age, gender or the appearance of the test-taker).

➢ A further example is a trial judge. The symbol of justice is of a female figure holding a sword and a pair of scales. The sword represents the power of the law to punish. The scales symbolise the way in which courts should operate, by judging according to the weight of evidence. But there is another feature of the figure: sometimes she is blindfolded. This emphasises what is supposed to be the neutrality of the law. Judgements should be made independently of anything but the evidence.

Think back to the Derek Bentley case: the Lord Chief Justice Goddard was described as giving an 'extraordinarily biased summing-up'. The same author who said this about him also made the following point:

> Lord Chief Justice Goddard ignored completely one of the most fundamental rules of a jury trial, that the judge must be impartial and balanced at all times.
>
> L Klein, *A Very English Hangman*, Corvo, 2006, p.117

Summing up, if we identify sources (whether a person, people, or an organisation) as neutral, then we are claiming that they have (or have had) no links with either side of a dispute that could affect their position.

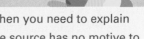

Exam tip

If you want to use the criterion of neutrality with a source, then you need to explain why this source is neutral. This will involve showing that the source has no motive to distort the truth.

The use of neutral evidence

The evidence of a source we can identify as neutral might still be used in a biased way. For example, we might find that evidence collected and analysed by a neutral source is selectively used in support of the position of another source.

Activity 7

As a group make a list of jobs, roles or materials that have neutrality as their key focus. Compare your list with the one on page 170.

Assessing possible perception

So far we have looked at the credibility criteria associated with a source having a motive to distort or present the truth accurately. We will now go on to look at whether they have what it takes to perceive and interpret the situation correctly.

Everyone has a filtering system by which they experience and interpret the world and this affects the credibility of their claims.

The credibility criteria associated with how a person perceives an event are:

➤ the **ability to perceive**, to see/hear/feel — in fact any of the senses

➤ expertise/experience

Key term

➤ **ability to perceive:** a source's ability to see, hear, touch, taste or smell when assessing an experience relevant to a claim.

Assessing possible perception: ability to perceive

The ability to perceive can also be described as the 'ability to observe'.

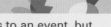

> **Exam tip**
>
> Ability to perceive can be applied not only to being an eye-witness to an event, but also to a source's access to reports, statistics or specialist materials.

How are we meant to use this criterion?

How much did they see?

The most obvious way when referring to someone who saw, heard, etc. something (especially an event) is to ask whether they were sufficiently close to it. You will often see on TV that, when a report is being given of an event such as an accident, the reporter will interview someone who claims to have seen it happen. That person's evidence is seen as especially important. In many ways, of course, it is.

However, there may be limitations with such evidence because even those who were sufficiently close to experience an event might have experienced only a part of it. They could also have been distracted by something during the event. They might even have been distressed or confused by things that were happening. All of these things can weaken or strengthen the credibility of a person's report.

How accurately did they remember it?

To make things potentially even more of a problem, someone might remember what they experienced in a selective way. These problems could seriously weaken the importance of the criterion of the ability to perceive.

The Derek Bentley case provides a very good example of this. Both Craig and Bentley, and the police officers, were there on the roof of the warehouse. So, in a very real sense, they were all able to tell the court what (really) happened. The fact that they disagreed so fundamentally shows that, even with a strong ability to perceive (in this case, to hear), other criteria might reduce the power of this criterion.

> **Exam tip**
>
> When using the criterion of the ability to perceive, you need to consider how strongly it can be applied. Just being in the vicinity of an incident does not mean that someone had a strong ability to perceive.

Here is another example that shows this.

As you probably know, the *Titanic* sank in 1912 with the loss of 1,517 lives. After the sinking, three inquiries were held into why the ship (which shouldn't have sunk) sank. One of the questions that the inquiries tried to answer was: 'Did the *Titanic* sink intact or did it break in two before it sank?' Here is the evidence given by two eye-witnesses, who give two very different and conflicting accounts of what happened.

Charles Herbert Lightoller, 2nd Officer on Collapsible B

Senator SMITH   Was the vessel broken in two in any manner, or intact?

Mr LIGHTOLLER   Absolutely intact.

Senator SMITH   On the decks?

Mr LIGHTOLLER   Intact, sir.

Frank Osman, Seaman in Lifeboat 2

Mr OSMAN   We pulled astern that way again, and after we got astern we lay on our oars and saw the ship go down. After she got to a certain angle she exploded, broke in halves, and it seemed to me as if all the engines and everything that was in the after part slid out into the forward part, and the after part came upright again, and as soon as it came upright down it went again.

In both cases confusion, fear and panic may have coloured the perception of the sources.

Activity 8

One hundred years after the sinking of the *Titanic*, in January 2012 a cruise ship, the *Costa Concordia*, sank off the coast of Tuscany during the night. Use the internet to find five accounts of what happened. Use a variety of sources, for example a passenger, a cruise crew member, a helicopter rescue pilot, a lifeboat crew member, a resident on the island.

Write down a key claim for each and apply the criterion of ability to perceive to find limitations or strengths in their accounts. You will need to consider what they could see and hear as well as what they could not see and hear; what possible frame of mind they were in at the time; and how the conditions of that night might have influenced their claims.

The capsized *Costa Concordia*

Assessing possible perception: expertise and experience

The second credibility criterion associated with ability to perceive is that of **expertise and experience** which includes training and knowledge. This is the mindset that helps the person or organisation to interpret the situation or materials in an expert manner.

This expertise is often seen as a very strong criterion, such that those who have it are likely to be more credible than those without it.

Relevant expertise

Here is an example:

> **Key term**
> ➤ **expertise and experience:** terms used to describe qualifications, knowledge, training, and understanding that are relevant to the issue, subject or claim being made. These inform the source's ability to interpret the situation or data correctly. Expertise and experience makes the claims more credible than if they had been made by someone without this knowledge.

> Johannes Doehmer, professor in genetics and biochemistry at the Technical University of Munich, told a conference in November 2008 that using animals in medical experiments to predict what would happen in humans was simply not scientifically valid. As he put it, there is 'no more place for animal studies'.

We have a clear example of relevant expertise here (Doehmer's qualifications are in genetics and biochemistry). One does not get to be professor at this university in Munich without qualifications and experience. Professor Doehmer is clearly an expert, so his views are likely to be informed and believable.

Lack of expertise

However, we can find many examples in newspapers in which people who write regular features feel comfortable in commenting on a wide range of topics. For example, columnists write for newspapers most weeks and feel entirely comfortable writing about the Church of England, vegetarianism, Josef Fritzl (the man who kept his daughter in a cellar for many years), politics, crime, education, poetry and any other subject they choose to comment on. So are they an expert in all these matters? This would be difficult to believe.

Expertise of the wrong kind

There is also the point that certain individuals or organisations might have lots of expertise that is not necessarily relevant to what they are commenting upon. Thus a medical doctor has expertise on health matters, but not necessarily on economics. A religious organisation might have expertise on the contents of religious books, but not necessarily on the theory of evolution. So when using expertise as a criterion to show strength of evidence, we need to make sure that it is relevant to the evidence.

Activity 9

Take a look at some advertisements. On television, celebrities are used to recommend shampoo, footballers to sell packets of crisps, and actresses to recommend stairlifts and adjustable beds. It is clear that they are likely to have little specialist expertise in these areas.

But what about adverts in magazines and newspapers? As a group collect five adverts and assess the expertise of the sources making the claims.

Exam tip

When using expertise as a criterion, you need to be clear that the expertise is relevant in the case you're examining. The fact that a source has expertise doesn't mean that it is relevant to the issue in hand.

Past paper practice 12

OCR Unit F501, June 2009

Look at the documents in this exam paper on the issue of money and happiness. In these you will find that there are several experts on both sides of the debate. As a group, work out which might have more expertise than the others, with each person taking one of the experts:

➤ Professor Elizabeth Dunn

➤ Researchers working for Professor Dunn

➤ Professor Stephen Joseph

➤ Professor Ruut Veenhoven.

Present a case claiming that this person's expertise/ability to see or know is superior.

Check your answers with those given on page 170.

Exercise 17

How far can the credibility criteria help in assessing Stop Huntingdon Animal Cruelty's claim that 'every three minutes an animal dies inside Huntingdon'?

Now check your answers against those on page 170.

Summary

➢ Bias can be used to assess a tendency to favour someone or a particular position or set of beliefs.

➢ This can involve being selective ('cherry-picking').

➢ Vested interest involves a motive to either represent the facts accurately or to misrepresent them in order to gain or to avoid losing something.

➢ Vested interest can therefore both strengthen and weaken credibility.

➢ The strength of a reputation depends upon the credibility of the person giving the reputation, whether by others or self-acclaimed.

➢ It also depends upon that feature still applying in the present.

➢ Neutrality involves having no motive to distort the truth.

➢ Ability to perceive can involve all the senses.

➢ It can refer to events and materials such as reports and data.

➢ It can be strengthened or weakened by range, memory, emotions etc.

➢ Expertise and experience may be relevant, irrelevant or lacking.

➢ When using each of these criteria, you need to explain why a source has bias etc. before you go on to give the consequence of this.

Chapter 12

Credibility of documents

Learning objectives

By the end of this chapter, you will be able to:

➢ distinguish between primary and secondary evidence

➢ apply credibility criteria to assess a document using the provenance and the document itself

Having looked at the range of credibility criteria that help us to assess believability, we can move on to apply them. First we look at assessing the credibility of a document.

You can apply all the credibility criteria to documents. In doing so, 'ability to perceive' can take on additional significance, as the source may be writing from personal experience (using primary evidence) or may be commenting on materials drawn from someone else's experience (using secondary evidence).

Primary and secondary evidence

Primary evidence is that given by those with the ability to perceive, such as eye-witnesses to criminal behaviour and those who actually perform research. This has the benefit of being first-hand evidence. However, even with primary evidence, there is huge potential for distortion. For example, a historical document written by an apparent eye-witness might be reporting on an event from a biased perspective (as the winner of a battle, say).

Key terms

➢ **primary evidence:** evidence from those with the ability to observe.

➢ **secondary evidence:** a report based on another's primary evidence.

Secondary evidence is the reporting of primary evidence by a second-hand source. Although distortions can arise even with primary evidence, they can be increased further with secondary evidence. For example, someone might selectively report the content of primary evidence because of vested interest. On the other hand, someone producing secondary evidence could produce a more balanced account by researching a range of primary sources.

Applying credibility criteria to assess a document

Using the provenance

To be able to assess a document we need to step outside of the document itself. How do we do this? On websites you will often be able to click on an icon that says 'About us'. This gives you background details about the organisation. On a book you can often find details about the author on the back cover or in a preface or biography. These tell us important details about how long the author or organisation has been in this field (experience); their qualifications (expertise); what other publications they have produced (expertise/reputation); how they have gathered their materials (ability to perceive); and which organisations they might be affiliated to (vested interest).

In the examination, the provenance is given underneath the document. It may simply be the name of the organisation, or it may have an 'About us' or 'Mission statement' section.

Using the document itself

The body of the document can sometimes be used to demonstrate balance/neutrality, where both sides of the argument are given equal treatment. However, as documents are more often presented to make a point, it is more likely to have been written by the source with selectivity in line with the position that it favours — that is, its natural bias.

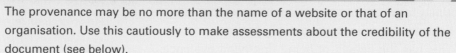

Exam tip

The provenance may be no more than the name of a website or that of an organisation. Use this cautiously to make assessments about the credibility of the document (see below).

Activity 10

Consider the following document. As a group look at its provenance and list the credibility criteria that you can apply. Check your answers with the guidance on page 171.

Stop the pylons

The recent proposal to build miles and miles of pylons across some of the most beautiful countryside in Britain has provoked considerable anger in all the areas that would be affected. The Government needs to see that the plans for lots more pylons have to be abandoned.

For one thing, beautiful landscapes will be spoiled. These include what's called 'Constable Country' in Suffolk (named after the 19th-century artist John Constable who lived there and many of whose famous paintings feature the area). This Suffolk landscape will be for ever ruined by these 40 metre-high monstrosities. The action group fighting this proposal includes people from most of the villages that would be affected.

Pylons spoil the landscape

As George Bell, a resident of Aldham (one of the villages that will be affected) has explained, 'These pylons will ruin our views and have a devastating effect on house prices in the village.'

In the same area, the well-known TV presenter, Griff Rhys-Jones, is campaigning strongly for the plans to be scrapped, describing them as 'despicable'. Mr Rhys-Jones has joined many local campaigns on environmental issues.

It's not just the negative effect on beautiful landscapes that's a problem. It's been shown that pylons are very bad for health. A major study has found that overhead power lines carried by pylons might increase the risk of childhood leukaemia. The study by Oxford University found that 64 children with leukaemia lived within 200 metres of overhead power lines. A study in San Francisco found that overhead power lines can also increase the risk of babies getting asthma.

In addition, a number of residents in Devon who lived near pylons said that they often experienced headaches, dizziness, aches and pains. They also said that their children suffered from headaches.

If like us you want to preserve the countryside we live in, join us today in opposing the plans for more pylons. See our website www.nomorepylons.co.uk

Here are some of the criteria that you probably listed and an explanation of how they can be applied or not applied.

Reputation — NO

As you can see, the source of the document is the organisation 'No more pylons'. Beyond what is said here, we have no further information about the organisation, so we cannot bring in criteria such as reputation to judge it.

Vested interest — YES

Because it is what is called a 'pressure group' (a group that works to benefit some individuals or to bring about — or stop — certain policies), we would expect it to present claims in a way that makes a particular case. The organisation therefore has a vested interest to be selective and to present those points that support its case.

Bias

The organisation favours the position against pylons as it is a pressure group against them, so the document is likely to be biased. There is no information on whether the plans for more pylons are supported by others (such as people who don't live in the affected areas), and whether there are very good reasons to have the pylons built. The sources quoted in the document are all from one side of the debate. (These are George Bell, Griff Rhys-Jones, and the 'residents from Devon'.)

We can see then that the document can be assessed as a biased account of the proposal to build more pylons in various parts of the country.

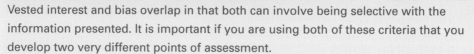

Exam tip

Vested interest and bias overlap in that both can involve being selective with the information presented. It is important if you are using both of these criteria that you develop two very different points of assessment.

Expertise/experience — YES

It is possible that being a pressure group related to pylons, it will have acquired expertise in knowing the issues and the relevant statistics, or even have used the expertise of others to have made its case stronger. Certainly it uses a study from Oxford University which cites the relationship between overhead power lines and childhood leukaemia.

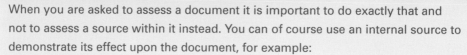

Exam tip

When you are asked to assess a document it is important to do exactly that and not to assess a source within it instead. You can of course use an internal source to demonstrate its effect upon the document, for example:

'The expertise of…strengthens the expertise of the document because…'

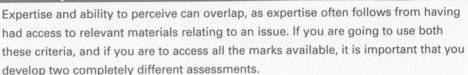

Ability to perceive — YES

The pressure group has access to studies on the effects of pylons, so it has the ability to perceive the possible effects that they may have.

Exam tip

Expertise and ability to perceive can overlap, as expertise often follows from having had access to relevant materials relating to an issue. If you are going to use both these criteria, and if you are to access all the marks available, it is important that you develop two completely different assessments.

Including a reference to the text

When assessing a document in the exam, you are asked to support your answer with reference to the text. You should be looking for a reference that justifies why the credibility is strengthened or weakened by specific criteria. The most useful place to find this reference will be in the provenance, as this tells you about the source. The following activity guides you through making an assessment and justifying this with a reference.

Activity 11

Here is the provenance from a drug company and a little information so that you can see what its documents might contain. See how many credibility criteria you can apply and note down references that would justify these. Check your answers against the text that follows.

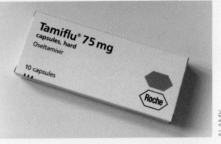

Roche claims high levels of effectiveness for the Tamiflu drug

Roche

Roche, the manufacturer of the drug Tamiflu, claims that the drug reduces complications of 'flu (including bronchitis and pneumonia) by 67% in otherwise healthy people.

Roche is a Swiss-based global pharmaceutical company.

Its website www.roche.co.uk makes the following claims about itself:

'At Roche we focus on developing medicines and diagnostics that will help patients live longer, better lives.

We strive to address unmet medical needs through excellence in science — from early detection and prevention of diseases to diagnosis, treatment and treatment monitoring.'

You could have used all the credibility criteria here:

➤ Roche would have the **ability to perceive** the results of its own research on the effectiveness of Tamiflu, as it 'develops medicines'.

➤ Roche has **vested interest** in claiming high levels of effectiveness for Tamiflu, because then it would be able to sell more of its drugs — as it says, 'we focus on developing medicines'.

The above assessment could alternatively be expressed:

➤ Roche is **not neutral** in its promotion of the benefits of the drug Tamiflu. It has a vested interest in selling its product as it is 'a Swiss-based global pharmaceutical company'.

➤ Roche has a **vested interest** to report results of its research accurately to maintain the public confidence in its 'diagnostics that will help patients live longer, better lives'.

➤ Roche has **expertise** in the field of testing drugs as it says that it focuses on 'developing medicines...through excellence in science'.

As you can see, you don't have to refer to full sentences. Often snippets from the provenance are enough to justify the assessment.

Activity 12

Now try Activity 11 with the *British Medical Journal* (*BMJ*), using the following information. Check your answers against the text that follows.

The British Medical Journal

An investigation by the *British Medical Journal* (*BMJ*) claimed to show that the benefits of Tamiflu in reducing complications appear to be 'vanishingly small'. The BMJ website www.bmj.com identifies its 'vision':

'to be the world's most influential and widely-read medical journal'

and its 'mission':

'to lead the debate on health, and to engage, inform and stimulate doctors, researchers and other health professionals in ways that will improve outcomes for patients.'

The *BMJ* has been published since 1840.

You may have made some of the following assessments:

➤ The *BMJ* is a **neutral** source in the debate over Tamiflu because it seeks only to 'inform...doctors, researchers and other health professionals in ways that will improve outcomes for patients' and does not profit from recommending any drugs.

➤ The *BMJ* has **no obvious bias** in its reporting of results of medical research. Its wish to 'lead the debate on health, and to...inform...doctors' requires it not to be biased in its presentation of the evidence.

➤ The *BMJ* has high levels of **experience** in evaluating medical research, having been published since 1840. Its vision 'to be the world's most influential…medical journal' will require it to use a range of medical experts.

➤ The *BMJ* has a **vested interest to present accurate reports** in order to maintain public confidence in its publishing in the area of medical research, having been going 'since 1840'.

Past paper practice 13

OCR Unit F501, January 2012

Look at the documents in this exam paper on micro-chipping dogs.
Assess the credibility of Document 5: 'Loss of Liberty' written by www.bigbrotherwatch.org.uk.

Apply each of the credibility criteria, making sure you include a reference to the text. Then check your answers against those given on page 172.

Summary

➤ You can use all the credibility criteria (RAVEN) to help you to assess the credibility of documents. The ability to see can be developed to make use of primary and secondary evidence.

➤ You should assess the document and not a source within the document, nor a claim within the document.

➤ Neutrality and vested interest often overlap, as do expertise and ability to perceive, so if you are going to use both criteria each time, make sure that you assess two completely different points.

➤ When you are looking for a reference to justify your assessment, you are more likely to find it in the provenance.

➤ The reference need be only a few words.

Chapter 13

Credibility of claims

Learning objectives

By the end of this chapter, you will be able to:

➤ apply the credibility criteria to assess claims

➤ make a judgement about a source's credibility by weighing up the assessments of credibility

➤ assess the effect of additional information on the credibility of claims

Applying the credibility criteria to assess claims

Judging the credibility of a claim normally involves judging the credibility of the source and how far this affects the credibility of this particular claim.

Planning your answer

If the question asks you to assess whether the credibility of a source's claims is strong or weak, then there are several decisions that you will need to make:

➤ Choose a claim that is not a matter of fact — that is, choose something that might be contentious or at least debatable.

> **Exam tip**
>
> If you are assessing the credibility of a claim you need to refer to the specifics of the claim in your answer.

➤ Choose an appropriate credibility criterion.

➤ Choose assessments that do not overlap — that is, two clearly different assessments.

You need to plan your answer to make sure that you cover all the aspects of the question:

> The source has [*credibility criterion, e.g. vested interest, expertise, etc.*] to claim [*the specifics of the claim*] because [*the assessment explained*]. This [*strengthens/weakens*] the credibility of the claim.

Here is one way of doing this. Look back at the passage 'Stop the pylons' on page 93 to assess the claim of George Bell:

> As George Bell, a resident of Aldham (one of the villages that will be affected) has explained, 'These pylons will ruin our views and have a devastating effect on house prices in the village.'

An answer assessing this claim might read:

> George Bell might have a **vested interest** to exaggerate [*credibility criterion*] the consequences of pylons as having '**a devastating effect on house prices in the village**' [*reference to the claim*], because **he will want to make the outcome seem more extreme, so that people will be persuaded to stand against the pylons** [*assessment*]. This **weakens** [*strengthens/weakens*] the credibility of his claim.

Exam tip

You need to plan your answer to cover all the points required in the question.

Activity 13

Look at the claims of another survivor of the *Titanic* and see what assessments can be made using the credibility criteria 'ability to perceive' and 'neutrality'. When you have completed your answers, check them with those below.

Emily Bosie Ryerson, 1st Class passenger in Lifeboat 4

Then suddenly, when we still seemed very near, we saw the ship was sinking rapidly. I was in the bow of the boat with my daughter and turned to see the great ship take a plunge toward the bow, the two forward funnels seemed to lean and then she seemed to break in half as if cut with a knife, and as the bow went under, the lights went out; the stern stood up for several minutes, black against the stars, and then that, too, plunged down, and there was no sound for what seemed like hours.

Ability to perceive

Emily Ryerson had the ability to perceive that the *Titanic* 'seemed to break in half' before sinking because she was a survivor who was able to witness the actual sinking. (Indeed, if her specific claim that she was 'very near' is accepted, then this would emphasise the importance of the criterion of ability to perceive.) This would strengthen the credibility of her claim.

Neutrality

Emily Ryerson was probably neutral and had no motive to distort the claim that the *Titanic* 'seemed to break in half' before sinking, because she was not (as far as we know) linked to the shipping line or any other relevant organisation and it cannot be seen that she has anything to gain by making this claim. This strengthens the credibility of her claim.

(If you were to go on to give another assessment that described the last point in terms of lack of vested interest, you would be repeating yourself as you would already have described neutrality.)

Exam tip

You need to choose assessments that do not overlap.

If you want to use the same credibility criterion more than once when assessing a claim or source, then make sure that you have shown how it can be used differently.

For example, a source may have a vested interest to tell the truth to preserve their professionalism, but also a vested interest to misrepresent the truth to support their cause. This is often the case with organisations in the public eye. They need to tell the truth to maintain public confidence, but there is also the temptation to exaggerate or to leave out important considerations in order to convince the public.

Exercise 18

Using three different credibility criteria, assess any claim made below by Robert Taylor. Make sure that you target the required points above.

Robert (Bob) Taylor died in March 2007, aged 88. He is famous for having claimed to have been abducted by aliens.

This report of the incident uses his description, and includes snippets of his exact words which have been italicised.

An alien encounter

The incident happened in November 1979. Bob worked as a forester in West Lothian, Scotland, a job he had had all his working life. He was described as an unassuming man, steady, with a craggy outdoorsman's face. He had an occasional drink, but never while he was working.

Bob Taylor always stood by his story

On this November morning, he set out, with his red setter Lara, to check for stray sheep and cattle in the forest. Having walked for a while between the rows of fir trees, he then turned a corner into a clearing. It was 10.30. That's when he saw it.

It was a '*flying dome*', just over six metres wide, hovering above the grass. The dome was silent and didn't move. About halfway down, there was a circular platform like the brim of a hat. The dome looked solid one moment and transparent the next, such that Bob could see the fir trees through it.

Then two small spheres dropped out of the dome. They were covered in spikes and made a sucking sound as they came across the grass towards Bob. When they reached Bob, they grabbed his legs, resulting in a '*foul choking smell like burning brakes*'. He felt himself being pulled towards the dome and then passed out.

When he came to, the dome had gone. He staggered home to his wife with his dog, a graze on his chin, ripped trousers, covered in mud, and with a really bad headache. However, a doctor who examined him found no evidence of a head injury. After two days of a 'wild, craving thirst', he took the police to the scene.

They found a large circle of flattened grass, and 40 little holes coming away from the flattened circle. There was, however, no evidence of anything having gone into or out of the forest clearing.

The police opened a case of criminal assault, a case that remains open to this day. Bob Taylor never changed his story. Three years before he died, he was interviewed by a newspaper about the incident. He said, '*I stand by every word of my account. I told it as it happened and it's as clear as yesterday. It is the most amazing thing that ever happened to me. I know what I saw and it looked like a spaceship, a huge flying dome.*' He never sold his story, and moved house to escape the publicity that followed the story.

Although Bob Taylor's account might be questionable — both in the sense that what he said happened is very unlikely to have happened, and in the sense that it is unreasonable to believe it — when you assessed it using the credibility criteria you would have seen that the evidence had some possible strengths.

Now check your answers against those on page 172.

Exercise 19

Assess the credibility of these claims.

You might like to know these background details first.

Background

Research is carried out by drug companies on how effective their products are. An example is that of research on non-steroidal anti-inflammatory (NSAI) drugs. Having done this research, the companies want to have their results published.

Drug companies use research to back up their claims

Ben Goldacre

Ben is a medical doctor and academic who is well known for his books and for his newspaper column 'Bad Science' in which he looks critically at various apparently scientific claims that have been made. He claims to have looked at *all* the studies published by the drug companies where one NSAI was compared with another:

'In every single trial, the sponsoring company's drug was claimed to be either equivalent to, or better than, the drug it was compared with: all these companies' drugs were better than all the other drugs. Such a result is plainly impossible.'

Vincent Lawton

Vincent Lawton is a director of a pharmaceutical company, with many years of experience in the industry:

'Clinical trials are properly managed by a rigorous system of regulatory scrutiny throughout. Potential for conflict of interest, when clearly identified and controlled, is not unacceptable. The industry develops medicines through years of painstaking research by some of the best scientists in the world, often in collaboration with academic researchers.'

Now check your answers against those on page 173.

Making a judgement about a source's credibility

You may be asked to come to an overall judgement about the credibility of a claim made by a particular source. In this case you need to weigh up your individual assessments of the credibility of the claim, and to judge which credibility criterion was most important in this case. This is a bit like playing 'Top Trumps' where certain criteria will always trump, or out-perform, other criteria. In the case of credibility, a vested interest to lie will almost always trump expertise or ability to see, as no matter how good a source is at seeing and interpreting a situation, if they have a strong motive to lie, this will outweigh their good judgement.

Now let's see how this works.

Activity 14

Consider the following claim and come to an overall judgement, explaining which credibility criterion you consider to be the most important in this case.

This is a further example from the enquiries about the sinking of the *Titanic*, answering the question whether the *Titanic* sank intact or broke in two before it sank.

It might be helpful if you know the following background information:

Was the *Titanic* intact before it sank?

The White Star shipping line which owned the *Titanic* wanted the enquiry to accept that the ship had sunk intact. This was because this would show how strong their ship was. The senior officers tended to support this, whilst the junior seamen gave the broken-in-two version.

When you have made an answer, check your observations with the assessments on page 104.

Herbert John Pitman, 3rd Officer in Lifeboat 5

Senator SMITH   Did you see the *Titanic* go down?

Mr PITMAN   Yes, sir.

Senator SMITH   Describe, if you can, how she sank.

Mr PITMAN   Judging by what I could see from a distance, she gradually disappeared until the forecastle head was submerged to the bridge. Then she turned right on end and went down perpendicularly.

Senator SMITH   Did she seem to be broken in two?

Mr PITMAN   Oh, no.

At this stage we can note that credibility criteria gain strength or add to weakness by acting together.

Pitman:

➤ Relevant expertise + limited ability to perceive + vested interest.

➤ Judgement — the claim has weak credibility.

➤ Most important criterion — weighing up the relative importance of the above assessments — vested interest to misrepresent the truth, also weakened by lack of ability to see, even though he had relevant expertise

Taking the credibility of Pitman's claim, if you were to write out an answer, it might be something like this:

> Officer Pitman's claim has weak credibility because most importantly he has a vested interest to misrepresent the truth in order to support the shipping line which owned the *Titanic*, and wanted to claim that it had been a strong ship. The claim is further weakened by the fact that the officer was at a distance and so may not have been able to see what happened in the dark. These weaknesses outweigh his relevant expertise as an officer to know about ships, because whatever he saw he is likely to support the shipping line's interests.

Now see if you can make a judgement using a past exam question.

Past paper practice 14

OCR Unit F501, January 2012

Look at the documents in this exam paper on micro-chipping dogs.

1 Assess the credibility of a claim made by Dr Albrecht using three different credibility criteria.

2 Based on your assessments, come to an overall judgement about the credibility of the claim made by Dr Albrecht by:

➤ stating your judgement

➤ explaining which credibility criterion you consider to be the most important in this case

➤ weighing up the significance of the assessment you made about the claim

Check your answers against those given on page 173.

Assessing the effect of additional information on the credibility of claims

Now we need to consider the effect of additional information upon the credibility of a claim. With much of what we do in critical thinking, having further information can change the way in which we assess claims. Assessing the credibility of claims is no exception. We often want to know more.

For example, in Exercise 19 on page 102, about NSAI drugs, there were times when it would have been very helpful to know more about those making a claim. All you were told about Vincent Lawton is that 'he is a director of a pharmaceutical company, with many years of experience in the industry'.

Relevant additional information

Just to remind you, this is what he said:

> Clinical trials are properly managed by a rigorous system of regulatory scrutiny throughout. Potential for conflict of interest, when clearly identified and controlled, is not unacceptable.

Some of the things that would have helped you in assessing the credibility of his claims would be the following.
- Has his company been involved in research into NSAI drugs?
  relevant to — bias, expertise, ability to perceive, neutrality and reputation
- Has he ever been involved in research into NSAI drugs?
  relevant to — vested interest, expertise, ability to perceive and reputation
- Has he ever seen the detailed research carried out by companies into NSAI drugs?
  relevant to — expertise, ability to perceive, neutrality and reputation
- Does he earn money from being a director of his pharmaceutical company?
  relevant to — vested interest, neutrality and reputation

Additional information not relevant

There's plenty of information about Vincent Lawton that would not be relevant to assessing his claim. For example:
- Whether he is married or not would appear to make no difference.
- Whether he worked in Spain at any point would appear to be irrelevant.

Thus, you need to ask:
- What would be *relevant* to the credibility of the claim?
- What would make *a difference* to the credibility of a claim?

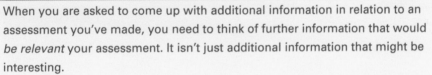

Exam tip
When you are asked to come up with additional information in relation to an assessment you've made, you need to think of further information that would *be relevant* your assessment. It isn't just additional information that might be interesting.

In the above, you have seen that additional information can often improve assessments of credibility.

Using additional hypothetical information

In the exam, you do not have access to this additional information, so you need to assess the impact of the additional information in a hypothetical way:

> Applying the credibility criterion x to claim y has the effect of strengthening/weakening the credibility of the claim if…

To illustrate this, we can go back to the Bob Taylor story.

If it could be shown that the police did carry out a detailed examination of the clearing to look for damage to the habitat, such that it were shown that there was no way a craft could have entered or exited the site, then this would have the effect of weakening the credibility of the claim made by Bob Taylor that there was a UFO in the forest, as it would challenge Bob's ability to have perceived a craft 6 metres wide coming into the forest clearing.

> **Exam tip**
>
> The same point can be made about hypothetical additional information as was made about additional information. You're looking to see how such hypothetical information could support your assessment, if it were true.

As with any hypothetical judgement, you need to remember that the judgement is only good so long as the possibility remains open that the 'if…' could be the case. For example, if we find evidence that the police didn't carry out a very detailed examination of the site that Bob Taylor showed them, then the hypothetical judgement above about the weakness of his ability to perceive has to be rejected.

> **Exam tip**
>
> Only use hypothetical reasoning if you are asked for the impact of further information. If you are asked to assess the credibility of claims, you are expected to make assessments on the information available in the passage.

You could also use additional hypothetical information with the evidence on the sinking of the *Titanic*:

> Applying the credibility criterion of vested interest to the claim made by the surviving officers of the *Titanic* that she sank intact has the effect of weakening the credibility of the claim if it could be shown that the officers had been told by the White Star Line that they would lose their jobs if they said she broke in two.

Past paper practice 15

OCR Unit F501, June 2009

Look at the documents in this exam paper on the issue of the relationship between money and happiness.

1 Assess the credibility of a claim made by Professor Steven Joseph.

2 Explain the impact that additional information would have on this assessment.

Check your answer against that given on page 174.

Summary

➢ When assessing the credibility of a claim, make sure that you plan your answer so that you include all the elements required, including a specific reference to the claim.

➢ When you are judging the overall credibility of a claim, make sure that you weigh up against each other the different credibility criteria that you applied.

➢ When you are judging the effect of possible additional information upon a credibility assessment, make sure that it is relevant.

Chapter 14

The wider picture: support and opposition

Learning objectives

By the end of this chapter, you will be able to:

➤ identify corroboration and conflict

➤ identify consistency and inconsistency

Using corroboration and conflict, consistency and inconsistency

In OCR Critical Thinking Unit 1 the credibility criteria of corroboration and consistency can be used in two very specific ways:

➤ **Identifying sides.** They can help you to look at the wider picture where several sources are involved to help you to identify which 'side' a source is on. If there is debate about an issue, these criteria will help to clarify whether a source can be counted to support or oppose the matter in question.

➤ **Identifying the relationship between claims.** You may also be asked to identify claims or pieces of evidence that support or oppose each other. These criteria will direct you to look for particular types of support or opposition.

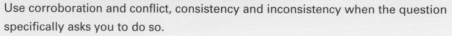

Exam tip

Use corroboration and conflict, consistency and inconsistency when the question specifically asks you to do so.

So what do these terms actually mean?

Identifying corroboration and conflict

Corroboration

This is a stronger form of support than consistency. **Corroboration** occurs where two sources make very similar observations that *directly* agree.

If you look again at the traffic accident on page 72, both the Renault car driver and the witness made a claim about the van driver:

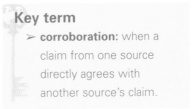

Key term

➤ **corroboration:** when a claim from one source directly agrees with another source's claim.

> **Renault car driver:** 'He just drove away.'
>
> **Witness:** 'The van driver just drove away.'

These directly support each other, so they can be said to be a very basic example of corroboration.

In criminal cases, a case is strong or weak depending on the way the evidence stacks up one way or the other. Thus Steve Wright, 'the Suffolk Strangler', was convicted on the basis of an accumulation of evidence from several independent sources (DNA evidence, fibres of clothing, photographic evidence, and so on) which all pointed in the direction of his guilt. Each separate type of evidence corroborated the others.

Conflicting evidence

Conflict is where claims are *directly* opposed. This points us in a different direction, to question which is likely to be the most credible claim.

If you look again at the traffic accident there are two claims there that are directly opposed.

The Renault car driver claimed:

Key term

➤ **conflict:** where sources make directly opposing claims, they are said to conflict.

> The driver of the van in front of me in the queue approaching the roundabout reversed into me with such sudden force that he split my number plate.

The van driver said:

> The Renault drove into the back of me when I stopped pulling onto the roundabout, as some silly fool sped out of the blind junction to my right.

These claims would be said to conflict and you would need to use other credibility criteria to work out which source/claim was more believable.

The Wilkins case in 2005 is another example of direct conflict. If you remember:

> The psychologist appointed by the defence reported to the court that Mr Wilkins had an IQ of 58 and so, because he did not understand the court proceedings, should not stand trial.
>
> However, the psychologist appointed by the prosecution reported to the court that Mr Wilkins had an IQ of 88 and so, because he understood the proceedings, should stand trial.

Here the claims were in direct conflict, as clearly Mr Wilkins could not have had an IQ of both 58 and 88.

Exam tip

If you're asked to find claims that corroborate other claims, make sure you check that the claims are talking about the same specific points, and include all the points.

Past paper practice 16

OCR Unit F501, January 2010

Look at the documents in this exam paper on street lighting. Question 7 asks you to identify a claim and its source that corroborates the claim of the Transport Minister:

'Experience shows that better street lighting helps improve road safety, as well as reducing crime and the fear of crime.'

Remember that you are looking for a claim that directly supports the detail of this claim.

Check your answer against that given on page 174.

Identifying consistency and inconsistency

These might be seen as giving us two credibility criteria, even though one is just the positive or negative of the other.

Consistency

In terms of credibility, claims that are **consistent** offer less strong support than those that corroborate each other, because with consistency they don't have to be directly related in the same precise detail.

> **Key term**
> ➤ **consistency:** refers to claims that are relevant to each other and can both be held to be true at the same time.

> **Exam tip**
>
> When looking for claims that are consistent, you are looking for claims that are relevant to each other.

Referring back to the traffic incident, the Renault car driver claimed:

It was 8.55am and I was already pressed for time because of the amount of traffic.

The witness said:

The queue had been stopping and starting for several minutes.

These two claims could both be said to be true at the same time. However, this is not as strong as corroboration, as the claims do not directly support each other. Stopping and starting is consistent with heavy traffic but not the same, as it could have been caused by other factors.

> **Exam tip**
>
> Claims that corroborate are also consistent, but it doesn't work the other way around. Claims that are consistent do not necessarily corroborate, as their connection is looser.

Past paper practice 17

OCR Unit F501, January 2012

Look at the documents in this exam paper on micro-chipping dogs in relation to the following question:

In 2010, vets only charged between £7 and £35 for micro-chipping a dog. Identify two claims and their sources from Documents 2 and 3 that would be consistent with this fact.

Here you are looking for claims that give support without confirming the precise details. When you think you have found the answers, check them against the guidance given on page 174.

Inconsistency

Claims that cannot both be true at the same time are **inconsistent**.

> **Key term**
>
> ➤ **inconsistency:** refers to claims that cannot both be true at the same time.

Past paper practice 18

OCR Unit F501, June 2011

Look at the documents in this exam paper on food and the carbon footprint and try answering this question:

Consider the different figures given about food waste in Documents 2 and 3. Identify two pieces of data that are inconsistent with each other.

Remember: you are looking for claims that cannot be held to be true at the same time. When you think you have found the answers, check them against the guidance give on page 175.

Summary

> Corroboration is stronger than consistency, because with corroboration the claims need to directly support each other.

> The criteria of corroboration and consistency can be used to help you to determine which sources support which side of the issue.

Chapter 15

Plausibility of claims

Learning objectives

By the end of this chapter, you will be able to:

➤ identify where plausibility can be used

➤ assess plausibility as 'likelihood'

➤ assess plausibility as 'reasonableness'

Identifying where plausibility can be used

You have seen that when we assess the credibility of a claim (or its source), various criteria can be used. Having applied them, we can then decide whether a claim and/or its source is more or less credible.

But using these credibility criteria on their own isn't always the full story. Often plausibility also has a part to play.

> **Key term**
>
> ➤ **plausibility:** in OCR critical thinking this is used to answer the questions: is it likely? Is it reasonable?

What is plausibility?

Look at the following example:

> In November 2008, an 8-year-old boy in Phoenix, Arizona confessed to murdering his 29-year-old father and his 39-year-old workmate, a male lodger. Although at first he denied killing them, after an hour of police questioning he admitted to the crime. He claimed that he found them already wounded, so shot his father to put him out of suffering.

Crucially, we have an eye-witness (someone who claimed to have the ability to perceive what had gone on in the house). So what makes this case a problem for plausibility? It's that it seems such a bizarre scenario.

➤ Would an 8-year-old shoot his father?

➤ Would an 8-year-old shoot the lodger?

➤ Would an 8-year-old shoot both his father and the lodger to put them out of their suffering, having already found them shot and wounded, by someone else, an unknown attacker?

This example shows that there is something else to consider. This is what we call plausibility.

To put it very simply, we are asking two things:

➤ How *likely* is it that an 8-year-old would do this, despite the fact that he said he did? If we say that it is very unlikely, then we are saying that it is not plausible (or that it is implausible).

➤ How reasonable is it that the police wanted the boy prosecuted as an adult, and to have him charged with premeditated murder? Many were opposed to this:

> Various legal experts have argued that the boy should not and indeed cannot be tried as an adult. His apparent 'confession' was obtained in circumstances that did not follow the correct procedure (there was no lawyer present during the questioning). In addition, as the director of a law-psychiatry programme at a US university has pointed out, 'I have never heard of an 8-year-old being tried as an adult. It would be more than extraordinary. It would be totally unique.'

In this passage, we read that there are reasons why the boy should not be tried as an adult. If we were to ask 'is this plausible?' we're not asking 'is this likely?' because the latter question makes no sense. We are asking 'is this *reasonable*?'

Exam tip

Plausibility is more likely to be seen in terms of the *likelihood,* when looking at events; that things that are supposed to have happened, might happen.

Plausibility can be seen in terms of *reasonableness,* when dealing with two different reasoned cases.

Activity 15

Consider the case of the Scottish jelly mystery that has been documented by the BBC Scotland Outdoors team — see www.bbc.co.uk/scotland/outdoors/articles/jelly/

Watch the video on their website to gain a clear understanding of what is causing the mystery.

Now that you have an understanding of how credibility and plausibility appear on the exam paper:

➤ credibility — how believable are the documents and claims?

➤ plausibility — how likely is this to have happened? How reasonable is this?

answer the following questions.

Questions

1 Assess the **credibility** of the following claims. Use two credibility criteria for each person's claims and make sure that you use the plan for assessing the credibility of claims developed on page 75.

Hans Sluiman — algae expert at the Royal Botanic Garden Edinburgh: told the BBC Scotland Outdoors programme that he was convinced that the gel was neither plant nor animal.

Dr Andy Taylor — studies fungi at the Macaulay Institute in Aberdeen: says that there are fungus filaments growing in the slime.

An Outdoors listener: 'Cleaning out my pond today, I pulled out a dead frog that has obviously broken open exposing a white "blob". Several of your programmes a few months ago were going on about strange "matter" lying about the countryside. Here is an actual specimen of the white matter of your discussion.'

2 Assess the **plausibility** of the following explanations. You may like to read 'Some listeners' comments' on the website to gain some idea of the evidence and explanations that have been suggested, for example:

- ➢ The jelly has something to do with frogspawn.
- ➢ It is star jelly (as described by seventeenth-century poetry).
- ➢ The jelly is 'chem-trailing'.

You might think that this sounds like the game 'Balderdash' where players are given a word for which they have to write a plausible definition. Players then have to choose which one is true from those given alongside the correct definition. Here we are making a similar assessment — we are given explanations and we need to choose which sounds the closest to being plausible/reasonable.

Check your answers against the guidance on page 175.

Assessing plausibility as 'likelihood' and as 'reasonableness'

Plausibility as 'likelihood' — what happened?
The following story appeared in various media in August 2009:

In August 2009, 'dozens of people' reported seeing mermaids in the coastal town of Kirvat Yam in Israel. 'Many people are telling us they are sure they've seen a mermaid and they are all independent of each other,' said Natti Zilberman, a town council spokesman. 'People say it is half girl, half fish, jumping like a dolphin. It does all kinds of tricks, then disappears.' One of the witnesses was Shlomo Cohen. 'I was with friends when suddenly we saw a woman lying on the sand in a weird way. At first I thought she was just another sunbather, but when we approached she jumped into the water and disappeared. We were all in shock because we saw she had a tail. At least five of us saw it and we all couldn't believe it.'

Do mermaids exist?

The town council of Kirvat Yam is offering a $1m reward for anyone who can prove by a photo or capture that mermaids do exist.

Beyond the question of credibility, there is the question of the likelihood of what was said to have happened at Kirvat Yam. Do we see the whole report as plausible or not? Even if most of the relevant credibility criteria make this account appear to be credible, we might want to say that it doesn't appear to be plausible. We would want to say that there must be another explanation for what went on in this place. (Incidentally, the $1m reward has yet to be claimed.)

Plausibility as 'likelihood' — what might happen?

There is also the question of 'what might happen?' For example, is it the case that listening to loud music over time with headphones will seriously damage your hearing? There is considerable evidence that this is so. So we can say that it is very likely that hearing would be damaged by long-term listening to loud music with headphones.

Here's another example:

A study has been carried out by the University of Bristol on possible links between diet in early childhood and future IQ levels. Fourteen thousand children were studied, with their parents filling in questionnaires detailing what their children ate at different ages (2, 4, 7 and 8½ years). Each child was given a score ranging from a 'processed' diet (high in fats and sugars) to a 'health-conscious' one (rich in salad, fruit, vegetables, rice and pasta). These diets were then compared with the results of IQ tests taken when the children were 8½.

The study showed that a diet rich in processed food up to the age of 3 was associated with lower IQ five years later. A healthy diet at the age of 3 was associated with a higher IQ at the age of 8½.

So what is the most plausible conclusion we could draw from this study?

Credibility criteria would have given us expertise and reputation (the well-respected University of Bristol), as well as the same university's presumed neutrality.

Beyond the effect of credibility criteria, there's still the issue of plausibility. How plausible is it that diet in childhood will affect intelligence? Is it likely that this diet in itself could be the cause, or could there be other causes (such as amount of stimulation parents give to their children, or the quality of housing, or the quality of the schools that the children attend)?

So, based on an evaluation of plausibility (or likelihood) that diet affects intelligence, which of these two statements would you accept?

➢ It is likely that diet in infancy affects a child's future intelligence.
➢ It is unlikely that diet in infancy affects a child's future intelligence.

Plausibility as 'reasonableness' of a case

Plausibility as 'likelihood' tips towards plausibility as 'reasonableness' when we are dealing with disputes between two sides of a case where we have arguments on each side in which evidence is presented.

This evidence (and any other claims that are made) should be assessed for credibility. (For example, we should look at the sources of the evidence, any expertise involved on either side, any vested interest, and so on.) But we should also look at how plausible (reasonable) is either case.

Activity 16

Consider the following text and come to a judgement as to the plausibility of the theory that to lose weight you need to consider the type of the food that you eat as well as the quantity. You might like to divide into two groups, with one side arguing for the implausibility and the other side arguing for the plausibility. Check you answers against the guidance on page 175.

Do some foods contribute to weight loss?

The importance of diet

What you eat is just as important as how much you eat when it comes to keeping slim in the long term. This is the finding of research carried out by scientists at Harvard University.

A study of 120,000 people over 20 years found that the average person gained about 0.45 kg every year. Excess calories amounting to no more than a biscuit a day were enough to cause gradual weight gain in most people, according to the researchers.

Diet was found to be more important than exercise in keeping weight off, but the researchers found that calorie counting alone was not the main thing, showing that 'eat less and exercise more' messages are too simple to be useful.

Although some foods do, they found, contribute to weight gain (chips, crisps, sugary drinks, processed meat, potatoes, white bread and sweets), other foods actually contribute to weight loss. These include fruit, vegetables, nuts, and (especially) yoghurt. This is because, by and large, 'natural' foodstuffs (such as fruit and vegetables) take longer for the body to break down, which could reduce weight gain by leaving people with less appetite for high-calorific foods.

Note: Harvard University is one of the most important universities in the world, ranked very highly for the quality of its staff and their research.

Summary

➢ When asked to assess the plausibility of an outcome, see it in terms of 'likelihood' if it is more or less likely that one outcome rather than another is the case. Put very simply, what is more likely to have happened?

➢ When asked to assess the plausibility of a case, see it in terms of 'reasonableness' if it is more reasonable that one side has the better case than the other. Put very simply, which side has the better case?

Chapter 16

Judgement based on credibility and plausibility

Learning objectives

By the end of this chapter, you will be able to:

➤ assess relative credibility

➤ assess relative plausibility

➤ make a judgement by weighing the credibility against the plausibility

Having looked at the credibility of claims and the plausibility of outcomes, we now need to develop those skills that help you make an overall judgement that is based on assessing:

➤ the *opposing sides* of the issue and

➤ the *opposing possible outcomes*

Thus we need to look at things from a wider perspective.

Assessing relative credibility

We have seen how to assess a source's claim holistically, weighing up the impact of various relevant credibility criteria. Now we need to weigh up the overall credibility of the opposing *sides* and make a mini judgement about which side is more credible.

To remind you how the criteria line up, here they are, to be applied to the opposing sides in an issue:

Stronger credibility: relevant expertise + ability to perceive + neutrality + positive reputation.

Weaker credibility: lack of relevant expertise + lack of ability to perceive + bias (including vested interest) + negative reputation.

Of course reality isn't as clear-cut as this. There will be instances of weak credibility on a more credible side, and instances of strong credibility on a less credible side. The task is to weigh these up.

Exam tip

You need to assess like with like, so you need to compare the vested interest on one side with the vested interest on the other side. (It would not be a fair comparison to compare negative vested interest on one side with relevant expertise on the other side and conclude that the second side was more credible because of this.)

We begin with a mini comparison, where there is only one person on each side — but bear in mind that in an exam paper there is likely to be more than one person on each side.

Activity 17

Consider these claims made about probiotic drinks and yoghurts.

Probiotic drinks and yoghurts

Scientists at the European Food Safety Authority (EFSA) examined more than 800 claims made by food companies that probiotic drinks and yoghurts could strengthen the body's defences and reduce digestive problems. They concluded that none of these claims could be proved. It's clear that people should not be taken in by the claims made about these probiotic products.

Are probiotic products good for you?

Here we see the claims made by the food companies and the counter-claim made by the EFSA. It's worth noting what this organisation is (or at least what it claims to be):

The European Food Safety Authority is the keystone of European Union (EU) risk assessment regarding food and feed safety. The EFSA provides independent scientific advice and clear communication on existing and emerging risks.

OCR AS Critical Thinking

You can see that the words 'independent scientific advice' are going to be important for a credibility assessment.

As the claims are reported, you will have to extract them from the text.

- ➤ **The food companies** — probiotic drinks and yoghurts could strengthen the body's defences and reduce digestive problems.
- ➤ **Scientists at the EFSA** — none of these claims could be proved.

What about the credibility of the claims being made here?

Which side is the more credible? We will apply the same two criteria to each side.

Write down your initial responses before reading what follows.

Ability to perceive

Food companies: this strengthens the credibility of the food companies' claims because they would have access to the research they have done on this issue.

EFSA: this strengthens the credibility of its claims because it would have access to the research it has done on this issue.

The credibility criterion of ability to see therefore does not give us much to choose between the two, as both have access to their research.

Vested interest/neutrality

Food companies: possible vested interest to misrepresent the facts weakens credibility of the food companies' claims because they might want people to buy these probiotic products, and appealing to healthy consequences would be seen as a strong selling factor. (You could express this as lack of neutrality to weaken the credibility of this claim because they would benefit from people buying these probiotic products.)

However, vested interest to represent the facts accurately in order to keep the public's trust would strengthen the credibility of this claim, because they would not want to be shown to have distorted any claims about the effects of these probiotic products.

EFSA: vested interest to represent the facts accurately strengthens the credibility of this claim because the EFSA has no obvious benefit to be gained by disputing what the food companies claim.

Neutrality strengthens the credibility of this claim because the EFSA provides 'independent scientific advice' on 'risk assessment regarding food...safety'.

The criterion of vested interest tends to indicate that the EFSA possibly has more scope for neutrality than the food companies.

Mini conclusion about relative credibility

Therefore, using the two credibility criteria of ability to perceive and vested interest, the side claiming that there is no proof about the benefits (the EFSA) could be seen as more credible, because although both sides have access to research, the criterion of motive is the deciding factor here and the EFSA has no obvious motive to distort the facts.

We could go on to look at expertise, but with this limited material it can only be supposed that they both have expertise in their various areas.

Assessing relative plausibility

An example that we can look at here is the dispute over the planned (and now rejected) building of a third runway for Heathrow airport:

Activity 18

Read the following information.
1 Identify the plausibility of the opposing positions.
2 Make a preliminary judgement about which position is more plausible.

Check your answers against the text that follows.

A third runway for Heathrow airport

In 2009 the then Labour Government gave approval for the building of a third runway at Heathrow. In 2010, the Conservative-led Government cancelled this proposal.

What was being proposed?

➤ A new 2,195-metre runway to be built, allowing for an increase of take-offs and landings from 480,000 today to 605,000 by 2020 and 720,00 by 2030.

➤ The building of the runway would have taken place north of the existing airport.

➤ 700 homes would have been lost in the village of Sipson.

What arguments were presented on both sides?

➤ Businesses, trade unions and aviation firms said that the third runway was necessary for trade and tourism, as other European airports have more runways that attract more business.

➤ Environmental groups claimed that the new runway would fail European Union (EU) pollution limits. Local groups claimed that there would be excessive noise levels and that communities would be destroyed (as a result of where the runway would have been sited).

We need to look at the plausibility of the two sides. On the basis of what's presented, which side has the more plausible case? To judge between these two very different approaches requires that you look at the reasonableness of each.

You could say that those in favour of the third runway had a plausible case if you want to stress trade, tourism and competition from other European airports. We do see increased business trade where communications are improved, so it is reasonable to suppose that this might have happened again.

Protesting against a third runway

You could then say that those against it would have the more plausible case if you want to stress environmental concerns (including quality of life of local people) and the preservation of local communities. For example, how reasonable is it that communities will be 'destroyed' because of increased noise levels? Going on past examples of developments impacting on residents, they may move out of these areas and house prices may drop, but we don't usually hear of whole areas being completely abandoned. However, 700 homes would have been lost to make way for the development.

Mini conclusion about relative plausibility

Here you need to weigh up one set of issues against the other. One conclusion might be:

➢ Taking these two strands of support for each case, it seems more plausible that the extra runway would have brought benefits in terms of trade and tourism than it would have been detrimental. More people would be affected by the benefits in terms of businesses and tourists than would be negatively affected in their homes.

However, another conclusion could equally be drawn:

➢ As the proposal was eventually rejected, it seems more plausible that the extra runway would have been more detrimental to the surrounding residential area than it would have been beneficial in terms of extra business.

There is no single correct answer. You could draw the conclusion in favour of either position. However, it is important that your reasoning supports this.

Making a judgement

It will be useful to unpack further this relationship between credibility and plausibility.

- If both the credibility and plausibility that x is the case are *strong*, then the judgement must be that it is *likely* that x is the case.
- If both the credibility and plausibility that x is the case are *weak,* then the judgement must be that it is *unlikely* that x is the case.

These judgements did not require much thought.

But what if you have a strength and a weakness?

- low credibility + high plausibility = ?

This might fit with the claim by local groups that a third runway would increase noise levels. They have a vested interest to say this to try to prevent the runway affecting their communities, but it is common sense that increased noise levels will occur.

- high credibility + low plausibility = ?

This might fit with the Bob Taylor case about alien abduction. Although the credibility criteria might push us in the direction of believing his story, many of you would see that its plausibility is too low to be believable.

In both cases, then, plausibility is likely to trump credibility.

> **Exam tip**
>
> In a difficult judgement where there is both weakness and strength on one side when weighing credibility against plausibility, the plausibility judgement is likely to override that of credibility.

In this example, you were judging the credibility and plausibility of the outcome of some research. This is obviously different from judging whether a particular thing happened at a particular time but, importantly, you were doing the same thing.

> **Exam tip**
>
> In coming to a judgement about the credibility and plausibility of what's presented to you, you need to remember to cover both of these. This means that you should look at the credibility of both sides, and the plausibility of both sides. From this fourfold assessment will come your judgement.

We have so far looked at credibility and plausibility of claims and sources within a single report or document. However, you also need to be able to compare credibility and plausibility *between* different accounts. This is your task in the next exercise.

Exercise 20

The following two reports are concerned with the Government's proposal to build a new High Speed Rail network (commonly referred to as HS2) over the next 15 years. HS2 will provide faster rail links between London and Birmingham, and then between London, Manchester and Leeds (with connections to other northern cities). The company HS2 Ltd was set up to develop proposals for the new rail network.

HS2 will provide a modern, high-speed rail network

➤ Read each document.
➤ Assess the relative credibility and relative plausibility of each side.
➤ Make an overall judgement about which is the most likely outcome.

Then compare your answers with those on page 176.

Document 1
Say Yes to rail progress

The HS2 plan has many supporters including:

➤ **The Campaign for High Speed Rail:** this organisation describes itself as 'independent from the Government and HS2 Ltd, representing employers from across the country who believe Britain needs a modern, high speed rail network to meet the challenges of the 21st century'. It is supported by business people across the country because it can see huge benefits in the faster rail times. These benefits include making it easier for companies to recruit staff and find customers.

➤ **Centro**, an organisation that promotes and develops public transport in the West Midlands and is a big supporter of HS2. It points out that HS2 will lead to increases in wages of people in the area and, by encouraging more people to use public transport, will reduce road congestion and carbon emissions, and improve air quality.

➤ **Rail travellers** have voiced their support for the HS2. One of them, Jason Roberts, is a frequent traveller between London and Birmingham. He makes the point in a letter to his local paper: 'I am often forced to stand all the way from London to Birmingham because of the overcrowding on the train. With more and faster trains on the HS2, this is much less likely to happen.'

For the sake of the economy, the environment, and rail passengers, join the campaign for HS2.

Document 2
Say No to HS2

The building of HS2 cannot be justified in terms of its huge cost, the benefits that are claimed for it, and the impact on the environment.

Two leading **transport economists**, Chris Castles and David Parish, have argued that the existing rail line could easily take three times the amount of rail traffic. Furthermore, there will massive disruption caused by the building of the new line.

Various official bodies have also criticised the HS2 plan:

> **Natural England** is the Government's adviser on the environment. It has stated that the proposed route will have 'a severe, significant effect on the natural beauty of the Chilterns'.
> Another Government advisory body, the **Environment Agency**, is concerned about the 'potentially significant risks' to water resources if the building of the line goes ahead.
> **Local councils affected by the planned route** are also opposed to the plan, as are many **MPs** (including many Government supporters) whose constituencies are in the affected areas.

Other opponents of the plan include:

> Michael O'Leary, the **boss of Ryanair**, has criticised the idea of replacing short-haul flights with high speed rail as 'insane'.
> **The Taxpayers' Alliance** has also condemned the HS2 plan, pointing out that it will cost each family in the country over £1,000.
> This worry about cost is supported by the *Financial Times* newspaper which questions the value for money from a plan that would cost £130 million for each mile.

HS2 must be opposed.

Notes

The Taxpayers' Alliance describes itself as 'Britain's independent grassroots campaign for lower taxes'.

The *Financial Times* is a UK newspaper which specialises in reporting on financial and economic affairs.

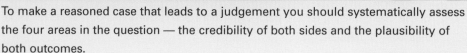

Exam tip

To make a reasoned case that leads to a judgement you should systematically assess the four areas in the question — the credibility of both sides and the plausibility of both outcomes.

There are sample answers in the OCR mark schemes demonstrating how to answer this question. Look at the level 3 descriptors in the mark scheme to identify how you should target the marks.

Exam tip

Refer to the text to support your assessments in each of the four areas.

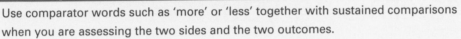

Exam tip

Use comparator words such as 'more' or 'less' together with sustained comparisons when you are assessing the two sides and the two outcomes.

Summary

> When assessing relative credibility you should use the same credibility criterion to assess both sides.

> When assessing relative plausibility, make sure that you assess both the stated outcomes and not just the positive of one side and then the negative of that side.

Chapter 17

Maximising your marks on Unit 1

Learning objectives

By the end of this chapter, you will:

➢ be familiar with the types of questions typically asked in the Unit 1 paper

➢ understand what these questions are asking you to do

➢ understand how to answer these questions, maximising your marks in doing so

The question paper

Exam materials

In the examination you will be given:

➢ a **Resource Booklet** containing several 'documents' and any background information that you are likely to need in order to understand the topic

➢ **a question and answer booklet** which will be divided into Section A and Section B, with a total of 75 marks available.

Exam timing

You will have a total of 1 hour 30 minutes to do the paper. You are advised on the front of the question paper to divide this time into three parts:

➢ 'about **10 minutes**' in reading the Resource Booklet

➢ 'about **35 minutes**' in answering the questions in Section A — 35 marks

➢ 'about **40 minutes**' in answering the questions in Section B — 40 marks.

> ### Exam tip
> You can see that this is about a minute a mark. This should give you a useful guide to how to manage your time in the exam.

OCR AS Critical Thinking

Practice exam-style paper

This chapter has been organised so that you can try out the questions in a practice exam before reading about the answers.

In the practice exam you will find:

> **background information** that should answer any questions you might have about the content, followed by several **documents**

> **questions** based on these documents — the exam questions can vary from year to year, so we will look at a range of different questions that are typical of ones that have been asked previously.

Advice and guidance is given below about how to reach the correct answers and how to avoid many of the pitfalls.

Answers to the questions are given below, with some strong answers (to show you how to get full marks), and some less so. Advice and guidance is also given about how to reach the correct answers and how to avoid many of the pitfalls.

Unit 1 practice exam-style paper

Background information
Zoologists are biologists who study animals.

Kudus are a type of antelope.

Document 1
Zoos and animal conservation
It is often claimed by zoos that, without them, many species, including tigers and rhinos, would disappear, because their conservation and captive-breeding programmes help to preserve endangered species. However, zoos should not be seen as being concerned with the interests of animals, as their main purpose is to make money for their owners. Furthermore, animals in zoos often lead highly stressful lives by being restricted in small enclosures and deprived of stimulation. Even the apparently large enclosures sometimes provided for elephants cannot begin to provide the normal 30-mile-a-day range that these animals cover.

Document 2
Animals need zoos, say zoo organisations
The British and Irish Association of Zoos and Aquariums (BIAZA)
BIAZA sees the promotion of good welfare for zoo animals as a priority. Many of the members of BIAZA are world-famous zoos such as London Zoo and Whipsnade, and these specialise in conservation activities in areas where endangered species live. Some species, such as the African black rhino, would not survive without some degree of management, including taking some animals into captivity.

BIAZA insists that zoos 'meet the needs of the animals in their care by understanding what constitutes good welfare, and by providing appropriate housing and husbandry'.

BIAZA stresses that, in the wild, many animals suffer attacks by predators, starvation, disease, parasites, cold and heat. Well-designed zoo enclosures can minimise, even eliminate, all these factors.

In addition, BIAZA makes the point that the daily lives of zoo animals can be enriched by providing enhanced environments if zoos employ highly skilled and imaginative staff. Thus zoos, they argue, improve the welfare of animals compared to their lives in the wild.

The International Congress of Zookeepers (ICZ)

ICZ is active in improving standards of zoo-keeping and in developing conservation activities. A spokesman has said that ICZ has had a really 'positive effect on the development of the world's zookeepers'.

Document 3

PETA: Why zoos are bad for animals

There is important research that has been carried out by scientists at Oxford University that showed that animals suffer in zoos. They live in 'enclosures' that are so much smaller than they would have in the wild. Polar bears, lions, tigers, elephants, cheetahs and other animals who would roam for many miles in the wild, become stressed and miserable in their restricted enclosures.

We stress that, although zoos claim to contribute to conservation, they actually take money away from useful conservation projects in the wild. Instead of people paying money to see animals in cages and enclosures, they should be encouraged to give money to help animals survive in their natural habitats.

Lions need space to roam

We have discovered that the Dickerson Park Zoo in the US sold or 'donated' a giraffe, a kudu, five kangaroos and two deer to Buddy Johnson, an 'animal dealer who sells animals to exotic-animal auctions and breeders, unaccredited zoos, and even hunting ranches'.

People for the Ethical Treatment of Animals (PETA)

Mission statement: PETA is the largest animal rights organisation in the world, with more than 3 million members and supporters. PETA works through public education, cruelty investigations, research, animal rescue, legislation, special events, celebrity involvement, and protest campaigns.

Document 4

Zoos and elephants

Research published in the highly respected journal *Science* has shown that 'elephants kept in zoos die younger than in the wild'. The zoologists who did the research studied more than 4,500 African and Asian female elephants kept in zoos or living in the wild. The researchers showed that those elephants born in captivity had the lowest life expectancy of all, shorter even than those elephants that were captured in the wild and taken to zoos. They also showed that zoos need to have elephants taken from the wild in order to keep their breeding programmes going. As a result, it can be seen that elephants should not be kept in zoos.

Questions

Section A — The language of reasoning

1 (a) State the main conclusion of the argument presented in Document 1.

(b) State the two reasons that are given to support the main conclusion in Document 1.

(c) State the counter-argument presented in Document 1:

  (i) counter-conclusion

  (ii) counter-reason

(d) State one example that is used to support the argument in Document 1.

(e) State three argument indicator words that are used by the author in Document 1.

2 In paragraph 4 of Document 2, BIAZA claims that 'the daily lives of zoo animals can be enriched by providing enhanced environments if zoos employ highly skilled and imaginative staff'.

(a) Name the argument element used.

(b) Explain your answer to (a).

3 (a) Paragraph 1 of Document 2 gives the example of the African black rhino to support the claim that some species have to be managed (including taking some animals into captivity) in order to survive.

  Explain two ways in which this animal might or might not be representative of zoo animals.

(b)(i) Explain one way in which the photograph of the lion might give support to the caption, 'Lions need space to roam'.

  (ii) Explain one way in which the photograph of the lion might give only limited support to the caption, 'Lions need space to roam'.

(c) In paragraph 1 of Document 3 the research by scientists from Oxford University claimed that animals in zoos became 'stressed' and 'miserable' because of their 'restricted enclosures'. Suggest an alternative explanation for the animals suffering these feelings.

4 State one assumption that is needed for the conclusion in Document 2, that 'zoos improve the welfare of animals compared to their lives in the wild'.

5 Suggest one reason to support a claim that zoos are no longer necessary for the public to find out about animals.

6 Consider the argument in Document 1 against zoos. Assess how strongly the reasons support its conclusion. You should make two developed points that refer directly to the links between the reasons and the conclusion.

Section B — Credibility

7 Assess the credibility of Document 3 from PETA.

You should make two points. Each point should identify and use a relevant credibility criterion to assess the credibility of the document, supported by reference to the text.

8 (a) The last sentence of Document 4 includes the claim that 'elephants should not be kept in zoos'.

Identify a claim and its source in any of the other documents that would be consistent with this claim.

(b) In Document 3, PETA claims that 'although zoos claim to contribute to conservation, they actually take money away from useful conservation projects'.

Identify a claim and its source in any of the other documents that would be inconsistent with this claim.

9 (a) Assess the credibility of one claim made by BIAZA and one made by PETA.

Apply two credibility criteria to explain how these might strengthen or weaken the credibility of each claim.

(b) Explain what other information you would need to know in order to reach one of your points of assessment about the credibility of BIAZA's claim. You should make one precise point.

(c) Based on your assessments in 9(a), come to an overall judgement about the credibility of the claim made by BIAZA. You should explain which credibility criterion you consider to be important in this case and then weigh this against the other chosen criterion.

10 Referring to the material within the documents, come to a reasoned judgement as to whether zoos increase or reduce animal welfare. You should make a reasoned case with a judgement based on:
> the relative credibility of both sides
> the relative plausibility of both positions

Section A answers and discussion

The first few questions on the paper will normally focus on the analysis of an argument that has been presented. This means that you are likely to be asked to find argument elements such as the main conclusion, reasons, counter-assertions and so on.

In any of these analysis questions, you might be tempted to give what can be called the *gist* of the right answer. Giving only the gist means that you have paraphrased the wording of the passage. You are specifically told not to do this and there are two good reasons why you shouldn't.

➤ The first reason for this is that you're being asked to *state* the conclusion, reason, etc. You're being asked to state what the author has said, not to give a different version of it. Paraphrasing means that you give it differently, with the risk that you give an inaccurate version.

➤ The second is that paraphrasing takes more time than merely stating! You're having to give thought to how to put it differently, whereas you should be simply writing it down and moving on.

In the examples below, the correct student answers are flagged blue and the incorrect student answers are flagged red.

Question 1

> **1 (a)** State the main conclusion of the argument presented in Document 1.

 Zoos should not be seen as being concerned with the interests of animals.

In Chapter 2 you looked at ways of finding the conclusion of an argument.

➤ The word 'should' was one of these ways, so hopefully this helped you identify this sentence.

➤ In the same chapter, there was also the point that a word such as 'however' or 'but' often indicates that the author is starting his or her argument, having already given a counter-position.

You will see that the answer we gave satisfies the requirement to give the exact words. This is what the author says — no more and no less. (You might want to query whether the word 'however' in the sentence should have been included. The word isn't technically part of the conclusion, so you should not include it. But you'll be pleased to hear that you would not be penalised if you did.)

What about the following answers?

 ➤ Zoos are not concerned with the interests of animals.
➤ Zoos should not be seen as being concerned with animals.

In these answers, part of the original has been omitted, so they would lose marks. What about the next answer?

 Zoos aren't interested in animals.

This misunderstands the word 'interests' in the conclusion, although it still has the thrust of the anti-zoo conclusion.

What could count as a wrong answer?

Anything that gives the wrong part of the argument, such as a reason or evidence.

> **1 (b)** State the two reasons that are given to support the main conclusion in Document 1.

Student

> The main purpose of zoos is to make money for their owners.
>
> Animals in zoos often lead highly stressful lives by being restricted in small enclosures and deprived of stimulation.

Having found the conclusion correctly, you should be able to find the reasons using the 'because' or 'therefore' test, which you looked at in Chapter 2.

In each case, we have given only what is needed. In the second, you will see that we have missed out the word 'furthermore', because all that word is doing is *signalling* a further reason. As before, you would not be penalised if you included the word.

The two answers above are accurate. They give the words that the author uses. What would less successful answers look like?

Adding extra material: if you had given the reason correctly, but had added something that wasn't part of the reason, then you would lose marks, as in the next example:

Student

> Animals in zoos often lead highly stressful lives. They are restricted in small enclosures and deprived of stimulation. Even the apparently large enclosures sometimes provided for elephants cannot begin to provide the normal 30-mile-a-day range that these animals cover.

The obvious things that would distract you would be evidence, examples and development. There's plenty of this. For example, if you had put any of the following, you were providing material relevant to the reasons, but not the reasons themselves.

Student

> Captive breeding programmes help them to make money as a result of people wanting to see recently-born animals (such as elephants and rhinos).
>
> Even the apparently large enclosures sometimes provided for elephants cannot begin to provide the normal 30-mile-a-day range that these animals cover.

Missing out material: however, if you had put:

Student

> The main purpose of zoos is to make money.

then you have been accurate in one way (you've used the right wording) but inaccurate in another (having missed out part of the words of the reason).

> **1 (c)** State the counter-argument presented in Document 1:
>
> **(i)** counter-conclusion
>
> **(ii)** counter-reason

Student **(i) Counter-conclusion:** Without zoos, many species would disappear.

As you can see, we have had to re-jig the first sentence a little to get to this. We've done this because the author was presenting the conclusion in a way that fitted with introducing the subject. The following presents the full version, but shows the words not needed in brackets.

Student (It is often claimed by zoos that,) without them, many species would disappear.

What about the answer:

Student Without zoos, many species, including tigers and rhinos, would disappear.

As you would expect, adding in 'including tigers and rhinos' is less accurate, because these are examples and not part of the conclusion as such.

Student **(ii) Counter-reason:** (This is because) their conservation and captive breeding programmes help to preserve endangered species.

The words in brackets are not needed, but you will not be penalised for including them.

1 (d) State one example that is used to support the argument in Document 1.

Student (Recently-born) Elephants and rhinos.

This example is given to support the claim about captive breeding programmes.
The example of elephants given in the final sentence of Document 1 would be an alternative answer.
What about the answer:

Student Tigers and rhinos.

Why would 'tigers and rhinos' not be right? Because this example supports the counter-argument rather than the argument itself.
A similar question might ask you to identify evidence rather than give an example.

1 (e) State three argument indicator words that are used by the author in Document 1.

Student because, however, furthermore

'As' and 'including' would be equally correct but only three indicator words are given as only three were asked for in the answer.
You will know that, in such questions, you're looking for both conclusion indicator words (such as 'so', 'thus', 'therefore' and 'in consequence') and reason indicator words (such as 'because', 'as' and 'since'). You will also remember that, in Document 1, the

word 'however' (or an equivalent) can be used to indicate the author's response to a counter-assertion or a counter-argument. Indicator words for examples might be 'such as', 'including' and 'for instance'.

In question 1 you have gained marks for quite straightforward analysis of argument. The watchword for getting these marks, as for any analysis questions, is *accuracy*. You're largely stating what's there, so be careful that you don't lose marks by being inaccurate (which includes being incomplete).

Exam tips

➢ Use the exact words of the author in your answers.

➢ Do not miss out any words.

➢ Do not add any embellishments.

➢ Do not add on any other argument elements.

Question 2

A further type of analysis question is to ask you to name an argument element. Here's an example of such a question.

> **2** In paragraph 4 of Document 2, BIAZA claims that 'the daily lives of zoo animals can be enriched by providing enhanced environments if zoos employ highly skilled and imaginative staff'.
>
> **(a)** Name the argument element used.

Student Hypothetical reason.

As you can see, you're doing no more than 'naming' an argument element, so you don't need to write very much in order to be right.

How might your answer be less well-focused?

By being incomplete: for example, if you just put 'reason' then, although you are in one important sense right (that's what it is in the sequence of the argument), you haven't described it sufficiently fully.

Similarly, if you just put 'hypothetical', then your answer is incomplete.

By being inaccurate: you would be inaccurate to say that it's a 'hypothetical argument' because this sentence is not the full argument.

To be entirely inaccurate, you would have to be describing it wrongly (e.g. as 'evidence' or 'conclusion').

> **2 (b)** Explain your answer to (a).

Student It is a reason that includes a condition and a consequence.

A definition is all that is required. You do not need to refer to the text for this answer. You will remember that we looked at hypothetical forms in Chapter 3.

What about the answer:

 Student | It has the 'if…then' form of hypothetical reasoning.

From your understanding of these, you might think that this is all you need to say. But you need to develop this point further. You will remember that this was concerned with consequences and conditions.

> **Exam tip**
>
> The argument element will be one of those listed in the exam specification.
> A definition of the element is all that is required for the explanation.

Question 3

3 (a) Paragraph 1 of Document 2 gives the example of the African black rhino to support the claim that some species have to be managed (including taking some animals into captivity) in order to survive.

Explain two ways in which this animal might or might not be representative of zoo animals.

Two example answers of being representative:

 Student
> ➤ The African black rhino might not be typical of other species because it is so endangered, whereas many other zoo animals are more likely to be able to survive in the wild, such as penguins and kangaroos.
> ➤ The African black rhino may not be typical because they can be looked after satisfactorily in captivity, whereas other animals such as polar bears can become distressed in captivity.

An example answer of being unrepresentative:

 Student | The African black rhino might be typical of animals that are at particular risk of poaching, such as giant pandas and snow leopards, so managing them (including having them in zoos) is the only solution to ensure their survival.

This is an example of a possible evaluation question.

Sometimes you are asked to come up with one way in which an example or evidence might be representative and one which way in which it might not be. Alternatively you might be asked to come up with two ways in which it might or might not be. Let's look at the answers that were given to the question above.

As you can see, we have provided a clear explanation of why the rhino is representative or not:

➤ We've focused upon a characteristic, being 'so endangered'; ability to 'be looked after satisfactorily in captivity' and 'risk of poaching'...

➤ and then applied it to both the African black rhino and other animals in zoos that may or may not fall into this category.

What about less well-developed answers?

 Black rhinos are typical of the problem of helping large animals.

This is insufficiently developed in that it doesn't explain why rhinos are typical. It doesn't identify a particular characteristic. If you look again at our first answer above, you can see how this is done.

 The African black rhino might not be typical of other species *because it is **so endangered**, whereas many other zoo animals are more likely to be able to survive in the wild, such as penguins and kangaroos.*

3 (b) (i) Explain one way in which the photograph of the lion might give support to the caption, 'Lions need space to roam'.

(ii) Explain one way in which the photograph of the lion might give only limited support to the caption, 'Lions need space to roam'.

 (i) The photograph emphasises the problem of zoos in forcing lions to live in ways that are completely unnatural, by being very restricted in their movements behind bars, being unable to roam far.

(ii) The photograph shows only a lion behind bars. It doesn't show how much space the lion has to roam — the enclosure might be very large, enabling the lion to roam quite a long way.

This type of question refers you to an image and an accompanying caption, which will be the focus of the question.

You will see that the answers focus directly upon the image and what it gives as evidence of the lion's ability to roam or not to roam.

What would less successful answers look like?

An unfocused answer to 3(b)(i):

 The lion is in a cage.

This answer does not go on to *explain* how this restricts the ability of the lion to roam.

A vague answer to 3(b)(ii):

We don't know enough about the space that the lion has.

This answer does not *explain* the impact of the possibilities of the space available upon the lion's ability to roam.

> **3 (c)** In paragraph 1 of Document 3 the research by scientists from Oxford University claimed that animals in zoos became 'stressed' and 'miserable' because of their 'restricted enclosures'. Suggest an alternative explanation for the animals suffering these feelings.

Three possible example answers, although you only need to give one of these:

> ➤ The animals might be stressed and miserable because the climate is not the same as in their natural habitat, so they may be either too hot or too cold or the air might be too moist or too dry.
> ➤ The animals may be sociable animals and so they may be stressed and miserable because they are missing either their family group or the feeling of being with larger numbers of their species.
> ➤ The animals may appear to be stressed and miserable because of a natural instinct or the need to defend their territory.

This is another type of evaluation question. This time you are expected to give a different reason from that given in the text as to why something is the case. Here the 'something' is the suffering of the animals in terms of being stressed and miserable.

The answers above give the reasons of different *climate*, lack of *social group* and *natural instinct* as to why the animals are suffering or appear to be unhappy. These are plausible explanations — that is, they could be considered to be *likely* explanations.

You might think that anything you could give as an explanation could be credited. So how would you not get some or any of the marks available?

A weak explanation:

The animals are depressed and miserable because they are too cold.

This does not go on to explain why they might be too cold on a regular basis.

An explanation that is not different:

The animals are depressed and miserable because they are not running around on open ground.

This simply develops the explanation given in the text of the restricted enclosures.

An implausible explanation:

The animals are depressed and miserable because the zookeepers treat them cruelly and they should not do this.

Zoos have to comply with strict codes of conduct towards the animals, so it would be unlikely that many zoos have cruel zookeepers. This answer goes on to give an opinion about the situation, which was not asked for in the question. It simply asks for an alternative explanation.

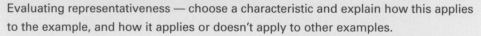

Exam tips

Evaluating representativeness — choose a characteristic and explain how this applies to the example, and how it applies or doesn't apply to other examples.

Alternative explanation — this must be plausible (likely) and completely different from the explanation given.

Question 4

> **4** State one assumption that is needed for the conclusion in Document 2, that 'zoos improve the welfare of animals compared to their lives in the wild'.

Four sample answers (although you would only need to give one answer):

Student
- ➤ Zoo enclosures are well designed.
- ➤ Zoos employ highly skilled and imaginative staff.
- ➤ Zoos provide enhanced environments for their animals.
- ➤ The welfare of wild animals consists only in minimising or eliminating attacks by predators, starvation, disease, parasites, cold and heat.

This is another analysis question, in that you are identifying a gap in the reasoning.

All the above are necessary assumptions for this conclusion to be drawn. Use the negative test to check. (You will have noticed that the hypothetical reasoning we looked at earlier required that the 'if' part of it *was actually the case*. This is always worth looking out for. When an author moves from a hypothetical reason to a conclusion that is not hypothetical, he or she must assume that the 'if' part of the 'if...then' is the case. This gives us both the second and the third of the above statements.)

To get the full marks for this question you need to have identified an assumption and to have expressed it carefully (indeed, not just carefully but exactly).

So how might you get fewer than the full marks available?

A less accurate statement of what is assumed:

Student All zoos are well designed.

A condensed version of what is assumed:

Student All zoos employ good staff.

A challenge:

Student Just because some zoos provide well-designed enclosures doesn't mean that all do.

Finding assumptions is not an exercise in saying whether or not an argument is strong or weak.

What sort of answer is straightforwardly wrong?

To write something that's already stated by the author:

 The daily lives of zoo animals can be enriched by providing enhanced environments.

An assumption is a gap in the reasoning, so it can **never** be something that the author states.

To seriously misinterpret what the author is saying:

 Animals in zoos can't be compared with those in the wild.

Exam tips

➤ Take care to express the assumption exactly.

➤ What is stated in the text (or a paraphrase of it) will never be the assumption.

➤ Use the negative test to see if your assumption works.

Question 5

5 Suggest one reason to support a claim that zoos are no longer necessary for the public to find out about animals.

Three sample answers (although you only need to give one answer):

 ➤ People can see lots of films on TV about animals in their natural habitats.

➤ People can get hold of lots of information about animals from the internet.

➤ People can learn about animals by going on safari holidays.

As you can see:

➤ This question is asking you to produce an argument, with the conclusion already given.

➤ The claim that you're asked to support will be relevant to the material in the documents, but will not be one already argued for in the documents.

➤ The claim that is given is likely to be quite specific in what it is stating.

In questions like this, you need to ensure that you focus on the specific nature of the claim that needs supporting. In this example, the claim is not simply an anti-zoo one, but is concerned with one specific aspect — that is, information/education. Many years ago, seeing exotic animals like elephants and tigers would have been possible only in a zoo. The key words are therefore:

➤ no longer

➤ necessary

➤ to find out

These are the areas that your reason should focus upon.

You will see that the above reasons are well focused to these specific points. We can check this by putting the reason and the claim together:

> **Student** People can see lots of films on TV about animals in their natural habitats.

So zoos are no longer *necessary* for the public to *find out about* animals.
Less well-focused answers:

> **Student** People can't learn much about animals by just looking at them in cages.

This doesn't address the specific point about zoos no longer being '*necessary* for the public to find out about animals'. This suggested reason goes way beyond the claim by suggesting that, by their very nature, zoos cannot inform the public about animals.

> **Student** People aren't likely to be interested in all the animals in a zoo.

Like the previous one, this doesn't support the specific claim that zoos are no longer '*necessary*' to inform people about animals. It might support a version of an anti-zoo argument which is concerned with how 'unglamorous' animals (like small snails) are going to be ignored by zoos. But it doesn't do what you are asked to do: give a reason to support the claim that's given.

Answers that go beyond a reason: you might come up with a well-focused reason only to lose marks by extending it with evidence or examples or even another conclusion.

> **Student** People can see lots of films on TV about animals in their natural habitats, such as the documentary on gorillas by David Attenborough.

The example of David Attenborough would be relevant if you were writing an extended argument on this subject. But, if you're asked to produce a reason, that's all you should produce.

Here is an answer that gives a focused reason but extends this by adding a further conclusion. In effect it is giving an argument in itself.

> **Student** People can see lots of films on TV about animals in their natural habitats, so there are obviously other ways that this can be done.

Exam tips

➤ Give only a reason and no extra argument elements.

➤ Make sure the reason is directly focused upon the claim that is given for you to support.

Question 6

6 Consider the argument in Document 1 against zoos. Assess how strongly the reasons support its conclusion. You should make two developed points that refer directly to the links between the reasons and the conclusion.

Two possible answers. As the question asks for two points you would need two answers here.

> The reason 'animals in zoos often lead highly stressful lives by being restricted in small enclosures and deprived of stimulation' may not support the conclusion that 'zoos should not be seen as being concerned with the interests of animals', because it could well be that the stress is due to normal aspects of an animal's life, such as the need to defend territory. If this is the case, then an animal looking stressed is not a relevant indicator of a zoo's lack of concern for their animals, and the reason gives only weak support.

> Even if 'the main purpose of zoos is to make money for their owners', this doesn't mean that 'zoos should not be seen as being concerned with the interests of animals'. By trying to make money, zoo owners will have to make their zoos appealing. This will involve ensuring that their animals are well cared for and housed in appropriate enclosures, otherwise people won't want to come and visit a zoo. So making money is not a relevant indicator of a zoo's lack of concern for their animals and the reason gives only weak support.

This is an example of a question type that asks you evaluate the link between the reasons and the conclusion.

> You can do this by looking at *relevance* and any *missing links*/assumptions.
> You need to refer explicitly to both a reason and the conclusion.
> If you are given a choice as to whether to make assessments about strength or weakness you will need to indicate which you have chosen. You may be given these words to circle to indicate your choice.

Above there are two possible answers (both in the 'weak link' category).

They both show how what is chosen in the reasons *making money* and *animal stress* may not be relevant indicators of lack of concern for the animals.

What would less successful answers look like?

A weak point of challenge with no reference to the reason or conclusion:

Captive breeding programmes could still be good because they could help to keep species like rhinos going.

In this point of evaluation, there is no explicit reference to either a reason or the conclusion. The answer challenges the argument rather than evaluating the link between a reason and the conclusion.

An answer with reference to a reason and the conclusion with very weak evaluation:

It is obvious that the reason 'animals in zoos often lead highly stressful lives' very strongly supports the conclusion, 'zoos should not be seen as being concerned with the interests of animals' because it is about the same thing.

This answer does very little more than identify the reason and the conclusion. It does not explain why the reason is relevant to the conclusion.

> **Exam tips**
> ➢ Explicitly identify the reason and the conclusion.
> ➢ You can assess the link between them using relevance and assumptions.
> ➢ Make clear whether you are assessing a weakness or a strength.

Section B answers and discussion

The questions in Section B are all concerned with the problem of credibility, so in these questions you need to apply the credibility criteria that we looked at in Chapter 11.

Question 7

> **7** Assess the credibility of Document 3 from PETA.
>
> You should make two points. Each point should identify and use a relevant credibility criterion to assess the credibility of the document, supported by reference to the text.

The first question is likely to ask you to evaluate the credibility of a report (which could well be one of the documents). In doing this, you will need (and be asked) to apply credibility criteria that you think are relevant in assessing the credibility of the report and to show why you think they are relevant.

Two answers:

 ➢ Document 3 from PETA could be seen as having a vested interest to present information that shows that zoos are a problem for the animal rights position because PETA is 'the largest animal rights organisation in the world' and this would make it select only those studies that would support the position of animal rights.
➢ Document 3 from PETA could be seen as credible because it uses experts. It quotes from a study by 'scientists at Oxford University'. This study and therefore the document must be based on expertise, because scientists at Oxford University are likely to have considerable expertise.

It is very clear from the question what you're being asked to do. You need to do three things:
➢ Identify a relevant credibility criterion.
➢ Apply it to the document.
➢ Refer to the document and/or its source.

Here is how the answers above targeted these points:

OCR AS Critical Thinking

> ➤ PETA could be seen as having a vested interest to present information which shows that zoos are a problem for the animal rights position (*identifying a relevant criterion*) because PETA is 'the largest animal rights organisation in the world' (*referring to the text to show why the criterion is relevant*) and this would make it select only those studies that would support the position of animal rights (*explanation of why the criterion is relevant*).
> ➤ Document 3 from PETA could be seen as credible because it uses experts. It quotes from a study by 'scientists at Oxford University' (*referring to the text to show why the criterion is relevant*). This study and therefore the document must be based on expertise (*identifying a relevant criterion*) because scientists at Oxford University are likely to have considerable expertise (*explanation of why the criterion is relevant*).

You might have noticed that the first answer took its reference from the provenance, whereas the second took it from the body of the text. Both gave support to why the credibility criteria should be applied to the document.

The second assessment used a source within the document to show why the document itself exhibited expertise. It is important that you assess the document and not just a source within it. If the answer had assessed the study and not the document, then its marks would have been restricted.

What will less well-developed answers look like? These will miss out at least one of the three things.

No reference and no development of relevance:

Document 3 shows bias in the way it selects only that evidence that supports its position.

In this answer, there is no reference to the text and no development to show why the credibility criterion is relevant.

No clear development of the credibility criterion:

Document 3 must be biased because it refers only to a study by scientists at Oxford University.

In this answer, there is no useful explanation of why Document 3 is biased. Just because PETA refers to this study and no other study does not in itself show bias. You would need to show why referring to just this study is possible evidence of bias (that it fits with PETA's anti-zoo position).

Exam tips

You need to:

➤ explicitly name and apply a credibility criterion

➤ make explicit reference to the text or its provenance to show why the credibility criterion is relevant

➤ assess the document and not a source within the document

Question 8

8 (a) The last sentence of Document 4 includes the claim that 'elephants should not be kept in zoos'.

Identify a claim and its source in any of the other documents that would be consistent with this claim.

Two possible answers:

 ➤ As PETA says, elephants are one example of animals that 'become stressed and miserable in their restricted enclosures'.

➤ In Document 1 we are told that 'Even the apparently large enclosures sometimes provided for elephants cannot begin to provide the normal 30-mile-a-day range that these animals cover'.

This type of question uses the criteria of consistency, inconsistency and corroboration. It may give you a claim, possibly but not necessarily one that has been made in one of the documents. It may then ask you to find claims that are consistent and inconsistent with it, or to find a claim that corroborates it.

In the above answers we have given both the accurate relevant claim (quoted) and the correct source. It is important to remember that the claims should be relevant to each other.

How might you not get full marks in this question?

To give a correct claim without a source:

 'Even the apparently large enclosures sometimes provided for elephants cannot begin to provide the normal 30-mile-a-day range that these animals cover.'

Here there is the correct claim, so you would expect to gain some of the marks.

To give a source without a claim:

 PETA gives a consistent claim.

Although the source is correct, without a correct claim this cannot be credited, as this source made many claims, some of which would be incorrect for this answer.

To give a correct claim from a wrong document:

Student 'elephants kept in zoos die younger than in the wild'

Although this claim is consistent with the claim given in the question, it is from the same document, so it cannot be credited.

> **8 (b)** In Document 3, PETA claims that 'although zoos claim to contribute to conservation, they actually take money away from useful conservation projects'.
>
> Identify a claim and its source in any of the other documents that would be inconsistent with this claim.

Student BIAZA claims that many of its members 'specialise in conservation activities in areas where endangered species live'.

This question focuses on the counterpart of consistency, inconsistency. As before, two things are needed to answer this question. In the answer above both the correct source and the relevant accurate claim (quoted) are given.

We've given the source (BIAZA) and the relevant claim. It needs to be stressed that, in both questions on consistency/inconsistency, you need to be very specific about the source of the claim. You should quote the document as the source only if the name of the source is not given.

Claims from opposing sides are not always inconsistent.

What about the answer:

Student BIAZA claims that zoos 'improve the welfare of animals compared to their lives in the wild'.

Although PETA and BIAZA disagree fundamentally with each other over whether or not zoos are a good thing, this claim by BIAZA is not inconsistent with the specific claim of PETA in the question.

You need to be careful about this. Just because sources are on different sides doesn't mean that any of their claims is inconsistent with any made by the other side. You need to match the consistency and the inconsistency closely to the specific claim given.

Exam tips

- ➢ Give both parts of what the question requires – the source and the claim.
- ➢ Quote the claim accurately.
- ➢ Give the name of the specific source if it is known, rather than the document number.
- ➢ Make sure you draw your answer from the specific documents required by the question.

Question 9

This type of question uses the RAVEN credibility criteria that you used in the document question. You can choose not only which criteria you apply but also which claim you assess.

> Assess the credibility of one claim made by x (in Document A) and one made by y (in Document B).
>
> Apply two credibility criteria to explain how these might strengthen or weaken the credibility of each of their claims.

You will need to do the following:

➤ Identify a claim.
➤ Identify a credibility criterion.
➤ Explain how this applies to the claim.
➤ Judge whether the criterion strengthens or weakens the claim.

You may be asked to assess the claim by applying several different credibility criteria.

So now you're clear about the task in this question, let's see how it applies to the specific question below.

> **9 (a)** Assess the credibility of one claim made by BIAZA and one made by PETA.
>
> Apply two credibility criteria to explain how these might strengthen or weaken the credibility of each claim.

BIAZA

Claim: Zoos 'meet the needs of the animals in their care by understanding what constitutes good welfare, and by providing appropriate housing and husbandry' (*correct identification of a claim*).

Assessment: As the organisation that represents zoos in Britain and Ireland, it would have the ability to perceive *(explicit credibility criterion)* what's happening on a day-to-day basis in zoos in order to form a judgement as to whether or not the 'good welfare' *(reference to the specifics of the claim chosen)* of the animals was met. This would therefore strengthen the credibility *(the effect of the criterion)* of this claim. *(The whole of the first sentence applies the criterion.)*

Here are further assessments of the same claim, one that strengthens and one that weakens the credibility of the claim, although you are only asked for two assessments:

Assessment: As the organisation that represents zoos in Britain and Ireland, it would have the expertise needed to understand what is involved in meeting the 'good welfare' needs of zoo animals, in that its members have considerable experience of working with such animals. This would therefore strengthen the credibility of this claim.

Assessment: As the organisation that represents zoos in Britain and Ireland, it would have a vested interest to be selective and only present zoos in a good light by claiming that zoos provide the animals with appropriate 'housing and husbandry'. If people thought they weren't, they would be less likely to visit, thus lowering profits. In this way, we can see that vested interest weakens the credibility of this claim.

In this last answer, we've spelled out the possible negative vested interest in enough detail for it to be clear that the situation may have been misrepresented.

Now we need to assess the claims of the other organisation, PETA.

Student | **PETA**

Claim: PETA has 'discovered that the Dickerson Park Zoo in the US sold or "donated" a giraffe, a kudu, five kangaroos and two deer to Buddy Johnson, an "animal dealer who sells animals to exotic-animal auctions and breeders, unaccredited zoos, and even hunting ranches".'

Assessment: As the largest animal rights organisation in the world, PETA will have expertise in researching and understanding information about animal welfare. This will mean that it will be able to find out what is going on in zoos, including any sale of zoo animals to an 'animal dealer'. As a result, the credibility of this claim would be strengthened.

Let's just consider the claim before moving on to look at the answer on credibility. The claim has been accurately given, so that would be credited. Now we'll check the application of the credibility criterion.

Student | **Assessment:** As the largest animal rights organisation in the world, PETA will have expertise *(explicit credibility criterion)* in researching and understanding information about animal welfare. This will mean that it will be able to find out what is going on in zoos, including any sale of zoo animals to an 'animal dealer' *(reference to the specifics of the claim chosen)*. As a result, the credibility of this claim would be strengthened *(the effect of the credibility criterion)*. *(The whole of the first two sentences apply the credibility criterion.)*

We'll now use the same criterion in a slightly different way, although with the same result. As above, only two assessments are required.

Student | **Assessment:** As the largest animal rights organisation in the world, PETA will have expertise in researching and understanding information about animal welfare. This will mean that it will know about what goes on in zoos like Dickerson Park and about 'animal dealers' like 'Buddy Johnson'. As a result, the credibility of this claim would be strengthened.

Here is an answer applying a criterion to weaken the claim:

Assessment: As the largest animal rights organisation in the world, PETA will have a vested interest to show zoos in a bad light. This will mean that it is likely to present a very selective picture of what goes on with the animals in zoos, such that 'Dickerson Park Zoo' might be a very unusual example. As a result, the credibility of its claim is weakened.

We noted earlier that you can use the same criterion in two different ways, with therefore two different outcomes. Here's an example of how this can be done.

 Assessment: As the largest animal rights organisation in the world, PETA will have a vested interest to present correct information on what zoos are doing with their animals and their association with 'animal dealers', so that it will be taken seriously by its supporters and those it wants to influence. As a result, the credibility of its claim is strengthened.

What would less successful answers look like?
Missing out an explicit credibility criterion:

 As the largest animal rights organisation in the world, PETA will want to present correct information on what zoos are doing with their animals and their association with 'animal dealers', so that it will be taken seriously by its supporters and those it wants to influence. As a result, the credibility of its claim is strengthened.

This answer sounds like a complete answer but it misses out the credibility criterion.
Missing out the explanation:

 PETA will be biased in its reporting of 'Dickerson Park Zoo' and 'Buddy Johnson', so its claim is weakened.

In the above answer, there is no explanation of why PETA will be biased, so it is an incomplete answer.
Missing out a reference to the claim:

 As the largest animal rights organisation in the world, PETA will want to present correct information, so that it will be taken seriously by its supporters and those it wants to influence. As a result, the credibility of its claim is strengthened.

Again, this sounds complete, but it is a generic answer. It could apply to any of its claims. The answer needs to assess the specific claim that has been chosen by referring to it.
Missing out 'strengthen' or 'weaken' the credibility of the claim:

 PETA will be biased in its reporting of 'Dickerson Park Zoo' and 'Buddy Johnson' because, being the biggest animal rights organisation, it will want to select only that evidence that looks bad for zoos.

In the answer above, all the work has been done except to say why the bias, which has been explained, will weaken the claim.

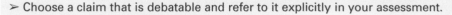

Exam tips

➤ Choose a claim that is debatable and refer to it explicitly in your assessment.

➤ Explicitly state a credibility criterion.

➤ Make sure that you explain why the credibility criterion can be applied.

➤ Make an explicit judgement whether your assessment weakens or strengthens the credibility of the claim.

We'll now move on to look at a question that's linked to the previous one.

This question asks you to look again at an assessment you have made in the previous question and to consider how you could make this assessment stronger by having more information.

Explain what other information you would need to know in order to reach one of your points of assessment (in question (a)) about the credibility of X's claim. You should make one precise point.

What is this asking? Think of it like this: 'What other information do you need to have in order to make your assessment of the claim stronger?' Let's see how it applies to the specific questions below.

9 (b) Explain what other information you would need to know in order to reach one of your points of assessment about the credibility of BIAZA's claim. You should make one precise point.

> **Student**
> You would need to know whether the claim was based on information that BIAZA got from the staff who actually work day-to-day with the animals, rather than just from the owners and senior managers who might have little to do with the animals.

Let's look again at two of the assessments that we did in the previous question. Here's the first.

> **Student**
> As the organisation that represents zoos in Britain and Ireland, it would have the expertise needed to understand what is involved in meeting the 'good welfare' needs of zoo animals, in that its members work with such animals. This would therefore strengthen the credibility of this claim.

Remember that the question is effectively asking you, 'What further information do you need in order to make your assessment stronger?' You already know some things about BIAZA and this was enough to make some assessment of any claim they make. But what else would it be useful to know?

In the above answer, we've done two things. We've not only said what other information we need, but we've explained why we need to have this.

Here's another one of our assessments in 9(a):

 Student As the largest animal rights organisation in the world, PETA will have a vested interest to show zoos in a bad light. This will mean that it is likely to present a very selective picture of what goes on with the animals in zoos, such that 'Dickerson Park Zoo' might be a very unusual example. As a result, the credibility of its claim is weakened.

What else do we need to know to make this assessment stronger?

 Student We need to know whether the sale or 'donation' of animals by Dickerson Park Zoo to Buddy Johnson was indeed a very unusual example and whether PETA's claim about this zoo is accurate — that is, that it wasn't in any way unrepresentative of how zoos operate.

In this answer we have focused on the need to know whether PETA was being over-selective in its use of evidence. If you had this information, then the assessment that PETA's claim was weakened would itself be strengthened.

What would less successful answers look like?

Additional information that questions the criterion:

Student We would need to know if PETA has a vested interest to show zoos in a bad light. We need to know this in order to help us to see if its claim is weakened.

In this answer, we're not really getting anywhere. We're just asking for information on something we've already stated is the case. We need information to strengthen this.

Additional information on the claim rather than on the assessment of it:

Student We need to know how BIAZA defines 'good welfare' because it might be using the term to include just physical health and so excluding mental well-being.

This answer is explaining why we need more information to assess the claim that's made. In other words it is doing some assessment of the claim itself rather than on one of your assessments of it. This is a good point! But unfortunately it isn't an answer to the specific requirements of this question. You need to remember to focus your answer on one of your assessments given in the previous question.

Here is another type of question that you may be asked:

9 (c) Based on your assessments in 9(a), come to an overall judgement about the credibility of the claim made by BIAZA. You should explain which credibility criterion you consider to be important in this case and then weigh this against the other chosen criterion.

Let's see how we covered the requirements in the question:

> **Student** The credibility of the claim made by BIAZA can be considered to be weak *(overall judgement about the credibility of the chosen claim)*. The most important credibility criterion is vested interest *(most important credibility criterion)*. This is because their motive to selectively present the best things about zoos, because they are the organisation representing zoos in Britain and Ireland and so would want to show them in the best light, outweighs their ability to see what goes on in zoos and their expertise to know what represents 'the good welfare' of animals in zoos *(explanation weighing up the most important credibility criterion against the others)*.

Basically what you are doing is weighing up your assessments to decide which was the most important, and why, and then deciding how this affects the overall credibility of the claim. In the answers above we have weighed up three credibility criteria, because these were the ones we applied. If you were asked to have made only two assessments, then you would only be able to weigh up two criteria.

What would a less successful answer look like?

Missing out the overall judgement:

> **Student** The most important credibility criterion is vested interest. This is because their motive to selectively present the best things about zoos (because they are the organisation representing zoos in Britain and Ireland and so would want to show them in the best light) outweighs their ability to see what goes on in zoos and their expertise to know what represents 'the good welfare' of animals in zoos.

Here all the work has been done, but the final judgement has not been reached.

Missing out a decision as to which criterion is the most important:

> **Student** The credibility of the claim made by BIAZA can be considered to be weak. Their motive to selectively present the best things about zoos (because they are the organisation representing zoos in Britain and Ireland and so would want to show them in the best light) outweighs their ability to see what goes on in zoos and their expertise to know what represents 'the good welfare' of animals in zoos.

Here the most important credibility criterion can be implied, as the answer does the weighing up, but it is not explicitly stated.

Missing out the weighing up:

> **Student** The credibility of the claim made by BIAZA can be considered to be weak. The most important credibility criterion is vested interest. This is because their motive to selectively present the best things about zoos (because they are the organisation representing zoos in Britain and Ireland and so would want to show them in the best light) will mean that they do not give a balanced viewpoint.

This answer simply assesses the claim once again with one credibility criterion.

Exam tips

Make sure that you cover all three requirements of the question:

➤ a weighing-up of the credibility criteria against each other

➤ the most important credibility criterion

➤ the overall judgement

Question 10

10 Referring to the material within the documents, come to a reasoned judgement as to whether zoos increase or reduce animal welfare. You should make a reasoned case with a judgement based on:

➤ the relative credibility of both sides

➤ the relative plausibility of both positions

This question asks you to look at both sides of the dispute and to compare them in terms of their credibility and their plausibility. In the end, you'll need to make an overall decision as to which side is the more credible and plausible.

You'll remember that we looked at plausibility in some detail in Chapter 15. It's worth just reminding yourself about the difference between credibility and plausibility.

Look at the answer below. Blue text has been added to help you to see what is being tackled. Specialist terms, signposting and comparator words have been emboldened. References to the text have been italicised.

First we will look at the relative credibility of both sides.

The case for zoos is represented by BIAZA, which has lots of **expertise** and **experience**. Its members include what are described as *'world-famous zoos'*. It **also** has day-to-day experience, **because** it looks after thousands of animals, and its staff will include those who have specialist training. This expertise is added to by that of ICZ. **Because** this is an international organisation of zookeepers, it will have lots of expertise and experience in dealing with many different types of animals.
[Expertise explained for two sources on the side that zoos increase animal welfare]

On the other side of the argument we **also** have **expertise**. PETA will have much knowledge and experience in animal welfare. **In addition**, PETA refers to *'research carried out by scientists at Oxford University'* on the suffering of zoo animals. Oxford is one of the most important universities in the world. There is **also** expertise in research published in 'the highly respected journal *Science*'.
[Expertise explained for two sources on the side that zoos reduce animal welfare]

Thus both sides have relevant expertise and experience in this area.
[Conclusion reached using the criterion of expertise]

However, in terms of day-to-day experience, it would appear that those who think zoos increase animal welfare have **more** of this, thus strengthening their credibility.

BIAZA and ICZ will have a clear **vested interest** in getting people to believe that animals in zoos don't suffer, to continue to attract visitors. **However**, PETA could also be seen as having a **vested interest** in presenting only anti-zoo information, given that PETA is an important animal rights organisation. **However**, PETA (unlike BIAZA and ICZ) will survive without the zoo issue. Neither the Oxford University study nor the one published in *Science* can be shown to be based on any anti-zoo **vested interest**.
[Comparison of two sides using vested interest and at least two sources on each side]

This shows that those who think zoos increase animal welfare have **greater vested interest** to present their evidence in a good light, thereby weakening their credibility.
[Conclusion reached using the criterion of vested interest]

ICZ work with zoo animals on a day-to-day basis. PETA might have some **ability to perceive** but must be at a **lower** level than that of BIAZA and ICZ. **However**, the research published in *Science* was based on more than 4,500 elephants both in the wild and in zoos. Though this is a big study, it is of only one type of zoo animals. BIAZA and ICZ will have **far greater ability to perceive** how animals in zoos live.
[Comparison of the two sides using ability to see reaching a conclusion]

The side that argues that zoos increase animal welfare appears to have **greater expertise**, **experience** and **the ability to perceive**, than the side that argues that zoos reduce animal welfare. **However**, the strong **vested interest** to present zoos in a good light acts to reduce the credibility of those who think zoos increase animal welfare relative to those who think zoos reduce animal welfare.
[Overall conclusion about the relative credibility]

Now we need to look at the **plausibility** of both outcomes.

If animal welfare is to be seen in terms of protecting animals from the problems of their everyday life in the wild **such as** *'attacks by predators, starvation, disease, parasites, cold and heat'*, **then** zoos could be seen as increasing their welfare. **Also** BIAZA sees zoos as contributing to conservation, claiming that *'some species would not survive without some degree of management, including taking some animals into captivity'*, **so** this can be argued to increase their welfare as it is enabling the species to survive.
[Plausibility of the side that zoos increase animal welfare]

However, animals in zoos have had their welfare reduced **because** they have had to exchange their freedom to roam, forage, hunt and breed, for what the zoo offers. **Also** PETA makes the point that zoos *'actually take money away from useful conservation projects'*. Ideally, animals would presumably prefer to live their lives in the wild, **so** it would seem more plausible that animal welfare is increased by using resources to keep them there rather than to require them to survive only by living unnaturally restricted lives.
[Plausibility of the side that zoos reduce the welfare of other animals]

If zoos are there for the animals (as BIAZA itself seems to be arguing, with its emphasis on animal welfare), **then** the case of those who think zoos increase animal welfare is **less plausible** than the case of those who think zoos reduce animal welfare.
[Conclusion weighing up plausibility of both sides]

Thus in terms of both credibility and **plausibility**, it can be concluded that zoos reduce animal welfare.
[Overall conclusion weighing up credibility and plausibility]

Giving a reasoned case

You need to be clear about what you have to do. You must produce 'a reasoned case with a judgement' and 'come to a reasoned judgement'. In other words, *this question is asking you to write an argument.* With that in mind, you'll be clear that there needs to be a sequence of points leading to a conclusion/judgement.

What should the sequence include?

➢ **The material in the documents:** this is not an opportunity for you to just write an argument of your own on the subject in question. You'll have an opportunity to write an argument on a topic in the Unit 2 paper. Here you should write an argument based on the credibility and plausibility of the material that's given for each side. This involves you in making some reference to the material in the documents and assessing its credibility and plausibility.

➢ **The credibility criteria by name, to assess the credibility of each side:** this involves assessing the credibility of *more than one source* on each side. You might have been tempted to simply reproduce part of your answer to the question on the credibility of claims in question 9(a), but in a very important way this would not be answering question 10 as it requires you to assess the collective *credibility of a side.* You need to ask such questions as:

— Does one *side* have more expertise than the other?

— Is one side heavier on the *side* of vested interest than the other?

— To what extent do the two *sides* balance or outweigh each other?

➢ **A weighing-up of the plausibility of the two outcomes:** looking at the outcomes given in the question, which is the more likely to be the case or is the more reasonable? You can start with the claims given in the text, but you need to develop these with ideas of your own on the issue.

➢ **A sustained comparison within each of these tasks:** an answer that is assessed to be in the top level is described as one that provides 'strong, relative and sustained assessment'. ('Relative' here means a comparison between the two sides.) You can see from this that four areas of evaluation are necessary in order to arrive at a judgement:

— credibility of side X

— plausibility of outcome X

— credibility of side Y

— plausibility of outcome Y

➢ **The specific judgement required by the question:** in question 10 above this was 'come to a reasoned judgement as to whether zoos increase or reduce animal welfare'. Thus your judgement couldn't be 'zoos are necessary' or 'zoos should be better controlled' because these don't fit with what's being asked. In our example, the judgement will have to be either 'zoos increase animal welfare' or 'zoos reduce animal welfare'.

How did we do in the answer above?

➢ The relative credibility of *each* side was assessed, so that a comparison could be drawn between the two sides.

> The relative plausibility of *each* side was assessed, so that a comparison could be drawn between the two sides.
> A clear and explicit judgement was made based on the comparisons of credibility and plausibility.
> Specialist terms (such as credibility criteria) were used.
> Relevant reference was made to the documents.
> The answer included 'signposting' used in argument. This 'signposting' included words like 'however', 'in addition', 'if...then' and helped the reader to follow the way in which the argument progressed.
> Grammar, spelling and punctuation were used accurately.

Summary

You should now be able to see that success in the Unit 1 exam requires you to do a number of things:

> **Read the documents with the types of questions that you're going to be asked in mind** — this will include identifying the sides taken in the issue and thinking about which outcomes are more likely.
> **Read the question carefully** to see exactly what's being asked for. This will include checking:
>> which document you are being referred to
>> what the marks are being given for
>> how many things are being asked for in the question
> **Use terminology appropriately**, especially credibility criteria.
> **Manage your time properly**, ensuring in particular that you have sufficient time for the final big-mark question.
> **Write with clarity and precision** — after all, this is critical thinking.

The final big-mark question

To gain marks in the top band for the final big-mark question, make sure you target the requirements given in the mark scheme. Your answer should show:

> four areas that are strong
> direct points of comparison
> effective reference to the text in at least three areas
> a clear and explicit overall judgement drawn from an assessment of both credibility and plausibility
> effective use of specialist terms and argument indicator words
> accurate grammar, spelling and punctuation

Unit 1 *answers*

Chapter 1

Activities 1–4

Classroom and revision activities.

Exercise 1

Dialogue 1
A is the character presenting an argument. A gives two assertions, which are connected (even if poorly) in the following way.

Conclusion It doesn't matter where Topshop gets its T-shirts made.

because

Reason They're really cheap and good quality.

(or the other way round: reason so conclusion)

B's disagreement is not in itself an argument. We don't know which of A's assertions B disagrees with (it does matter where Topshop gets its T-shirts from/they're not really cheap/they're not good quality/all of these?) Nor does B give A a reason to show why he or she disagrees.

Dialogue 2
Again, only A presents an argument.

B's question 'why' is key here. A's conclusion ('People should get a lot of their clothes...') is then supported by the reason ('They're good quality and not too expensive').

Although B gives A two pieces of information, these are not linked in such a way that an argument is going on.

You might also want to say that A's reason is actually two separate reasons:

Topshop's clothes are good quality. Topshop's clothes are not too expensive.

Technically, you're right, so well done for spotting that.

Dialogue 3
In this dialogue there are two arguments: one from A and the other from B.

This is A's:

Reason Some species of animals might not survive without zoos — like tigers and rhinos.

so

Conclusion This must mean that zoos aren't a bad thing.

This is B's:

Reason Zoos keep animals in artificial environments that are often far too limiting for the animals' needs.

so

Conclusion This means that zoos cause animal suffering.

Past paper practice 1

The argument is in the last sentence.

Conclusion: 'The proposal for ecotowns should be welcomed'

Reason: 'because it would be a valuable step towards easing the housing crisis.'

There is a conclusion followed by a reason. This is the minimum that is required for an argument. You may have noticed that there are indicator words here which signal or signpost the argument elements. The first sentences are background information.

Chapter 2

Exercise 2

Argument 1   The second sentence provides the reason for the conclusion in the first.

Argument 2   The first sentence provides a reason for the conclusion in the second.

Argument 3   The first sentence provides a reason for the conclusion in the second.

Argument 4   The first sentence provides a reason for the conclusion in the second.

Exercise 3

Argument 1   **(C)** People need to see the eating of eggs differently from how they used to. **(R)** People used to think that eating more than a few eggs a week was bad for their health. **(R)** Eggs these days have low levels of cholesterol. **(R)** They have also been shown to have high levels of vitamins.

Argument 2   **(R)** Many parents are using allergy-testing kits on their children (bought online or on the high street) which simply don't work. **(C)** These unauthorised allergy-testing kits must be banned. **(R)** When the kits show a

positive result for an allergy, children are often put on an unnecessarily restricted diet. **(R)** This makes it more difficult for doctors to diagnose any possible allergies.

Argument 3   **(R)** Happily-married couples eat more healthily than other groups. **(R)** They also have more friends than others. **(R)** In addition, they take better care of each other than people who live unhappily with others. **(C)** It is important that schools tell young people about the benefits of a happy marriage.

Exercise 4

Passage 1   The first sentence is a counter-assertion (there is a claim but no argument). The subsequent argument responds to it.

Passage 2   The first two sentences make up a counter-argument (the first sentence is its conclusion and the second its reason). The rest of the passage is an argument in response to this.

Passage 3   The third sentence includes a counter-assertion (the Earth is 'unique in having well-developed life forms'). The rest of the passage is an argument against this claim.

Past paper practice 2

1 '(Consequently), as a response to saving money, energy and the planet, the blackout needs to be rethought.'

2 also, however, consequently, equally, needs, if

3 'Councils in England and Wales argue that a reduction in street lighting is necessary.'

4 There are two possible answers:

'If street lights are switched off in suburban areas at certain times, a council's carbon foot print can be reduced and its climate-change targets can be met.'

'(Councils also claim) the blackout could almost halve street lighting bills.'

You may have struggled at first to distinguish between the argument and the counter-argument. However on further reading it should have become clear that the author has introduced an opposition position in order to dismiss it.

Chapter 3

Exercise 5

Argument 1 The fourth sentence is a hypothetical reason.

Argument 2 The second sentence is a hypothetical conclusion.

Argument 3 The third sentence is a hypothetical reason.

Past paper practice 3

The hypothetical reason is:

'If street lights are switched off in suburban areas at certain times, a council's carbon foot print can be reduced and its climate-change targets can be met.'

You may have been helped by the argument indicator word 'if' which signposts the condition. However, although the indicator word 'then' isn't used in the text to signpost the consequence, by reading it in yourself, it should become obvious that the second half of the sentence is the consequence.

To gain all the marks available you would need to give both the condition and the consequence. You will notice here that there are two consequences.

Chapter 4

Exercise 6

Argument 1 This has both evidence and an example. The evidence is presented in the third sentence, and this evidence is illustrated by the example of 'donating blood'.

Argument 2 This has detailed evidence but there is no example.

Argument 3 This provides a small piece of evidence in the first sentence, with an example in the second.

Argument 4 This has evidence but no example. (Yakult could have been given as an example.)

Argument 5 This is an odd one. The evidence on the significance of wearing red provides an example of how 'the colour of the clothes we wear can significantly affect how other people see us'. But, as it's presented, we would take this as evidence rather than an example.

Past paper practice 4

The examples are: 'accommodation', 'transport', 'safety equipment', 'food', 'medical care'

You may have been tempted by 'funding-raising', 'marketing' and 'office costs', but this is given as the entirety of how the rest of the money is spent.

Chapter 5

Exercise 7

The following are assumed:

- (Many) children wouldn't be allergic to Omega-3 supplements.

- Omega-3 supplements don't have unacceptable negative side effects.

You will see that, in each case, without stating it, the author must believe it in order to draw the conclusion.

Exercise 8

If we take the answers we provided for Exercise 7, then we need to apply the negative test to check if they are assumed.

The assumed claims now read like this.

- (Many) children would be allergic to Omega-3 supplements.

- Omega-3 supplements have unacceptable negative side effects.

In each case, you can see that when the negative (opposite) version is put into the argument, the conclusion cannot be drawn.

Exercise 9

The author must assume all the following:

- The number of doctors per head of population is the best way of measuring the quality of healthcare. (*Otherwise, the author can't move from number of doctors per head to a judgement on the quality of Cuba's healthcare system.*)

- The doctors in Cuba are trained to an acceptably high standard. (*If not, then the Cuban healthcare system can't be as good as the author claims.*)

- The doctors in Cuba are spread geographically to ensure that all the people in Cuba have adequate access to them. (*If not, then the statistic on number of doctors per head is of limited value because it would suggest that people couldn't get to see the doctors.*)

- Access to the doctors in Cuba is not significantly limited by financial barriers. (*This*

is essentially the same point as the previous one on geographical spread.)

- The doctors in Cuba have access to other medical facilities (drugs, health centres, hospitals, nurses, necessary equipment). (*This is necessary because, if it were not the case, then the number of doctors in Cuba wouldn't be a very good guide to the quality of the healthcare.*)

- All the doctors identified in the Cuban statistics are working (rather than retired). (*If the number of doctors in a country is taken as a guide to the quality of its healthcare, then the doctors who are included have to be working. If not, the significance of the figure is distorted.*)

- The doctors in Cuba cover the necessary range of medical specialties (such as obstetrics, surgery and so on). (*If the doctors in Cuba do not cover the range, then the quality of the healthcare available is likely to be reduced.*)

- The doctors identified in the Cuban statistics are all medical doctors. (*If the number of doctors in a country is taken as a guide to the quality of its healthcare, then the doctors who are included have to be medical doctors, rather than those with a non-medical doctorate qualification. If not, the significance of the figure is distorted.*)

- The collection of statistics on the number of doctors in Cuba is reliable. (*If the number of doctors in Cuba has been over-counted — for whatever reason — then the evidence cannot be used to support the author's conclusion.*)

Exercise 10

Claim A   This is not assumed. The author's conclusion would require that doctors were aware of their patients' sleeping problems (because, if not, how would they treat them?) So the author does not have to believe that patients don't report them. Interestingly, the negative test throws up something that looks as if it might itself be assumed: 'people with sleep problems do report these problems to their doctor'. It's certainly not inconsistent with the author's argument, but this version isn't required either. Perhaps doctors could simply ask their patients if they have any sleep problems!

Claim B   This is not assumed. The thrust of the author's argument is the other way round: sleep problems cause health problems, so the author will not see the causal relationship as in B. Indeed, you can see here something that is assumed: sleep problems can cause health problems. This is not stated but is necessary to connect the evidence in the first sentence with the claim in the second. Checking with the negative test, we find that 'poor health can't cause sleep problems' to be something that the author might or might not believe to be true, without the argument being affected.

Claim C   This is assumed. The recommendation (the conclusion) that doctors should do more must be based on the belief that sleep problems can be treated by doctors. If not, then why would the author conclude in this way? Checking the negative test, we find that 'sleep problems cannot be treated by doctors' to be a devastating problem for the argument.

Claim D   This is not assumed. Although the author sees not sleeping well as a cause of health problems, he or she is not required to see sleeping well to be correlated with *no* health problems. (People who sleep well might have fewer problems or different problems.) Checking with the negative test gives us 'people who sleep well have health problems'. Just as the author is not required to believe that people who sleep well have no health problems, it is not necessary to believe that they will have them.

Exercise 11

Remember we're looking for what's *not* assumed.

Claim A   This is assumed. The evidence indicates that fake smiling leads to reduced efficiency and the conclusion is that employers should employ people who smile a lot. For this conclusion to be drawn, the author must assume that people who smile a lot are not faking their smiles (otherwise why employ them?)

Claim B   This is not assumed. Although people who fake smiles at work have their mood worsened as a result (with possible reductions in their efficiency), the author does not have to believe that those who are inefficient are unhappy. The inefficient will include those who fake smiles but it will also include those who are simply not good workers (happy or not). (The happy workers could still be inefficient, but just not as inefficient as the unhappy, forced-smiling ones.)

Claim C   This is assumed. It's obvious that employers would want to employ efficient people, but the author still has to assume this (it isn't stated).

Claim D   This is assumed. The conclusion that employers should employ people who smile a lot must be based on the belief that those who do so are happy and so more efficient. (Otherwise why should employers want to employ them?)

Past paper practice 5

Here are some of the assumptions necessary:
- The information given by the computers will be acted upon to reduce energy use.
- There is a potential to be more energy efficient.
- The energy involved in monitoring will not be more than the energy that can be saved.

It is important that you choose your words carefully. If you go too far with the assumption, for example if you expressed the first bullet as 'everyone will always act on this information', you would not gain all the marks available. Similarly, if you expressed the assumption as a challenge you would also gain limited marks, for example,

'Just because the information is monitored, doesn't mean that it will be acted upon.'

Chapter 6

Exercise 12

The first thing to consider is whether 2,400 students in each country will give a representative picture of all young people in the age groups in each country.

- Is 2,400 a big enough number? (It would normally be taken as a big enough sample size. Public opinion polls, which are often used around election time to predict the level of support for parties, normally use about half that number, and they're normally fairly accurate.)

The next thing to consider is the male/female issue.

- Spreading evenly between males and females should increase the representativeness of the sample (unless, of course, the total numbers in a population are not similar).

What about using teenagers in schools?

- Using teenagers in schools might be a problem for representativeness. It would depend what percentage of this group (especially 17–18-year-olds) were in education. This will vary from country to country (and, within countries, between towns and cities).

Does using whole classes in schools increase the representativeness?

- The survey designers see this as increasing it. They claim that, if all the students in a class complete the questionnaire, this will discourage the young people from being dishonest (and encourage them to take the task seriously).

Is the completion rate of between 83% and 95% one that will provide a representative sample?

- This is a very high return, and so one would expect it to provide an accurate picture. However, you might want to consider whether missing those who are absent due to sickness somehow distorts the sample.

Is it significant that the actual numbers used varied from the expected 2,400?

- This should make no difference, except if the increase/decrease in the numbers somehow skewed the sample. Latvia's 1,640 is still a relatively large sample (especially when we see that the population of this country is only 2.3 million). Italy's 5,130 should also be seen in terms of the size of its total population of 58.9 million.

Exercise 13

Passage 1
- The source of the evidence is a very large sample (11,430), which should help to avoid the charge of over-generalisation.
- The age range is also very large, so again this will increase the chance of this being a representative group.
- The study was carried out over 6 weeks, giving what should be an adequate amount of time for any results to be apparent.
- Perhaps the under-18s and the over-60s should also have been included, otherwise some useful effects of the programmes might have been missed making it unrepresentative.
- We cannot be sure that the 6-week brain-training programme was typical of those used by Nintendo and similar companies.

Passage 2
- The author generalises from the north-east to the whole of the UK. There might be factors that make the north-east not typical of at least some of the other parts of the country.

- The vague 'several of them' creates problems for generalisation. How many is this? What percentage?

- The author generalises from 'social networking sites such as Facebook' to just Facebook (in the conclusion). This might be a problem in itself for generalisation.

- The evidence that 'young people in the north-east were 25% more likely to log on to social networking sites than are those in the rest of the country' is itself a problem for the author's conclusion. It shows that it is difficult to generalise from this obviously very unrepresentative group to the rest of the UK.

Passage 3
- 400 nine-year-olds is a usefully large number for a study to make it representative.

- There might be a problem generalising from nine-year-olds to other children (although it would need to be explained why).

- The author generalises from the six words to all such expressions of praise. (Perhaps this is a problem, although it could be responded that the six words are usefully representative of the problem of over-praising.)

- The author generalises from a particular test situation to all situations in which children perform. This could be a problem. For example, perhaps over-praising works well with children and activities such as sport and drama. (Although, why it might would have to be explained.)

- The author also generalises from 400 nine-year-olds in *New York*. You might see this as a problem, but you would have to explain why.

- We would want to know that the children had been selected to represent different sexes, ethnicities, social classes, etc. in the right proportions.

Passage 4
- In this argument, the conclusion is drawn from whole populations (rather than small samples of them), making it more likely that the results are respresentative.

- With both sets of figures, regional differences might be disguised, making it unrepresentative. Perhaps, in some parts of the country, the figures vary. (This is merely raised as an issue — there is no obviously compelling reason why this should be the case.)

- As a result, the evidence does seem capable of being usefully generalised to all women (except, of course, for the over-75 single woman still searching for Mr Right).

Passage 5
- The 18-month timescale of the study makes the evidence more reliable for any generalisation.

- The large numbers involved (69,000 jury verdicts, etc.) also make the evidence more reliable for any generalisation.

- We would take it that the number of female jurors was sufficiently representative out of the 800 total.

- We would also take it that the study looked at a sufficiently large number of courts in different areas of the country to make it representative.

- The author gives four examples (Teesside, etc.) but does not generalise from these as such. The author generalises from the whole evidence to say that 'the chances of a defendant being convicted can vary from place to place'.

Exercise 14

Perhaps surprisingly, all but number 7 have been used as definitions of binge drinking.

Past paper practice 6

You may have made the following points:

- If the bar worker's salary is significantly less than the average smoker's salary, then what he finds expensive may not be typical of smokers in general who may feel that they can afford this gadget.
- If the bar worker is a smoker, with the same priorities in relation to disposable income, other smokers would also find this gadget expensive.

To gain all the marks available, you need to identify the characteristic first, here being a smoker, or earning similar amounts or having similar disposable income. Second, you need to decide whether the general group, here smokers, would also share this characteristic.

Chapter 7

Exercise 15

Claim 1 This historical information might play some part in showing why the practice of changing the clocks was introduced but, as it is, it cannot be used one way or the other with the conclusion.

Claim 2 This provides a useful reason why we should not put the clocks back by 1 hour (assuming, of course, that the change in the clocks is the cause of the increased road accidents).

Claim 3 As it stands, it's difficult to see how this will fit with the conclusion. However, you might see this as relevant if getting dark earlier is the cause or part of the cause for people exercising less in winter. It's feasible that darker afternoons reduce the number of people walking or running on streets. But, of course, there could be other explanations for the claim. (After all, the opening hours of gyms are unaffected by the change in the clocks.)

Claim 4 The issue of UK time being out of line with the rest of Europe is one that could be used to support the conclusion but, again, would need more information. The latter would focus on any disadvantages that would follow (especially economic issues for businesses).

Claim 5 This is straightforwardly irrelevant to the conclusion: whatever happens with the clocks, there are some people who are 'larks' and some who are 'owls'.

Claim 6 Given that dusk comes earlier in the afternoon when the clocks are put back, this point of reasoning can be seen as relevant to the conclusion. It provides a reason for the conclusion.

Claim 7 This can also be seen as relevant to the conclusion, in that it provides a reason for the conclusion. However, for it to work as a reason, there would have to be assumptions slotted in. These would include:

- It is preferable for children to walk home after school in the light.
- Children are more at risk of harm if they walk home after school in the dark.

Past paper practice 7

Here are two points that you could have made:
- There is a weakness in the link. Just because there are advantages to allotment-grown food, it doesn't mean that it is the 'best way to eat locally'. The allotment growers haven't explained how this food compares to other locally-grown produce, such as food grown from your own garden or fruit from local markets, which might also be 'picked at the peak of ripeness'. The reasoning therefore isn't adequate to draw the conclusion about allotment-grown food being the 'best way to eat locally'.
- There is a weakness in the link. It assumes that the 'chemical input' in allotments is less than in conventional agriculture. Without this being stated, it is not possible to draw the

conclusion that allotment-grown food is the 'best way to eat locally'.

In each of the above answers clear reference was made to the parts of the reasoning that were being linked and this link was assessed. If you assess the reasoning in isolation from the conclusion, you will not be able to access all of the marks.

Chapter 8

Past paper practice 8

The following would have gained full marks because the points are relevant and do not include extra argument elements:

- You may have to travel further to an allotment.
- It is easier for thieves to steal produce and implements from an allotment.
- The scale of the commitment to allotment growing is more demanding.

The following gives a reason without any extra argument elements, but would not have accessed all the marks, because it focuses on growing food in general. The reason is therefore not directly relevant to the comparison drawn in the conclusion.

- Growing your own food requires a lot of knowledge about plants.

The following gives a relevant reason, but adds an extra argument element:

- Growing your own food in allotments requires more commitment, such as harvesting bigger crops in a short time span.

Chapter 9

Section A practice exam-style questions

Analysing argument

1 Main conclusion: *You shouldn't drive any vehicle while using a mobile phone.*

This gains full marks, whereas if you had included in the example 'including cars and lorries', you would have gained partial performance marks, because you would have included an extra argument element.

2 Choose two from: *as, despite, including, among.* Also acceptable are *should* and *and.*

'As' indicates a reason, 'despite' indicates counter-argument and 'including' and 'among' both indicate examples.

You might have been tempted by 'while', but it is used in the passage with the meaning 'at the same time as', rather than indicating counter-argument. This shows that it is important to look at how the words are used, rather than just learning a list of words that are usually argument indicator words.

'Should' here flags up that a conclusion is being used, although it could be present in an assertion, a reason, a principle and counter-reasoning. 'And' indicates additional reasoning in the second sentence, although this could be used in the sense of an additional item in a list.

3 Reason given in the counter-argument: *as they do it every day without any problems.*

If you gave the answer 'as your full attention can't be given to both phoning and driving at the same time' you would gain no marks, as you would have identified a reason to support the main conclusion.

4 Evidence: *AA reports show that that they are called out to a growing number of mobile phone-related accidents on a weekly basis.*

This is evidence that is given to support the claim that mobile phones are the cause of many accidents. Although there are no numerical data, you may have identified it as evidence by recognising that it was part of a report.

5 (a) Argument element: *example.*

(b) Explanation: *It gives a specific instance which illustrates the evidence.*

The key words are 'specific', 'instance' and 'illustrates.' All that you need to do here is to give a definition.

Identifying assumptions

Assumption: *There will be another frost tomorrow morning.*

If you had said, 'there are frosts every day', this would be going beyond the claim that recommends only closing the greenhouse tonight.

If you had said, 'greenhouses keep out frost', they do, but then you would also have to assume that there was going to be a frost that needed to be kept out.

Assessing evidence

An answer is given below for each of the criteria to illustrate how they can be applied, even though the question asks you to choose just two of them.

Representativeness
The experience of university students using the toothpaste may not be representative of that of the general public if the students' tooth brushing is normally minimal. Being part of a trial that regularises tooth brushing might mean that students would notice the difference more than the general public. Therefore the evidence in support of this toothpaste is weak.

Here the task was to identify why the students' *experience of the toothpaste* might be not be typical of that of other groups.

If you had answered, 'University students are more highly educated than the average person', this compares the university students to the general public without referring to their experience of the toothpaste and misses the point.

Relevance
The claim is that this toothpaste will make your teeth 'look cleaner for longer', but the evidence given is that the students' 'mouths felt fresher for a greater part of the day'. Feeling fresher is different from whether teeth look cleaner, as a mouth-freshener additive could give a pleasant feeling without having any effect on the appearance of the teeth. The evidence is therefore weak.

Relevance looks to see if claims are tightly linked, or to put it another way, are talking about the same thing. Here the claim and the evidence used to support it are clearly talking about different things: freshness and looking cleaner.

Alternative interpretation of statistics
It may not have been 'Staybright' toothpaste in particular that made their mouths feel fresher for longer, if, as part of the trial, the students were brushing their teeth more frequently than they would normally do. The increase in amount of cleaning may have done this, regardless of the brand.

This answer has identified the conditions of a trial which often makes people behave in a way that is different from usual. An alternative explanation is simply asking for a different reason to account for the evidence.

Assessing the link between reasoning and conclusion

In each of the answers below you will notice that both the reasoning and the conclusion are referred to. To assess the link, you need to indicate that you have correctly identified the conclusion and which part of the reasoning you are using to link to it.

The following answers would have gained full marks. To gain less than full marks, you might have identified the conclusion and the reasoning but not have assessed it. Or you might have assessed the reasoning instead of its link to the conclusion.

1 Canteen food

There is a strong link between the reasoning that the canteen 'now offers low-fat options' and the conclusion 'If employees want to eat healthy food they should buy their meals from the canteen', because low-fat meals are one way of eating healthily, as it can help to keep cholesterol low and help to keep people at an appropriate weight.

Here the answer has identified the relevance of the reasoning. Low-fat options and healthy eating are directly linked.

The reasoning 'There are also more tables to accommodate the larger workforce' and 'the menus are very competitively priced' gives weak support to the conclusion 'If employees want to eat healthy food they should buy their meals from the canteen'. Although they give good reasons why employees should eat there — good prices and comfortable eating — these factors are not relevant to eating healthily.

Here cost and being comfortable are not directly linked to eating healthily.

2 Sleep trials

There is a weakness in the link between the reasoning 'teenagers need 8 hours' sleep a night' and the conclusion 'So, students clearly need to restrict having late nights out to the weekend' because potentially two different sets of people are involved, teenagers and students. As not all students are teenagers, not all students would need the 8 hours' sleep or the advice about restricting late nights.

Here teenagers' needs are not necessarily directly linked to students' needs.

There is a relevant link between the reasoning 'teenagers need 8 hours' sleep a night in order for their brains to function at their best' and the conclusion 'So, students clearly need to restrict having late nights out to the weekend' because teenagers who are students need functioning brains to be able to cope with teaching situations during the week, whereas at weekends the demands on their concentration may be less, so they can afford to have less sleep then.

Here there is a direct link between when teenagers who are students need to concentrate most and need most sleep.

(This of course makes the assumptions that they don't have jobs that demand concentration at the weekend; that they don't need to concentrate for several hours at the weekend to do homework/coursework and that they couldn't alter their sleeping habits during the week to sleep from midnight to 8 a.m. or to break the 8 hours into 6 hours and 2 hours, and to take the 2 hours sleep before they went out.)

Chapter 10

Activity 5

There is guidance in the text following Activity 5 about how the types of the assessment will be developed in the book, but here are some specific points that you might have considered.

Looking at the document itself

Did you home in on the fact that the document was written by a pressure group, 'littlebrook. campaignforsaferroads.co.uk'? This might have made you think that the document was less believable, because they might exaggerate the facts to persuade you to support their cause.

Or it may have led you to think that, as a pressure group, they may have considerable experience in collecting the data available, making their claims more credible.

Either would be justifiable, but an important point to remember is that you argued this from the information about the source at the bottom of their document.

Looking at the claims within the document

You may have decided to believe the witness in the queue because they were not involved in the accident and they saw what actually happened. Or you might have thought that because they knew the Renault car driver that they might be biased towards them, which might weaken their believability.

The important points are that you were using specific criteria/standards with which to judge believability and that you recognised that there are strengths and weaknesses in the claims of the same source. These will help you to decide who to believe where the evidence is disputed, as with the claims of the two drivers about who was at fault.

Making an overall judgement

Here you would have to had looked at the claims of all the sources and balanced them against each other. You might have felt that, on balance, the claims of the Renault car driver and the witness in the queue were more credible than the van driver and his company manager, as the latter had more to lose if they were found at fault.

You might then have gone on to look at how likely it is that someone would reverse back from a roundabout as opposed to the other vehicle driving forward into a stationary vehicle.

Whatever you decided, you would then have needed to weigh up the believability of the claims against the likelihood of what might have happened. This may have led you to conclude that it is more likely that the Renault car driver was at fault, as it would be very rare that a vehicle would reverse into the stream of traffic behind them.

The document for this activity was based on a real-life incident, where the van driver did in fact reverse to avoid an oncoming lorry. However, in the examination there is no right or wrong

judgement, simply one that can be justified by a reasoned case.

Past paper practice 9

You should have identified that the following skills were required:

- Question 7 — assessing the credibility of a document
- Question 8 — assessing consistency
- Question 9 (a) — assessing the credibility of a claim made by one of the sources
- Question 9 (b) — weighing up the overall credibility of the source's claim

Chapter 11

Activity 6

Bias activity — answers will vary according to the organisation or pressure group used.

Exercise 16

Bias

The judge was biased in favour of the police officers. He raises the question of why we would expect 'brave' police officers to lie (with the strong implication that we wouldn't).

Vested interest

Bentley was seen to have a vested interest to lie to literally save his life. The judge said about Bentley's denial of having said 'let him have it, Chris', that it 'is the denial of a man in grievous peril'.

Past paper practice 10

The Town and Country Planning Association are making claims about their past performance to 'inspire' and to 'take a fresh perspective on major issues'. This is a self-acclaimed reputation, which *if true* would strengthen the credibility of their document, as the government and other bodies are more likely to listen to and act on ideas that are well founded.

Your assessment will be stronger if it recognises that this claim cannot be taken at face value.

Past paper practice 11

The two problems are that:
- this is self-acclaimed
- the long pedigree may not assure us of present care and expertise

To strengthen your assessments, you would have to make the following additions:

- The self-acclaimed reputation of being 'looked to by government' *if true* would strengthen the credibility of their document, as the government and other bodies are more likely to listen and act upon ideas that are well founded.
- The 'long pedigree in motoring affairs' might indicate that they have a reputation for guidance in policy, which is more likely to be credible *if their present ideas live up to their pedigree.*

Activity 7

Examples of supposed neutrality might be:
- referees or umpires in sport
- judges in courts, but also judges in competitions such as a 'best dog' competition
- mediators such as those involved in disputes between married couples and those who mediate between companies and trade unions

- researchers investigating something, with no connection to getting a result favourable to one side or the other
- government officials, such as civil servants, who have to work with whatever political party is in power

Activity 8

Costa Concordia activity— answers will vary according to the sources used.

Activity 9

Advertisements activity— answers will vary according to the examples used.

Past paper practice 12

Use the following to check your answers:
- Do they have expertise in this precise field?
- What is the depth of their knowledge in this field?
- Have they been directly involved with the experiments?
- How long have they been involved in the field?
- If you have access to the internet you might be able to find out extra information to make your case more convincing.

Exercise 17

Let's see how the credibility criteria RAVEN could be used to assess both sides.

SHAC
- **R**eputation: it has a reputation as an active campaigning organisation against what it sees as animal cruelty. This could mean that it has to present information in a way that preserves this reputation.

- **A**bility to perceive: it is difficult to know whether SHAC had been able to see inside the HLS buildings, or whether it had had access to documents that provided this information. If it had, then the credibility of the claim is strengthened; if not, it would be weakened.

- **V**ested interest: SHAC has an obvious vested interest in showing HLS in a very bad light, in that it exists to have HLS closed down. This could lead it to distort the evidence about HLS. It could also, however, have a vested interest to report accurately otherwise its supporters might switch off their support.

- **E**xpertise: it is not obvious what expertise SHAC has that would be relevant to this claim. We would need to know more about its membership and/or advisors.

- **N**eutrality: SHAC would not, of course, claim neutrality here. Its lack of neutrality might lead it to exaggerate the claim, but we can't tell.

Bias: SHAC will clearly be biased against animal experimentation and so may have cherry-picked evidence to arrive at this claim.

HLS

- **R**eputation: HLS has a scientific reputation to maintain, as doing useful (indeed, it might argue, necessary) work. It will therefore want to protect this reputation so that its status is maintained.

- **A**bility to perceive: it is obvious that HLS is in a very good position to see what happens inside its buildings. It will presumably keep records of the number of animals it processes, including how many die and how frequently deaths occur.

- **V**ested interest: HLS will have a vested interest to present its work in the best possible light. It will want to avoid criticism as a result of claims of cruelty to animals, and it would therefore want reports of numbers of animal deaths to be minimised. It might also have a vested interest to report information accurately, so that its customers and official

bodies are not embarrassed by reports that can be shown to be distorted.

- **E**xpertise: again, it is obvious that HLS staff are trained and experienced in working with animals in experiments. However, this expertise is not necessarily significant in deciding whether the claim on how many animals die is a particular number.

- **N**eutrality: whatever its response to the claim, it is not based on a neutral position.

Bias: HLS is obviously biased in the direction of the value of animal experiments. This might lead it to see the issue of animal deaths as not that significant.

Chapter 12

Activity 10

You might have identified the following credibility criteria:
- vested interest
- bias
- expertise
- ability to see

See the text on page 93 for an explanation as to why these credibility apply.

Activity 11

Roche and Tamiflu activity — answers discussed in the text.

Activity 12

BMJ and Tamiflu activity — answers discussed in the text.

Past paper practice 13

You might have identified some of the following assessment points:

- *Reputation:* we do not know about the reputation of BBW, but they would have a professionalism to maintain. As a pressure group 'bigbrotherwatch.org.uk' would want to appear credible in the eyes of the public to attract their support, so they would have a vested interest to make a realistic assessment of the negative impact of the effects of the micro-chipping of dogs to maintain their professionalism.

- *Ability to perceive:* as a pressure group 'bigbrotherwatch.org.uk' would want to monitor the government use of data first hand, so is likely to have the ability to perceive negative impacts on personal liberty, to be able to predict realistically the impact of the micro-chipping of dogs on personal freedom.

- *Vested interest:* Big Brother Watch may have a vested interest to exaggerate the negative effects of micro-chipping dogs on personal liberty, because of their aim to protect personal freedom by looking 'for the sly, slow seizure of control by the state — of power, of information and of our lives'. (This could be also expressed as lack of *neutrality*.)

- *Experience:* because Big Brother Watch is a pressure group with an aim to protect personal freedom by looking 'for the sly, slow seizure of control by the state — of power, of information and of our lives', they may have the experience to know about how the government collects, and uses, data, to be able to realistically predict the negative effects of the micro-chipping of dogs on personal liberty.

You will have noticed that when BBW was referred to as a pressure group, the name of their website could be used as a reference to the text.

Chapter 13

Activity 13

Titanic activity — answers discussed in the text.

Activity 14

Titanic activity (overall credibility) — answers discussed in the text.

Exercise 18

Let's take his claim, 'I know what I saw and it looked like a spaceship, a huge flying dome.'

- *Vested interest:* Bob Taylor made no financial gain from his story and sought to avoid publicity so he would have had no vested interest to invent a story about seeing 'a huge flying dome'. This strengthens the credibility of his claim. (This assessment could also be expressed as neutrality.)

- *Reputation:* Bob Taylor had a reputation for being 'steady'. This may mean that he would be unlikely to exaggerate what he saw. This strengthens his claim that he saw 'a huge flying dome'.

- *Ability to perceive:* Bob Taylor was reported to have had a really bad headache and a wild craving thirst. If these were symptoms of a virus, it may be that he hallucinated. If this were so, it would weaken the credibility of his claim that he saw 'a huge flying dome'.

Is Bob Taylor's experience as a 'forester' relevant? Probably not. However he would certainly know the forest well, and would therefore be familiar with any oddities of light coming through the trees. This however would not help him to identify the flying dome as such.

Exercise 19

Ben Goldacre

Let's take his claim, 'In every single trial, the sponsoring company's drug was claimed to be either equivalent to, or better than, the drug it was compared with'.

In the assessments that follow, you will notice that the reference to the specific claim (as this is what you are assessing) can be very brief.

- *Expertise:* Ben Goldacre's claim about the 'trials' into NSAI drugs is based on his expertise as a medical doctor. Reading about clinical trials to judge which drugs to give is part of a doctor's work, so this background will strengthen the credibility of his claim.

- *Vested interest:* Ben Goldacre might have a vested interest to show that the results of the medical research 'trials' are questionable. He writes a newspaper column on the subject of 'Bad Science' and also has a website promoting himself and his products (such as T-shirts). The publicity that could follow from his claim might greatly benefit him, which weakens its credibility.

- *Reputation:* Ben Goldacre has a reputation for reporting on 'Bad Science', and he would not want this reputation to be damaged by making a false claim about the 'trials'. In this way, the credibility of his claim is strengthened.

Vincent Lawton

Let's take his claim, 'Clinical trials are properly managed by a rigorous system of regulatory scrutiny throughout.'

- *Experience:* Vincent Lawton has had considerable experience for many years in the pharmaceutical industry. This experience is likely to enable him to know how 'the clinical trials are managed'. In this way, the credibility of his claim is strengthened.

- *Vested interest:* as a result of his long (and present) association with the pharmaceutical industry, Vincent Lawton has a vested interest to show the industry in a good light in terms of how 'the clinical trials are managed'. This weakens the credibility of his claim.

- *Ability to observe:* as a result of his long (and present) association with the pharmaceutical industry, Vincent Lawton will have had the ability to observe how its research is carried out, including its 'regulatory scrutiny'. This will strengthen his credibility of his claim. You could also turn this around. For example, Vincent Lawton might not have the ability to observe the actual research that has been carried out into NSAI drugs.

- *Neutrality:* Vincent Lawton could be seen as neutral with regard to the research on NSAI drugs, if his work (and his present company) has not been involved in the production of NSAI drugs. This would strengthen his credibility of his claim about 'regulatory scrutiny'.

Past paper practice 14

1 Let's take the claim 'These findings therefore warn that there are dangers in the continued use of micro-chips in both animals and human beings.'

- *Vested interest/neutrality:* as a seasoned campaigner against micro-chips, she might have a vested interest to preserve her public standing by making an accurate claim about the dangers of the continued use of micro-chips. This would strengthen the credibility of her warning about their 'continued use'.

- *Bias:* as a seasoned campaigner against micro-chips and having helped to create the website ChipMeNot, she favours that side and this is likely to influence the selection of the 'findings', which would weaken the credibility of her warning about their 'continued use'.

- *Expertise:* with a doctorate in education she may not have the relevant expertise required to accurately assess the degree of the link between micro-chips and cancer. This would weaken the credibility of her warning about their 'continued use'.

2 Here is one possible judgement that you could have made:

Overall, the credibility of her warning about the 'continued use' use of micro-chips *is weak. The most important credibility criterion is* lack of relevant expertise, as if her doctorate in education is not supported by a relevant degree in science and if she has no direct experience of the experiments, then *this would outweigh her vested interest to be accurate* in what she says. No matter how genuine she intended to be, she may have a limited picture of the research or the effects that micro-chips may have upon animals and human beings. This judgement would also be supported by her natural bias against micro-chips given her campaign against them.

Past paper practice 15

1 Let's take his claim 'Telling people how to spend their money, even if it is for worthwhile causes, is a very dangerous path to go down.' You might have made the following assessment:

Neutrality: as a source that is independent of the research, he would have no motive to interpret the implication of the findings in any particular way. This would strengthen the credibility of his claim about not 'telling people how to spend their money'.

2 You would need to know that he had nothing to gain from discrediting the suggestions made by the researchers, such as funding for the opportunity to research further into this field.

What we have done here is to think about the wider situation. We are told that he did not take part in the research, so he would have no motive in connection with it, but we are not told whether he was, or was likely to be, involved in research that might be in the same area.

Chapter 14

Past paper practice 16

Source: Derek Barnett of the Police Superintendent's Association.

Claim: 'Good street lighting reduces crime; it makes the public feel safe and reduces the risk of traffic accidents.'

You will see that these are specific claims about both crime and road safety that support those made by the transport minister.

If you had answered 'changes in street lighting could increase the number of road accidents', this is an opinion rather than a claim about what is the case and it deals only with road safety, not commenting on crime.

Past paper practice 17

Source 1: MP.

Claim 1: 'It would not represent a financial barrier to dog ownership for vulnerable groups.'

Source 2: the Dogs Trust.

Claim 2: 'It involves a small one-off fee.'

Here you were given a claim that was not included in the text. You will notice that the answers include a reference to the size of the fee: 'not a financial barrier' and 'small'. The following answers would be incorrect as they do not do this:

'It would provide a lifetime of security for a one-off payment.'

'Micro-chipping which would involve a one-off fee.'

Past paper practice 18

Claim: 'The average household needlessly throws away 18% of all food purchased and families with children throw away 27%.'

Claim: 'Around a third of all the food bought in the UK ends up being thrown away.'

In this question you were given the documents as the sources, so you only needed to find the claims. From these you can see that a third or 33.33% is higher than 18% or 27%. If you had included the raw figure, '6.7 million tonnes each year of food bought in the UK ends up being thrown away', instead of the percentage, this would have been incorrect, as by itself the raw number cannot be compared to the percentage.

Chapter 15

Activity 15

Here are some key ideas to check your answers against.

Credibility

Hans Sluiman

- *Relevant expertise:* as an algae expert to discount that the jelly was 'plant' life — strengthens the credibility.

- *Vested interest:* to be accurate that it was not 'plant' life to maintain professionalism as an algae expert — strengthens the credibility.

- *Ability to perceive:* if he saw the jelly first hand to identify that it was not 'plant' life — strengthens the credibility.

Andy Taylor

- *Relevant expertise:* as one who studies fungi to identify that the jelly contained 'fungus filaments' — strengthens the credibility.

- *Vested interest:* to be accurate that the jelly contained 'fungus filaments' to maintain

professionalism as one who studies fungi — strengthens the credibility.

- *Ability to perceive:* if he saw the jelly first hand to identify that the jelly contained 'fungus filaments' — strengthens the credibility.

Radio listener

- *Lack of relevant expertise:* to recognise whether the 'blob' was the same substance as the jelly — weakens the credibility.

- *Vested interest:* to make the connection between the jelly and the 'blob' to attract attention to themselves — weakens the credibility.

- *Ability to perceive:* saw the 'blob' first hand to know that it was a jelly-like substance — strengthens the credibility.

Plausibility

Any assessment of plausibility is likely to be speculative. You may have discounted the 'star jelly' as an earlier poetic attempt to explain its unknown origin. It is likely that if it had anything to do with frogspawn, that the experts would have picked this up, although the two experts cited were not experts in animal life. It might be as a result of chem-trailing, although again, if it were, an expert would most likely have made a positive identification.

Activity 16

You may have considered some of the following points:

- This is a long-term (often called 'longitudinal') study using evidence taken over 20 years. In addition, the number of participants is unusually high (120,000). With such a massive longitudinal study, it is likely that the results are a good indication of the relationship between type of food and weight loss/gain.

- The explanation given for why some foods contribute to weight loss (natural foods taking longer than high-calorific foods for the body to process) appears to be a likely explanation because the longer the processing, the longer a person will feel sustained and therefore not feel the need to eat more.

It is difficult to see why the theory might not be plausible, but here is an argument that might be put forward:

- Although not feeling hungry would stop most people from eating more, for those who are addictive eaters, this would not stop them. Thus in the case of compulsive eaters, considering the type of food they eat might not help them to lose weight.

Overall judgement: Since the research and explanation makes sense, and compulsive eaters are in the minority, it is highly likely that it is important to consider what you eat as well as how much you eat when it comes to keeping slim in the long term.

Chapter 16

Activity 17

Probiotic drinks and yoghurts activity — answers discussed in the text.

Activity 18

Third runway at Heathrow activity — answers discussed in the text.

Exercise 20

Let's take vested interest as the criterion to compare the credibility of both sides. You could use any criterion, but it is important to remember to apply the same criterion to both sides.

Credibility of the side that supports the HS2

You probably spotted that there is a great deal of vested interest on this side as each source will have a direct gain if the HS2 goes ahead.

- *The Campaign for High Speed Rail* describes itself as 'independent from the Government and HS2 Ltd'. However this doesn't mean that it has no vested interest. As it represents employers who believe that Britain needs a high speed network, it will want to promote their interests and will strengthen their support if it is seen to do this.

- *Centro* has a vested interest in more people using public transport, because it promotes public transport in the West Midlands, so the success of its cause may be the main reason why it supports HS2.

- *The rail traveller, Jason Roberts,* would also have vested interest in wanting rail travel to be improved as 'a frequent traveller' who has to stand on the train because of overcrowding. His gain would be a quicker and more comfortable journey.

Credibility of the side that opposes the HS2

- *The 'two leading transport economists'* will have a vested interest to maintain their good reputation for the quality of their work, by making sure that their research here is of high quality.

- The two named official bodies, *Natural England* and the *Environment Agency* may have a vested interest to promote the interests of their own areas, which could be seen as increasing the chance of them reporting honestly on the impact of HS2.

- *The local councils* can be seen as having an obvious vested interest in opposing HS2. The rail line will run through their areas so, if there is local opposition to the plans, they will want to be seen as supporting this opposition in order to keep local votes. The same point applies to the local MPs.

- *The boss of Ryanair* has clear vested interest in opposing the HS2 because of the possible threat to the short-haul domestic flight market.

- *The Taxpayers' Alliance* has a vested interest to oppose any plans that will cost the taxpayers what it considers to be an unnecessary expense. Given that the HS2 plan is so expensive, they have a motive to oppose it.
- The *Financial Times* can be seen as neutral as it is not linked to either side in this debate.

Judgement of credibility

Using the criterion of vested interest, the side that opposes the HS2 would seem to be the more credible. It has more sources with a vested interest to report honestly on the subject and one source that is not linked to either side of the debate. Whereas the side that supports the HS2 all have direct gains if it goes ahead.

Plausibility of the side that supports HS2

How likely is it that the HS2 plan will produce benefits that can be justified? The supporters point to a number of benefits — advantages to businesses, more people using public transport, reduction in road congestion, reduced carbon emissions, improved air quality and more comfortable conditions on trains.

If the HS2 can lead to considerable benefits to business in terms of recruitment and sales, as claimed by the Campaign for High Speed Rail, then these benefits are likely to be significant for the whole country, as employment would increase and the national economy would improve. Also, if these improvements could be gained at the same time as reductions in road congestion and pollution, then the benefits would be very significant. This would depend, however, on a great number of people choosing rail travel over the car.

Plausibility of the side that opposes HS2

On the other hand, these claimed benefits have to be considered alongside the claimed costs of the HS2. Apart from the financial costs, there is the issue of the impact on areas of the country and the possible risks to water supplies. If the same benefits claimed by business people for the HS2 could be delivered, as Chris Castles and David Parish claim, by simply using the existing line more intensively, then the case for the HS2 loses considerable plausibility.

Judgement of plausibility

We have to consider whether the case for benefits or costs has been made. The case for HS2 rests largely on various claimed benefits to business and thus jobs, the environment in terms of pollution, and the convenience of the travelling public with 'more and faster trains' and reduced road congestion. These benefits seem very plausible, whereas the financial costs will be recouped over time and the impact upon the environment could be mitigated with landscaping. It would therefore seem that the plausibility of the side that supports HS2 is greater than that which opposes it.

Overall judgement

We have to weigh credibility and plausibility. Although the side that opposes HS2 appears to be more credible in terms of less vested interest to gain by the plans, the plausibility of the benefits of HS2 seems greater than the costs. Thus in spite of the weaker credibility of those that support HS2, in view of the likelihood of an improved economy, it could be seen that those who support HS2 have the stronger case.

Unit 2

Assessing and developing argument

Unit 2

The Unit 2 examination

As with the Unit 1 examination, Unit 2 can be taken in January or May/June and it is assessed by a written paper of 1 hour 30 minutes. Unit 2 is divided into three sections:

➢ **Section A:** Multiple choice (15 marks)
➢ **Section B:** Analysing and evaluating argument (30 marks)
➢ **Section C:** Developing your own argument (30 marks)

There is no coursework or controlled assessment.

Unit 2 examines the same three key reasoning skills as Unit 1:

➢ analysing argument (deconstructing argument into its component parts)
➢ evaluating argument (identifying strengths and weakness)
➢ developing argument (constructing your own reasoning)

It builds on the skills learned in Unit 1, adding extra argument elements to identify and assess; looking deeper into the evaluation of argument; and extending your own reasoning into a whole argument.

In Unit 2 there are fewer marks for analysis and evaluation and more marks (40%) for constructing your own reasoning, so this is a skill that it is particularly important not to neglect when tackling this unit.

Section A, multiple choice, is answered on an OMR sheet which is marked mechanically, whereas sections B and C are answered in a question-and-answer booklet similar to that of Unit 1.

Track your progress

Unit 2 builds on the skills you have already developed for Unit 1. The new elements are listed on the chart below. As with Unit 1, use the chart to keep track of your progress and to note down your levels of confidence in each particular skill. That way, you will have a record of the areas that may need further attention.

As you work through the skills required for Unit 2, use the traffic light system to record your confidence levels:

■ I feel confident with this skill

▢ I need a little more practice

■ I need more guidance and practice

Re-visit those skills which you have identified in red as needing further practice. Read the relevant examples in this book to see if you can gain a firmer grasp of these skills. The third column shows which chapter you can go to for explanation, exercises and guidance.

Section A topic	Skills required	Chapter	Confidence level		
Multiple choice	Analysis Evaluation	29			

Section B: Analysing argument	Skills required	Chapter	Confidence level		
Explanation	• Explain function • Distinguish between explanation and argument • Identify within an argument	18			
Intermediate conclusion	• Explain function • Identify within an argument	19			
Analogy	• Identify within an argument • Explain the analogy (the precise situations being compared)	20			
Principle	• Explain function • Identify within an argument	21			

Section B: Evaluating argument	Skills required	Chapter	Confidence level		
Evidence	• The significance of evidence • Alternative explanation	22			
Flaws	• Identify specific flaws • Explain specific flaws with reference to their context	23			
Appeals	• Identify specific appeals • Explain specific appeals with reference to their context	24			
Analogy	• Assess the analogy itself • Assess the support it gives to the conclusion	25			
Principle	• Assess the use of the principle • Assess where the principle would and would not apply	26			
Hypothetical reasoning	• Assess the hypothetical reasoning itself • Assess the support it gives to the conclusion	27			

Section C: Developing argument	Skills required	Chapter	Confidence level		
Individual argument elements	• Produce a range of individual argument elements	28			
Own argument	• Use an intermediate conclusion • Use counter-argument and respond to it	29			

Using a range of critical thinking terms

In Unit 2, as well as mastering the skills listed above, you are expected to use a range of specific terms relevant to critical thinking. Here are some of the most important terms you will need to learn.

Implication and inference

Consider the following:

> London's murder count reaches 90.

This was the headline of *thelondonpaper* on 28 July 2008.

As people grabbed the paper on their way to catch a train, they were meant to see this headline as telling them something beyond a message about numbers. This was, of course, that the number 90 was a cause for concern, indeed that it was alarming.

In this way, the reader was meant to draw something from the claim. To read it and say 'So?' was not the point. In addition, of course, to read it and say 'Is that all?' was also not expected.

One way of thinking of **implication** is as a ripe apple on a tree. The apple hasn't been picked yet, but will be when you come along and take it. A picked apple becomes an **inference**; an unpicked one has the potential to become one; it has 'implication' on it.

> ## Key terms
>
> ➤ **implication:** it is what the author means you to draw from what they say, without them explicitly saying this. Literally it means what is intended but not actually stated.
>
> ➤ **inference**: this is a conclusion drawn from the claims that are given or a conclusion that could be drawn from the claims given.

You might have heard the term implication used when people are arguing:

> 'I saw you looking at my boyfriend.'

> 'What are you implying by that?'

The inference could then be drawn.

'That you fancy him.'

'What, him?'

So, leaving them to sort that out, let's return to this claim:

London's murder count reaches 90.

There's an interesting sting in the tail here. We've seen that the implication intended by the author of the headline was that this was a cause for concern. However, someone who drew the inference 'Is that all?' would have actually been drawing a more accurate conclusion.

In a recent study, it has been shown that, although each murder is, in an important way, unpredictable, the overall number of murders is very predictable. The authors of the study have shown that, in any one year, we would have expected 93 murders in London by 28 July. So the inference that should be drawn from 'London's murder count reaches 90' is either '2008 is looking to be a normal year then' or 'Not too bad then'.

Misunderstandings often happen because people don't explicitly say what they mean, and there is a difference between what the speaker implies and the listener infers. You may recognise the following misunderstanding:

Parent shouts up the stairs	'It's 8 o'clock.'
implies	'You should be out of bed and dressed.' (They are to leave at 8.20 am.)
Child draws the inference	'That's OK then. I've got 10 more minutes before I need to get up.'

Such misunderstandings result because what is said can be interpreted in different ways — different inferences can be drawn.

Exam tip

If you're asked 'What inference does the author of the passage expect you to draw?' you need to look at the direction the author's claims are going in. What does the author intend that you draw from what's been said?

Use this past paper question to help you to develop the skill of drawing relevant inferences:

Past paper practice 19

OCR Unit F502, January 2012

State an inference that can be drawn from the use of the example below, which was included in an argument against parks being owned by councils.

Councils' attempts to regulate behaviour through by-laws have gone too far. For example one council in the Midlands banned ball games in a playing field, despite being in an area where there is a high level of child obesity.

Check your answer with the one given on page 339.

Contradiction

Contradiction is used in critical thinking in the same way as anywhere else. An author is guilty of contradiction if he or she simultaneously makes two claims that go against each other:

> The country with the lowest infant mortality rate is Singapore, although it needs to be remembered that Iceland's rate is even lower.

Key term

➤ **contradiction:** this is where two claims 'go against' each other. They conflict such that both cannot be held to be true at the same time.

It's obvious that, if Singapore has the lowest rate, Iceland's can't be even lower. But what about the next example?

> In July 2009, the European Parliament voted to ban the importation of all seal products. This ban was directed specifically at seal products from Canada where, every spring, thousands of seal cubs are killed by hunters as the cubs lie with their mothers on the ice. This is seen as cruel and thus unacceptable. However, the communities in Canada that carry out the seal-killing see the European Parliament as guilty of double standards. British, Swedish and Finnish fishermen are allowed to kill seals in order to protect (they argue) fish stocks. In addition, a few years ago, the European Union (EU) encouraged people to eat seal-meat, even funding a cookery book for this (with herb-stuffed seal schnitzel being an example of the dishes).

Is the EU being contradictory?

It's one of those arguments where we need more information:

➤ Is the EU opposed to the Canadian seal-hunt because of the method of killing the cubs (by clubbing them with long sticks)?

➤ Is the EU opposed to the Canadian seal-hunt because of the numbers involved (thousands)?

➤ Is the EU opposed to the Canadian seal-hunt because it's unconvinced of the need to kill the seals in Canada, but convinced of the need in Europe?

If any of these is the case, then the EU is not being contradictory, as there are special reasons why seal-killing should be allowed in one area but not in the other.

Refutation and repudiation

An author who claims to have **refuted** someone else's argument is saying that he or she has demonstrated that it isn't true. This can be a very demanding requirement. For example, how could one refute the principle 'theft is always wrong'?

Key terms

> **refute:** to refute an argument is to show it cannot be true because the claims cannot be accepted – that is, to clearly demonstrate that the argument is unsound. This is much stronger than just evaluating an argument.

> **repudiation:** this is where the opponent of an argument rejects it without giving reasons. They simply say that it isn't so.

However, refuting a factual claim is much more straightforward:

The number of murders in London in 2008 was much higher than in previous years.

It would be possible, by looking at the evidence, to show whether or not this is true.

But there are other claims in which refutation is made impossible by the language used:

Like a plague, murder by knife has taken London by storm.

This claim appears in an article on teenage knife crime. The problem is that the words 'like a plague' and 'taken London by storm' force us to get caught up with the meaning of words. Has knife crime taken London 'by storm'? What does it mean anyway? How many knife crimes do there need to be to make them a 'plague'?

Whereas refutation says 'you can't claim that because here's some opposing evidence', **repudiation** just wades in and says 'you can't claim that'.

If someone claimed that:

Allowing genetically modified (GM) food to be grown on a big scale will be a disaster for the world.

a reply that repudiated that claim would be no more than:

Allowing GM food to be grown on a big scale will not be a disaster for the world.

However, someone who wanted to refute the claim could argue like this:

> GM food could solve the major food production problems of the world. It can deliver crops that will survive severe droughts; it can provide crops that are resistant to disease and pests; it can deliver foods that are higher in nutrition than existing varieties.

Coherence

Coherence is the aim of developing your own argument in Section C: it should form one coherent whole, rather than a series of staccato claims that do not quite follow from each other.

Having set the scene for Unit 2, we now need to turn to four new argument elements: explanation, intermediate conclusion, analogy and principle.

Key term

> **coherence:** where a set of claims fit together closely so that they form a rationally ordered argument.

Chapter 18

Explanations

Learning objectives

By the end of this chapter you will be able to:

➢ explain the function of arguments and explanations

➢ identify explanations within arguments

➢ distinguish between explanations and arguments

Explaining the function of arguments and explanations

Arguments

In Unit 1, you found that **arguments** have three main characteristics:

1 They have at least one reason supporting a conclusion.
2 They seek to persuade you to accept something.
  ➢ Whatever we might think of an argument, there is little point to its having been produced if the author didn't think it stood a good chance of persuading us.
  ➢ Even if an argument doesn't persuade us, it still has that function of seeking to persuade.
  ➢ Even if we're already persuaded, it still has that function of seeking to persuade (perhaps to make us even more supportive of that position).
3 They don't have to involve a disagreement or dispute, as evidenced in this simple argument in Chapter 2:

When young children are using mobile phones and computers for communicating, they're not interacting with anyone face to face. Therefore parents need to limit the time young children use electronic media.

Explanations

Having seen what arguments are intended to do, what function do **explanations** have?

Let's look at the following explanation:

Key term

➤ **explanation:** an explanation seeks to show why *something which is accepted* is/was/will be the case, i.e. it seeks to throw light on the case (unlike an argument which *requires reasons to establish/persuade* the reader that this is so).

(a) Although July is often the hottest month of the year, it can also be very wet.

(b) These wetter conditions can frequently be the result of the warm temperatures: the ground heats up and sends parcels of hot air upwards. This warm air cools as it rises and the moisture it contains condenses into cumulus clouds that result in heavy showers.

July can be very wet

Although it has the look and form of an argument (as (b) could have a 'because' in front of it), it isn't one. This is because the author is not seeking to persuade you that (a) is the case: 'Although July is often the hottest month of the year, it can also be very wet' is taken to be accepted. So here we have an explanation.

You can see that an explanation has a central difference from an argument: what is being explained doesn't itself have to be justified, because it's just taken to be the case. Here's another example:

(a) By the end of 2010, the population of the UK was 62.3 million, the highest total ever (and three million more than it was ten years before).

(b) Natural increase (the difference between births and deaths) was the cause of 52% of the increase, with new immigrants contributing the other 48%.

It should be clear that (a) is being explained in this passage. This figure of 62.3 million isn't being argued for, as it's not as if there's someone arguing for a different figure. It is being explained.

Look at the next example:

(a) The Wilkins Ice Shelf in Antarctica began to collapse in 2008 such that only half of it remains.

(b) Recent research using tagged elephant seals has thrown light on why this ice shelf has started to collapse. The seals showed that the depth of the ocean in this area was not 400m (as expected) but almost a kilometre, showing that there were very deep water channels. These channels allow warmer water to reach far below glaciers and ice shelves. In this way, the ice would have been melted, with the rest of the Wilkins Ice Shelf expected to disintegrate over the next few years.

What is accepted that needs explanation?
- (a) The collapse of half of the Wilkins Ice Shelf in 2008.

What is the explanation?
- The existence of very deep water channels that 'allow warmer water to reach far below glaciers and ice shelves'.
- How these deep water channels were discovered: using tagged elephant seals.

Not that you need these for your AS in Critical Thinking but, if you like technical terms:
- that which is accepted and is being explained (a) is called the 'explanandum'
- the explanation itself, i.e. that which seeks to show why or to throw light on the accepted (b) is called the 'explanans'

These might help you to refer to the different parts when you are practising the skill.

Identifying explanations within arguments

So far, you have looked at explanations on their own, appearing as something separate from arguments. However, explanations can often appear within an argument.

The passage above has been extended to make it into an argument. The argument is the last two sentences, with the conclusion being the recommendation ('should be done'). You can see that the explanation provided the necessary support for the conclusion about using elephant seals for mapping the ocean floor.

The Wilkins Ice Shelf in Antarctica began to collapse in 2008 such that only half of it remains.

Explanation Recent research using tagged elephant seals has thrown light on why this ice shelf has started to collapse. The seals showed that the depth of the ocean in this area was not 400m (as expected) but almost a kilometre, showing that there were very deep water channels. These channels allow warmer water to reach far below glaciers and ice shelves. In this way, the ice would have been melted, with the rest of the Wilkins Ice Shelf expected to disintegrate over the next few years.

Reason It would be very useful to be able to predict what will happen to Antarctic glaciers and ice shelves.

Conclusion So, using elephant seals, mapping the ocean floor in the difficult waters of Antarctica should be done more extensively in order to predict better what will happen to the ice shelves.

Exam tip

You might well be asked to identify an explanation within an argument/passage. Remember that you're looking for something that shows why something is/was/will be the case.

> ### Exam tip
>
> If asked to justify why part of the text given is an explanation, you need to refer back to the definition of an explanation above and apply this to the text. For example, deep water channels that allow warmer water to reach far below glaciers and ice shelves *shows why/sheds light on why an accepted occurrence happened*, i.e. why half of the Wilkins Ice Shelf collapsed in 2008.
>
> ➤ The key words are 'shows why' and 'accepted'.
>
> ➤ You should not use the word 'explains' as this is saying nothing more than 'explanation'.
>
> ➤ You should not use the words 'reason' or 'conclusion' to justify an explanation as these elements belong to an argument.

Distinguishing between explanations and arguments

Exercise 21

For each of the following passages, decide whether it is an argument, an explanation (or more than one), or an argument that includes an explanation.

1 Many animals dance in order to attract a mate. These include scorpions, some birds and, of course, humans. Recent research has shown how, for humans, this is best achieved. Humans move in three planes: the head and the trunk can move backwards and forwards, side to side, or twisted. In the study, women were asked to rate men dancing (with features disguised to prevent other factors affecting the result). The women rated most highly those dancers who made large moves in all three planes. Such moves obviously showed both strength and suppleness, therefore indicating a genetically fit male.

2 Cases of lead poisoning in children have significantly declined. This is because of the banning of lead-based paint 20 years ago. However, many older buildings still have lead paint, and lead-contaminated dust from such buildings is still a cause of lead poisoning. This is particularly the case when redecorating goes on, with the old paint being sanded down or off. People need to take great care that children are kept away from rooms where such redecorating is being done.

Lead-based paint was banned 20 years ago

3 It is very important that young children get enough sleep. Evidence shows that those under five who don't get at least ten hours of sleep at night are almost twice

as likely to have weight problems as those who do. Sleep plays an important role in weight regulation, perhaps because tired children are not as active or because sleep affects hormones that influence hunger and appetite.

4 Research based on people in Finland shows that violent criminals are three times as likely to carry a specific abnormal gene as ordinary people. Although about one in a hundred people in Finland carries this gene, most are not aggressive and have never been convicted of a crime. What the gene does is to increase the risk of violent behaviour but only if various environmental factors are also present.

5 We should support plans to cut down 10 million more trees in the country each year in order to supply wood-burning stoves and boilers. Apart from providing fuel, the loss of so many trees would increase the amount of light falling on the forest floor in presently dark woodlands. The equivalent of 250,000 homes or 3,000 schools could be heated as a result, avoiding the burning of gas and oil.

Now check your answers against those on page 339.

Past paper practice 20

OCR Unit F502, January 2010

State the explanation used within the following argument:

Research carried out in Japan has shown that people who eat quickly are much more likely to become overweight. Fast-eating women were found to be twice as likely to become obese; for men this rose to three times as likely. Dietary experts say that eating too quickly reduces the ability of the body to respond to the 'feeling of fullness'. To avoid becoming obese, people should ensure they take more time over meals and eat slowly.

Check your answer with the one given on page 340.

Past paper practice 21

OCR Unit F502, January 2011

State whether the following is an argument or explanation and justify your answer with reference to the text.

Parks cost a lot to maintain and anti-social behaviour discourages people from using them, so things should be changed.

Check your answer with the one given on page 340.

Exam tip

When asked to justify your answer, you need to:

➤ give the definition of an explanation or argument

➤ illustrate this from the text

Activity 19

In groups, examine a set of newspapers to see which articles contain explanation or argument. Compare these with the letters to the editor page. Is there a difference? Be careful not to confuse explanation with description and accounts of events. These are also forms of non-argument, but they do not explain why something is as it is.

Keep these newspaper arguments, as you can use them in a different way in the next chapter.

Summary

➤ An explanation seeks to show why/throws light on why something that is already accepted is/was/will be the case.

➤ Unlike a conclusion, an explanation is not trying to persuade you.

➤ You should refer to the text when you are explaining why something is an explanation or argument.

Chapter 19

Intermediate conclusions

Learning objectives

By the end of this chapter, you will be able to:

➤ explain the function of intermediate conclusions

➤ identify intermediate conclusions in arguments

Explaining the function of intermediate conclusions

In Chapter 2, you saw how, in an argument, reasons provide support for a conclusion, and that there was no limit to the number of reasons in an argument. What we have not yet considered is whether an argument can have more than one conclusion.

The answer, at first glance, would appear to be a straightforward 'no'. A conclusion is, as you saw, where the argument is going, its final destination — it's the claim that its author wants others to accept.

Think of an argument like a journey, with the conclusion being your final destination. You know where you want to go, and you can see how you'll get there. But the final destination of a journey is sometimes achieved by going to other places on the way.

Have a look again at an argument you saw in Chapter 2:

Feeding children lots of processed food (such as sausages, burgers and sugary snacks) at a young age has been shown to lower their future intelligence. Giving them a diet rich in vitamins (including fruit, vegetables, rice and pasta) can make children more intelligent.

Conclusion Parents should be strongly encouraged to limit their children's consumption of processed food and to increase their consumption of vitamin-rich foods.

Can feeding children burgers reduce their intelligence?

FOTOLIA

The conclusion is, of course, the last sentence. But this last sentence could be used to take the argument further:

Intermediate conclusion	Parents should be strongly encouraged to limit their children's consumption of processed food and to increase their consumption of vitamin-rich foods.
Conclusion	Therefore there needs to be an information campaign to show parents which foods to avoid and which to use.

As you can see, what was the conclusion of the argument has now become a reason for a different conclusion. It's a reason with a special name: **intermediate conclusion** (IC).

It's an intermediate conclusion because it's a conclusion drawn on the way to the final or **main conclusion** (MC).

> **Key terms**
> ➤ **intermediate conclusion:** a conclusion drawn on the way to the main conclusion. It is drawn from at least one reason and becomes itself a reason for the main conclusion. Arguments can have no intermediate conclusion, or any number of them.
>
> ➤ **main conclusion:** the main conclusion of an argument is its final conclusion. An argument will therefore have only one main conclusion, with all the rest of the reasoning supporting it, including the intermediate conclusion if there is one.

Although an intermediate conclusion is followed by a main conclusion, it's still a conclusion. In other words, it could be used to end an argument at that point, as in the original argument above.

Identifying intermediate conclusions

How can you tell which is the IC and which is the MC?
In order to see which of two conclusions is the intermediate and which the main, you need to use either the 'because' or the 'therefore' test. In the example above we have these two conclusions:

... Parents should be strongly encouraged to limit their children's consumption of processed food and to increase their consumption of vitamin-rich foods.

Therefore there needs to be an information campaign to show parents which foods to avoid and which to use.

As you can see, the first of these provides a reason for the second, whereas the second cannot be seen as a reason for the first.

An intermediate conclusion, then, is a strange entity. Physicists are used to the idea of entities being simultaneously two different things (waves and particles), and with intermediate conclusions, we have the same thing. They are both conclusions and reasons.

Where will you find an IC?

Just as the main conclusion can be anywhere in an argument (beginning, middle, or end), so too can intermediate conclusions. Look at the next example, where the intermediate conclusion is the first sentence:

IC Chilled ready meals are one of the worst examples of wasting energy in food production.

R Energy is required to cook the meal, then freeze it, then cook it again for you to eat.

C If we are to save energy, cutting out chilled ready meals would be a good thing to do.

We could even find them appearing after the main conclusion:

C People should choose plastic bags rather than paper ones.

IC (because) Paper bags cause more global warming than plastic bags do.

R (because) Taking up more space than plastic bags, they need more energy to transport them.

Exercise 22

Identify the intermediate conclusion and the conclusion in the following two arguments.

1 Children are being made unwelcome in various places such as hotels and holiday destinations. There's even a village in Scotland, called Firhall, which has banned children. They're allowed to visit but not to stay there. This anti-child attitude might discourage people from having children. This would be a big problem for our society. Children are, in a very real sense, our future. We need to change this anti-child attitude.

2 The UK population is predicted to increase from the present 62.3 million to 70 million by 2029 and 77 million by 2050. The significantly increasing birth rate will be the major cause of these huge increases, which, in turn, will lead to massive pressure on schools, universities, employment and housing. Having more than two children should be seen as being antisocial (like being a benefits

cheat). The Government should introduce a law to make people pay heavily for their third or further children (just as in China, where couples pay the 'family planning fine' for their second).

Check your answers against those on page 340.

What does an argument look like with more than one intermediate conclusion?

Although there can be only one main conclusion, there can be an unlimited number of intermediate ones. This emphasises the point about them being both reasons and conclusions.

In the next example, the argument is built up, step by step, with conclusions morphing into reasons:

> **R**   There are many people who say that they have seen fairies.
>
> ↓
>
> **IC1** So fairies must exist.
>
> ↓
>
> **IC2** We must therefore make sure that places where fairies have been seen are protected from disturbance.
>
> ↓
>
> **C**   Consequently, councils must be told that any applications to build houses on these places must be refused.

As you can see, with the two intermediate conclusions, the argument could have stopped at each point. But, moving on, they in turn became reasons.

Exam tip

Think of an intermediate conclusion as marking the end of part of an argument, such that the author could have stopped the argument at this point.

You'll need to look at intermediate conclusions again when you come to write your own arguments. They add a level of complexity to an argument, and you will be rewarded for being able to write arguments with some complexity in the Unit 2 paper.

Exam tip

To see if a conclusion is an intermediate or a main one, use either the 'because' or the 'therefore' test.

Exercise 23

Analyse the following argument, finding any intermediate conclusions in it.

There is still a pay gap between men and women

1 The pay gap between men and women has been narrowing, but very slowly. Recent pay increases for female managers have been only half a percentage point faster than for male managers. If the present trends continue, the pay gap will not close until 2067. Companies must be ignoring the law requiring that women's pay is equal to that of men. The existing law must not be strong enough. New stronger laws must be introduced as soon as possible.

Now analyse this version of the argument, again finding any intermediate conclusions in it.

2 The pay gap between men and women has been narrowing, but very slowly. Recent pay increases for female managers have been only half a percentage point faster than for male managers. If the present trends continue, the pay gap will not close until 2067. Companies must be ignoring the law requiring that women's pay is equal to that of men. The existing law must not be strong enough. It is wrong that women are still treated unfairly with regard to their levels of pay compared to those of men. New stronger laws must be introduced as soon as possible.

Check your answers against those on page 340.

Past paper practice 22

OCR Unit F502, January 2010

Bioethanol made by fermenting sugar crops or maize can be added to petrol. The Government should insist that all petrol contains at least 15% bioethanol. Replacing some of the petrol with bioethanol would cause less pollution, so insisting that bioethanol is added to petrol would be good for the environment.

Which of the following is the intermediate conclusion of the above argument?

(a) Insisting that bioethanol is added to petrol would be good for the environment.

(b) Replacing some of the petrol with bioethanol would cause less pollution.

(c) The Government should insist that all petrol contains at least 15% bioethanol.

(d) We should take steps to stop the environment being harmed.

Check your answers with those given on page 341.

Activity 20

Look again at the arguments you found in the newspaper articles in Activity 19. Find the conclusion and then try adding a further conclusion based on this. For example, you may find a conclusion that says:

So it is obvious that British primary school children need to learn about nutrition if we want to alter their eating habits in order to tackle the rising incidence of childhood obesity.

We could turn this into an intermediate conclusion, by adding a further conclusion:

Therefore the government needs to bring back food technology lessons into the primary school curriculum.

Now try three of your own. By developing arguments in this way, it should help to reinforce that ICs are conclusions on the way to a main conclusion.

Summary

➢ An IC marks the end of part of the argument.

➢ It acts as a reason for the main conclusion.

➢ There can be more than one IC in an argument.

➢ Like conclusions, they don't have a fixed position in an argument. They can appear anywhere in the argument.

➢ To identify which is the IC and which is the conclusion, put them together and apply the 'therefore' test.

➢ If asked to identify an IC and justify your answer, make sure that you explain both of its functions (as a reason for the conclusion, and as a conclusion/point of persuasion) and that you refer to the text.

Chapter 20

Analogies

Learning objectives

By the end of this chapter, you will be able to:

➤ explain the function of 'analogy' and 'disanalogy'

➤ identify precisely the situations being compared

Explaining the function of analogies

Sufficient similarity — same subject

Here's an example of an **analogy** being used in an article in the *Daily Mail* in 2008:

> A source close to Simon Cowell said: 'He thinks Alexandra Burke will be a big international star, if they get the music right. In many ways she is more versatile than Leona Lewis — she can really dance and there is a greater variety of things that she can do.'
>
> Asked **if he was worried about the similarities between Leona and Alexandra**, Cowell said: **'It is like asking would you want to sign up Whitney Houston when you already have Mariah Carey.** Of course you would. There is room for more than one female singer.'

Key term

➤ **analogy:** an analogy takes one situation or scenario to be sufficiently similar to another one (using parallels), such that the first situation or scenario can be used in an argument about the other.

Responding to the specific counter-assertion that Leona Lewis and Alexandra Burke are too similar, Simon Cowell makes the claim:

'It is like asking would you want to sign up Whitney Houston when you already have Mariah Carey.'

Here we have Cowell using an analogy. He takes this scenario to be sufficiently similar to the issue about Alexandra Burke and Leona Lewis to be able to use it to support his argument. In a nutshell, Cowell is arguing that, since nobody would turn down the opportunity to sign Whitney Houston if they already had Mariah Carey, he has no problem with signing up Alexandra Burke, even though he already has Leona Lewis. He is comparing the situation of Burke and Lewis with that of Houston and Carey.

Moving beyond this specific example, you can see what is going on when an analogy is being used in an argument.

Simon Cowell had no problem signing up Alexandra Burke

Situation/scenario 1 is (very) similar to situation/scenario 2, so situation/scenario 1 can be used in an argument about situation/scenario 2.

Sufficient similarity — different subjects but a common characteristic

In the example above, the two situations were very similar in that they were both about female pop singers. However, in most analogies, it isn't the subjects that are similar. We have to look for a common characteristic or issue. To illustrate this point, here are two analogies.

1 This one is based on letters written in 2011 to the *New York Times* in response to an article about the use of corporal punishment:

All 50 states in the US allow parents to use 'reasonable' corporal punishment on their children, with 20 states still allowing schools to use such punishment on their students. However, such punishment doesn't stop bad behaviour. It can make behaviour worse (for example, it's associated with delinquency and other antisocial activities).

In addition, there are effective alternatives. **By showing that it's not a good thing to be doing, its use will decline. For instance, as a result of health education campaigns, the percentage of people who smoke has been cut in half in the past 40 years. The same thing can be done with corporal punishment.** A ban on such punishment in both the home and the school in the US should be introduced as soon as possible.

The analogy is the evidence on the big decline in smoking 'as a result of health education campaigns'. The author believes that, although the two subjects (smoking and smacking) are very different, there is a common characteristic or issue:

> By showing that it's not a good thing to be doing, its use will decline.

You will see that the author isn't saying that smoking and smacking are very similar *in themselves*. It's that both smoking and smacking lead to future problems and that what happened with the campaign against smoking is relevant to his proposed campaign against smacking.

2   To emphasise the point that analogies often have very different subject matter from the thing being argued about, have a look at the next argument. It's based on one used by Rod Morgan, former Head of the Youth Justice Board, in 2006:

> **Locking up children who commit crimes is like building more coal-fired power stations. You create future problems by doing so. So we should stop locking up children who commit crimes.**

As you can see, there is a huge difference in the content of the analogy (coal-fired power stations) and the subject of the argument (locking up young criminals).

Analogies draw on consistency

Why do authors use analogies in arguments?

They are used to provide strength to an argument. In the analogy about smoking and smacking, the author is saying that the situations are sufficiently similar, so, for the sake of consistency, if education campaigns rather than punishment can cut smoking in half, then we should try the same approach for cutting down on corporal punishment.

Identifying precisely the situations being compared

Let's now unpack an analogy, so that you can see how to identify the two things that are being compared in an examination answer. Consider the following passage:

> A recent study has shown that the average teenager's iPod or digital music player contains almost 850 illegally copied songs. Each one of these illegally copied songs represents a loss of income for a large number of people (artist, company, producer, etc.). **This is no less than theft. It's just like stealing a CD from a shop,** so it's about time that young people started to realise that they're nothing but common thieves every time they download a track without paying for it.

Identifying an analogy is, at one level, fairly simple:

➤ You're always looking for a reference to a new scenario.
➤ Very often you're also looking for language such as 'this is like', 'just as', 'this would be the same as' and so on.

So in this passage we find that the new scenario, and the language used, take us straight to the analogy: 'It's just like stealing a CD from a shop.'

If asked to identify an analogy, you need to do more than just identify the words. You need to unpack what is being compared. In this example, the comparison is between *illegal downloading* and *stealing a CD*:

> The author sees the act of illegally downloading a song as just like stealing a CD from a shop.

Put very simply, an author who uses an analogy is arguing like this:

> *X* is very similar to *Y* so, if *Z* can be drawn from *X*, *Z* can also be drawn from *Y*.

In the downloading argument, the author is saying, in effect, that if we don't allow the theft of CDs from a shop, then we shouldn't allow illegal downloading of music. Consistency requires this.

Exam tip

When you're asked to find an analogy:

➤ Look for words such as 'this is like', 'just as', 'this would be the same as' and so on.

➤ Look for a sudden change in the subject matter.

When asked to state what is being compared in the analogy, you need to identify:

➤ the common characteristic and how it relates to both things being compared, rather than just stating the words of the analogy as they appear in the text

➤ several points of comparison between the two situations being compared by breaking down the analogy into a series of parallels

---

Disanalogies

You've seen that analogies are used by an author to argue that, given similarities between situations and scenarios, we can use one situation/scenario to support an argument about the other.

But there are times when an author will want to emphasise the difference between situations in order to argue from one to the other.

Here's an example to illustrate this.

In 2008, faced with the criticism that some of the attempts to land spacecraft on Mars had not succeeded, the US space agency (NASA) made this point:

> People should expect that some space missions don't succeed. Putting a spacecraft safely on Mars is hard and risky. It's not a trip to Grandma's house.

As you can see, in this example the author is doing the opposite to using an analogy. Instead of saying 'here's one scenario, here's another very similar to it', the author is saying, 'Here's one scenario (putting a spacecraft safely on Mars); here's another very different from it (making a trip to Grandma's house)'.

Here the **disanalogy** is used to emphasise the difficulty of putting a spacecraft on Mars, by showing that the two situations were so different.

The author is saying that you must understand the special difficulties of getting safely to Mars. You can't see it as a simple exercise. So you need to think of it differently from getting somewhere unremarkable, everyday and ordinary. To be consistent, you would have to think of it in terms of other very difficult activities.

> **Key term**
>
> ➤ **disanalogy:** a disanalogy takes one situation or scenario to be sufficiently different from another one, such that the first situation or scenario can be used in an argument about the other.

These issues of similarity and consistency will be developed further in Chapter 25. Whether or not an analogy is a good one depends on these issues of similarity (and therefore consistency). If there is insufficient similarity between the two scenarios, then the issue of consistency loses relevance.

Exercise 24

Identify precisely the situations being compared in the analogy in each of the following passages:

1 In 2006, a UK judge refused to impose an antisocial behaviour order on a man who was growing cannabis at his home. The local council had applied for the order and for possession of the man's council house. The judge threw the case out, making the point that cultivating cannabis is 'no more antisocial than having tomato plants'. He explained that he couldn't see how growing cannabis could ever be seen as a nuisance because, for the neighbours, it's no different to them than if tomato plants had been grown.

Is recycling paper a pointless exercise?

FOTOLIA

2 Recycling of paper is a largely pointless exercise. Quite simply, it doesn't save trees. All paper in Britain comes from tree plantations, trees grown *for* paper. Thus when it's pointed out that if every UK newspaper was printed on recycled paper, about 8 million trees a year could be saved, it needs to be stressed that they are trees that would not exist if it wasn't for the paper industry. As a result, recycling paper to save trees is like not eating bread to save wheat.

3 The commercial manager of the company Hewlett Packard has argued that the trend towards constant e-mailing and texting creates the problems of the 24-hour 'always on' society. However, we shouldn't take much notice of his concern. As Hewlett Packard produces the technology that allows this to happen, it's like a motor manufacturer making a 150 mph sports car and then telling drivers to stick to the speed limit.

Check your answers against those on page 341.

Now have a look at the following examination question. You can see that it is very similar to the tasks that you have just been doing, so you should not have too much of a problem in answering it.

Past paper practice 23

OCR Unit F502, January 2012

Under council ownership, parks are not being used to their full capacity. They should be a facility for all sectors of the community to enjoy. However, young people are often not provided for. Much more could be done with that amount of space. Just as muscles become wasted without exercise, so too with parks; they are under-used and have become unpleasant, neglected and worthless.

There is an analogy in the above paragraph. Identify precisely the situations being compared in the analogy.

Check your answer with the one given on page 341.

Summary

➤ Analogies compare two situations that are similar.

➤ They draw on consistency in that if the situations are similar, we should act in the same way towards each.

➤ When asked to state exactly what is being compared, you should look for the common characteristic and explain how this applies to both situations.

Chapter 21

Principles

Learning objectives

By the end of this chapter, you will be able to:

➢ explain the function of principles

➢ identify principles

Explaining the function of principles

This chapter looks at the **principle**, an argument element that can appear as a reason, a conclusion and can also be assumed.

> **Key term**
>
> ➢ **principle:** a general rule that can act as guidance in a specific relevant situation.

Principles as guidance

Principles are general statements that are intended to be accepted in all relevant specific situations. Because they are general statements (or guides to what should be done), the language of principles is often that of 'should', 'must', 'duty to' and so on, and the negatives ('shouldn't', 'must not', 'never' and so on).

Let's look at three examples of principles:

It is our duty to help the poor.

Causing unnecessary pain to animals cannot be justified.

The interests of future generations must always be considered.

As you can see, these are general statements that, when applied to specific situations, can help us to determine what should be the case (assuming that those making the decisions accept the principle).

Principles as guidance — both to require and to prohibit

Principles can be both positive and negative. They can require or prohibit certain behaviours. Consider the following:

Negative Causing unnecessary pain to animals cannot be justified.

Positive The interests of future generations must always be considered.

It is worth noting, however, that any negative principle has a positive version (and vice versa):

Positive The prevention of unnecessary pain to animals is always **justified**.

Negative The interests of future generations should **never** be ignored.

Exam tip

When looking for principles, look for general statements of what should or should not be done.

Words such as 'should', 'must', 'ought', 'duty to' and the negative forms 'shouldn't', 'must not', 'ought not' and 'never', can indicate a principle.

The distinction between principles and other types of claim is one that is important to understand. Look at the following claim.

Whales are intelligent animals.

This claim is a descriptive one, saying something about whales. It doesn't tell us anything about how whales should or shouldn't be treated. Thus it doesn't provide any general guidance which would be relevant to this.

Here's another claim.

Whales suffer dreadful pain when they are harpooned.

This claim is also a descriptive one. It gives us specific information about whales. You can see that there is a principle possibly hovering nearby but we haven't got one yet.

Here's another claim.

Whales should be protected from the Japanese whaling fleet.

This has now moved away from a descriptive claim, and is making a recommendation. But it is a very specific recommendation, in that it doesn't apply to whales which are not being hunted by the Japanese whaling fleet. Thus I couldn't use it if I was in the North Atlantic in order to tell a Norwegian whaling ship to stop hunting whales.

What we need then is a general recommendation, a general guide to action that will apply to all whale-hunting situations. Here it is.

Deliberately harming intelligent animals can never be justified.

This is straightforwardly a principle. Given that we can include whales in the category 'intelligent animals', it covers all whales and all situations in which people might hunt them. It could be used to oppose hunting by the Japanese, the Norwegians, the Danes, the South Koreans and so on. Of course, the principle also applies to a wide range of other animals too: dolphins, porpoises, chimpanzees, baboons, dogs...and humans.

Activity 21

The following are specific rules. In groups, try making them more general so that they turn into principles. Several different answers will be possible for each one. Try making them both positive and negative. Here is an example:

Specific rule: *The general public must not walk on the patch of grass underneath the flagpole in front of the civic centre.*

Possible principles:
➤ *It is our duty to respect public places.*
➤ *We should do nothing that would harm the public environment.*

Now try these:
1 You should not get up late for work and miss your bus.
2 Students should not wear jeans to the school prom in July.
3 Customers should make sure that they receive the correct amount of money when they use a cash machine in this area.
4 Able-bodied passengers should give up their seats to the elderly and infirm on the London Underground.
5 Patients should respect the staff in A&E (Accident and Emergency) in this hospital at all times.
6 Workers in C Block should switch off their computers at the end of the day.

Principles drawn from principles

Because principles can be both reasons and conclusions, you can find arguments in which a principle as a conclusion can be drawn from another one as a reason. The next example shows this:

R We should always seek to increase people's welfare.

C So we should support policies that give people longer holidays.

You can see that the first principle has a huge scope, and the second one has a much smaller one. Because of the large scope of the first, all sorts of other principles could be drawn from it:

R We should always seek to increase people's welfare.

C So we should support policies that improve people's incomes.

or

R We should always seek to increase people's welfare.

C So we should ensure that nobody goes without medical care when they need it.

or

R We should always seek to increase people's welfare.

C So we should build enough properties so that everyone has decent accommodation.

Principles and exceptions

Principles cannot tolerate exceptions unless these exceptions are included in them. Let's look at the following principle:

The death penalty is always wrong.

We can't say 'except for serial killers', unless we want to alter the principle so that it includes this exception.

Here are two principles that do include exceptions:

We should be allowed to behave as we choose, **except** when our behaviour adversely affects others.

The death penalty should be used **only in cases** of extreme and premeditated cruelty.

The second of these could have been used to justify the execution of those who ran the Auschwitz concentration camp (premeditated), without opening the doors to allowing the execution of someone who shoots her husband in a jealous rage (unpremeditated).

Identifying principles

Stated principles

Now that you know what a principle is, try identifying the principles in the next two exercises and then check your answers on pages 341–2. Remember: you are looking for a general rule that can apply to several situations, so you should be able to discount specific recommendations or statements.

Exercise 25

Which of the following claims is a principle?

1 The United Nations should intervene in Zimbabwe in order to overthrow Robert Mugabe's corrupt government.
2 The United Nations should always intervene in countries where the government is corrupt.
3 Child trafficking can never be justified.
4 Sheep are far more intelligent than people realise.
5 The veal trade is a very cruel one.
6 Swimming with dolphins by sick children is bad both for the dolphins and the children.

Check your answers against those on page 341.

Exercise 26

Identify a principle in each of the following arguments.

Should illegal downloaders be made to pay?

1 A recent study has shown that the average teenager's iPod or digital music player contains almost 850 illegally copied songs. Each one of these illegally copied songs represents a loss of income for a large number of people (artist, company, producer, etc.). So it is good that internet providers are now going to start taking tougher action against this illegal downloading. It's no less than theft. Since theft is always wrong, these illegal downloaders should be made to pay.

2 The cost to the NHS of smoking is £2.7 billion per year; the cost of alcohol to the NHS is the same. If smokers stopped smoking and people drank much less alcohol, then this money would be saved. People choosing to behave in what are in the end antisocial ways deprive others who, through no fault of their own, need medical care that the NHS can't afford to pay for. It's clear that people whose own behaviour results in their being ill must be made to pay for their own healthcare.

Check your answers against those on page 342.

Assumed principles

Because principles normally operate as reasons in an argument, they can be assumed rather than stated. In the next example, we use the argument above. In this version, we start towards the end of the previous argument.

> It is good that internet providers are now going to start taking tougher action against illegal downloading. It's no less than theft. So these illegal downloaders should be made to pay.

We can see that the principle has been omitted. But it remains a necessary part of the argument to link 'It's no less than theft' and 'So these illegal downloaders should be made to pay'. In this version, then, the principle 'theft is always wrong' is assumed. (You can see that it must be because, without it, the argument doesn't work. Try the negative test to check this.)

Exam tip

If you are asked to find a principle as an assumption, see your task in the same way as looking for any assumption — as a necessary but unstated reason.

Now try this multiple-choice question.

Exercise 27

There is often a debate as to which groups of sick people should be given priority when it comes to the allocation of resources. There are people with arthritis who complain that they're not allowed drugs to help them with their pain. There are families with someone with Alzheimer's who also complain that drugs aren't being made available to them. Yet people with other conditions are given what they need. It's obvious that the Government can't allow this situation to continue. It must increase taxes to pay for everyone who needs medical treatment to get it.

Which one of the following principles is assumed in the above argument?

1 The Government must always help the sick.
2 People should be made to pay taxes to help those in need.
3 The medical needs of sick people should always be met.
4 Sick people should be given priority over those who are well.

Check your answer against those on page 342.

What do the questions look like in the Unit 2 exam? Here are two for you to try. They are testing exactly the same skill that you have been practising.

Past paper practice 24

OCR Unit F502, January 2012

State the principle used in the following paragraph:

Furthermore, council ownership of parks is an inefficient use of taxpayers' money. It simply costs too much. In one London borough, £5.4 million was spent on parks in one year, which was roughly £20 for each man, woman and child that lived in that area. If councils no longer had to look after parks, then the money would be spent on better things, like schools or hospitals. People should only have to pay tax for the things that they use or which benefit them.

Check your answer with the one given on page 342.

Past paper practice 25

OCR Unit F502, January 2012

American football has become too violent. Even the sport's main governing body, the NFL, has started to worry about the effects of even bigger, faster players smashing into each other. The resulting concussions can cause memory loss and depression. The NFL's proposal to suspend or fine players who use their helmets to injure their opponents ought to be supported.

Which of the following is a principle that would best support the above argument?

1 Concussions can cause memory loss and depression.

2 Life without risks is boring.

3 People should be protected from unnecessary harm.

4 Players should be fined for using their helmets to injure their opponents.

Check your answers with those given on page 343.

Summary

➢ Principles are general rules, so they must be transferable to other situations. When looking to identify a principle, avoid specific recommendations.

➢ Principles also act as guidance, so look out for words such as 'ought', 'should', 'duty to' and their negatives.

➢ An assumed principle is one that is necessary to draw the conclusion, but is unstated.

Chapter 22

Use of evidence to draw a conclusion

Learning objectives

By the end of this chapter, you will be able to:

➤ identify alternative conclusions that can be drawn from the evidence that weaken the conclusion drawn

➤ identify false assumption in the use of evidence that weakens the conclusion drawn

➤ assess the significance of evidence using the wider context when raw numbers, percentage, fraction, average, rate and index are used to draw a conclusion

Identifying alternative conclusions that can be drawn from the evidence

Authors will often provide numerical evidence as support for a conclusion that they wish to draw. In evaluating an author's use of evidence, we can look for possible *alternative* explanations to the one that they have given. In this way we are identifying a weakness in the use of their evidence to draw their particular conclusion.

Let's look at the following argument:

Example 1

Evidence   Britain spends the highest amount on cosmetic surgery of any country in Europe. In 2006 this was £497m. The second highest was Italy with £158m. In fact, if we add up the total amount spent by the countries that were second, third (France), fourth (Germany), and fifth (Spain) in the league table of spending, this total is still less than the amount spent in Britain.

> **Conclusion** This shows that British people are the vainest in Europe.

In this argument, the author takes the evidence to have only one explanation:

> British people are the vainest in Europe.

Our task is to consider alternative explanations. How many other explanations can we find?

(i) British treatment costs more. An article in the *Metro* headed 'Vain UK's £1bn plastic surgery bill' (14 February 2008) referred to the figures quoted above and also to the prediction that, by 2011, the figure will be £1.5bn. However, a little way into the article, we read that:

> While more people are going under the knife in Britain, procedures are generally more expensive here than abroad.

So here we have another possible explanation, and one that weakens the conclusion concerning British vanity. Now it seems that one of the reasons that the British spend more in this area is because it costs more in Britain.

(ii) British definition of treatment is more inclusive. Perhaps the definition of cosmetic surgery varies from country to country. For example, perhaps Botox treatment is included in the figures in Britain but not in other European countries. In addition, perhaps figures for plastic surgery for people who have been injured or are disfigured are included in the British figures but not in those from other countries.

(iii) British availability of treatment attracts others. Perhaps people come to Britain from abroad to have their cosmetic surgery done because there are more clinics here.

(iv) British quality of treatment attracts others. Perhaps people come to Britain from abroad to have their cosmetic surgery done because the quality of the cosmetic surgery is very high.

As you can see, each different explanation creates a significant problem for the argument. It identifies a weakness in the use of evidence to draw the author's conclusion.

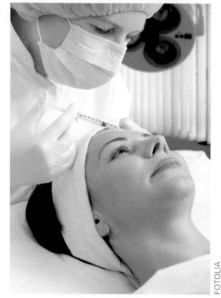

FOTOLIA

Britain spends more on cosmetic surgery than any other country in Europe

Here is another example where an alternative explanation can be drawn from the numerical evidence. You might remember the rescue of 33 miners in Chile in October 2010.

Example 2

There were 33 miners.

They were first located in the 33rd week of the year.

The rescue shaft was completed after exactly 33 days of drilling.

This rescue shaft was completed on the 66th (33 x 2) day of the miners' ordeal.

The day the miners were brought up was 13 October 2010: 13/10/10. Add 13 + 10 + 10, and you get, of course, 33.

It was said that the miners argued that they were convinced that they would be rescued because all the numbers showed they would (even though the whole operation was hugely difficult).

Coincidence. Sometimes we think that numbers have a significance when it is highly unlikely that they do. Here the alternative explanation was more likely to be simply one of coincidence.

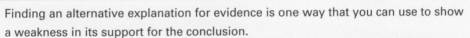

> **Exam tip**
>
> Finding an alternative explanation for evidence is one way that you can use to show a weakness in its support for the conclusion.
>
> You can be asked the question directly or you can use this in a more open question that asks you to find weakness in the use of evidence.

Identifying false assumption in the use of evidence

You might also have seen that looking for alternative explanations highlights the possible false assumption that the author of an argument must make — that is, that 'there is no other explanation than…'. Thus, in Example 1 the author had to assume that the *only* explanation for the high level of spending on cosmetic surgery in Britain is the vanity of British people.

> **Exam tip**
>
> This is another way of expressing the weakness in the author's use of evidence.

Assessing the significance of evidence to the conclusion

The next task is to look at the different kinds of evidence that can be provided to support an argument and how we can judge the strengths and weakness of the support that it gives. Numerical evidence can look impressive, but it is important to assess how far it is directly relevant to the reasoning and where it sits within the whole picture. Where the numbers have been interpreted to form statistics, we need to look carefully at that interpretation.

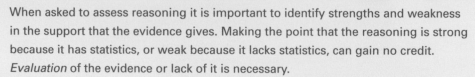

Exam tip

When asked to assess reasoning it is important to identify strengths and weakness in the support that the evidence gives. Making the point that the reasoning is strong because it has statistics, or weak because it lacks statistics, can gain no credit. *Evaluation* of the evidence or lack of it is necessary.

Raw figures

In Example 1 above, the numerical evidence was presented in a simple way — by simply reporting the raw figures without any attempt to present them in any proportional way (as, for example, a percentage). This can have many problems. Essentially, overall numbers alone do not normally provide enough information to allow us to judge their possible significance. We need to know the wider context to judge the significance.

Weakness: not knowing the whole context

In that example, you might want to question the significance of the figures in relation to population size.

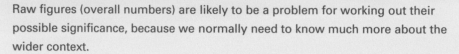

Exam tip

Raw figures (overall numbers) are likely to be a problem for working out their possible significance, because we normally need to know much more about the wider context.

Percentage and fraction

Much of the numerical evidence you'll look at will be presented in a proportional way. We'll look at a simple example to see how this works.

Example 1

About 10% of all US presidents have been assassinated while in office. This is about the same murder rate as that for street drug dealers in the US. It is therefore surprising that so many people in the US want to be president.

We take it, of course, that the figures are accurate. Does the similarity in the figures tell us anything? Specifically, can the author of the argument draw the conclusion? There are many things we could say. For example:

You cannot compare the experience of what's happened to 44 people over a period of 220 years with the death rate of thousands of people over a short period. This gets to the heart of the problem with the evidence. Although it takes the same thing and applies it to two groups, the two groups are different in all sorts of ways:

> The timescale of the US presidency goes from 1789 (George Washington) to the present. The timescale for street drug dealers will be much, much shorter.
> We're not told, but it could well be an *annual* murder rate for drug dealers. Perhaps 10% of all street drug dealers were murdered last year. If so, then the comparison fails completely.
> The chances of a street drug dealer being murdered this year are presumably something like 10%. But, based on the presidential assassination figures, there clearly isn't a 10% chance of Barack Obama being assassinated this year.
> The central problem is that, although there have been 44 US presidents, there is only ever one at any given time. With drug dealers in the US, there are normally thousands.
> We could add in further information, such as the last time a US president was assassinated was 1963 (J F Kennedy) and before that 1901, 1881 and 1865 (Abraham Lincoln).

We have thus shown that the significance of the evidence is not as great as the author suggests and that the conclusion from it is hugely overdrawn. In this example, you have seen that evidence can be hugely misleading if the groups being compared are so different as to make any useful comparison almost impossible.

In the next example, evidence is presented in two different ways. It is taken from findings from a June 2011 study commissioned by the Sea Cadets organisation. Two thousand adults in Britain were questioned for the study.

Example 2

> Three in ten said they were 'happy with how they are'.
> A quarter feel like they're stuck in a rut.
> The same number said they lacked motivation.
> One in ten of them blames their lack of success on the fact they have had no encouragement.
> A quarter said they aren't a risk-taker.
> 11% 'wouldn't know how to go about' changing their life.
> More than a third (35%) said they would give up trying to make it in life if they hadn't done so by the time they reach the age of 50.

(The first three bullet points are mutually exclusive answers to a single question.)

As you can see, it doesn't make much difference how the evidence is presented. It amounts to essentially the same thing whether we're looking at fractions or percentages.

The CEO of the Sea Cadets felt able to draw a conclusion from the findings, that the Sea Cadets were highly relevant to 'giving young people the life skills of commitment, discipline, courage and self-confidence to make the best of themselves and their future'.

Weakness: information is incomplete

This might well be the case, but the evidence is incomplete in the picture that we are given. For example, look again at the first three points:

> Three in ten said they were 'happy with how they are', a quarter feel like they're stuck in a rut and the same number said they lacked motivation.

If you add these up, we find that we know something about only eight in ten of the respondents. This might seem to be enough, but not in this case. If 80% of a group said X, then that's powerful evidence. But in this case it's different. Although we know something about 80% of the group, this percentage doesn't think in the same way.

Crucially we don't know if the missing fifth is happy with their life or not. Watch out for this. Some statistical evidence might seem quite strong, but be less so when you start evaluating its significance. The next two points further highlight this:

> One in ten of them blames their lack of success on the fact they have had no encouragement, a quarter said they aren't a risk-taker and 11% 'wouldn't know how to go about it'.

Add these up, and you'll find that we know something about less than half the group.

Exam tip

Look to see if you're given information about the whole group used in a survey. If not, the significance of the figures can be distorted.

This issue of incompleteness is important. It focuses us on looking for important gaps in the evidence. Here are some important questions to ask:

- **Left unknown.** What does the evidence not tell us?
- **Importance of the unknown.** Do we need to know what isn't given? For example, if we're told that 91% of people in a reliable survey wanted circuses with animals banned, then not knowing what the other 9% thought is not probably that significant.
- **Vagueness.** Does the evidence provide only rather vague information? For example, 'less than half the people thought that the death penalty should be reintroduced' — does this mean that 49% did, or 30%, or 1% ... or what?
- **Part picture.** Does the evidence provide only part of the picture for a particular finding? An example comes from yet another Sea Cadets survey. This was of 2,000 children in 2010. It showed all sorts of ignorance about British nautical history. For example, 'one in ten believed Horatio Nelson was a French footballer'. So did the other nine in ten know that he was one of the greatest British naval commanders of all time, the hero of the Battle of Trafalgar, and commemorated in Trafalgar Square? Did *you* know? Or what did the other 90% think? We don't know.

Exercise 28

An even more glaring example of incompleteness is the piece of evidence below.

Forty-four per cent of children aged between 10 and 16 said that they felt unsafe when their mother was driving.

What questions might you want to ask so that you could gain a more complete picture, in order to begin to draw a conclusion from the evidence?

Check your answers against those on page 343.

Averages or mean

Averages are calculated by adding up the separate numbers in a series and dividing the total by how many separate numbers there were. This gives us what is known as 'the mean'.

Although averages can be very useful evidence, this varies according to the nature of the evidence from which they are drawn:

> The average number of people in a UK household is 2.3. In 1971 it was 2.9; in 1981 it was 2.7; in 1991 it was 2.5; in 2003, it was 2.4. So UK households are getting smaller.

You might well have heard the tired jokes about figures like this ('I've never seen 2.3 people...'). But averages like this can be very useful in enabling us to make comparisons between different countries and between different years. In the example above, there is evidence that UK households are getting smaller. The number of households is 27 million, so it's a very large group from which to get an average.

Such an average also enables us to make comparisons between countries. For example, we can see that the average UK household size is smaller than that of many countries (for example: Argentina 3.7; Egypt 4.2; India 5.4), bigger than others (for example: Denmark 2.2; Finland and Germany 2.1), and the same as the Netherlands.

In the above example, average household size is a useful way of comparing the size over time and from place to place.

Weakness: extremes of high or low figures distorting the average

We have to be careful about seeing significance in averages.

The headline information about the Sea Cadet survey on 2,000 adults presented people's views of how they define success. These included the following:

> ➤ Driving a car worth £34,000
> ➤ Earning £50,000 a year

These are likely to be based on averages. Perhaps quite a few of the respondents said that success was having a car worth around £28,000 and a similar number said that it was having a car worth around £40,000, giving an average of £34,000. It could be that none of the 2,000 respondents actually defined success in terms of having a car worth £34,000.

This problem of how large figures can distort the significance of the average was strikingly described in a book published in 1971 by Jan Pen, *Income Distribution*. The book includes a memorable fable of watching a parade of the UK population march by. The population marches in order of size of income, so people's income is shown by their height. The shortest appear first. The whole parade lasts for only one hour.

Strikingly, it takes 48 minutes before we start to see people of average height (income). Here come the teachers, nurses, lots of civil servants, insurance sales people, and so on. This average group take six minutes to pass by, to be followed by those in the top 10%. Then in the last few minutes we see lawyers, doctors, judges and some accountants. In the final few seconds there are people whose heads are in the clouds. Here we have some Premiership footballers, Simon Cowell, some bankers and some members of the Royal Family.

In one hour, then, the UK population has flashed by. You can see how, in this case, the figure for average income has become almost meaningless. Many people were below it, but the few with very, very high incomes pushed up the average figure. It is not surprising that Jan Pen called his fable 'the parade of dwarfs'.

Now test out your skills in the following exercise.

> **Exam tip**
>
> When evaluating an average figure, consider what might distort its significance. This could include many low figures and a few very high figures. Look at the size of the extremes and the amount of spread within the range.

Exercise 29

House prices are often given as an average figure. Thus, in 2011, the average house price in England and Wales was given by the Land Registry as £161,823. Look at the figures below for average house prices (2011, as given by the Land Registry) in the different parts of England and Wales.

I Work out how useful this average is in giving us a picture of house prices.

House prices are often given as an average figure

OCR AS Critical Thinking

Region	Average house price
East Midlands	125,849
London	344,819
South East	206,980
North West	114,223
South West	173,083
East	171,531
Yorkshire & The Humber	122,311
West Midlands	131,282
North East	102,231
Wales	115,664

2 Consider how useful the average house price figure is in looking at what incomes should be for groups such as teachers, nurses, the police, and other groups whose pay is decided for the whole country. (Note that there is what's called a 'London weighting', giving people who work in that area a higher level of pay.)

Check your answers against those on page 343.

Rates

As you know, percentages show something as a **rate**. This is a rate per 100. But rates can be expressed in numbers per 1,000 or 10,000, and so on.

Here are some examples.

> **Key term**
>
> ➤ **rate:** a rate is always expressed as per a given number. This number could be anything, but is often used as per 1,000 or 10,000, and so on. If it is per 100, it is called a percentage.

Marriages per 1,000 population (2000)	
UK	5.1
Netherlands	4.2
France	3.9
Brazil	3.9

Divorces per 1,000 population (2000)	
UK	2.9
Netherlands	1.7
France	2.2
Brazil	0.8

What might these figures tell us?
> ➤ They are certainly more useful than giving us just the number of marriages and divorces, especially given the wide range of population size between these countries (Brazil 194.2m, Netherlands 16.5m).
> ➤ They enable us to compare marriage and divorce rates between countries. The UK has a relatively high marriage rate (compared with the other three) and (perhaps, in part, as a result) a relatively high divorce rate. You could also usefully compare

France and Brazil, which have the same marriage rate but very different divorce rates.

Rates can be used to show a wide range of information. For example, Israel has 122.1 computers per 100 people, whereas Bulgaria has only 11.0. This again tells us much more than simply knowing the numbers involved.

When the figures are very high, as with the Israeli rate for computers, then we can be more sure that we can draw useful conclusions:

Given that Israel has 122.1 computers for every 100 people, it's clear that the people of that country are very likely to use computers much more than people in Bulgaria.

Here are two other examples of drawing conclusions, using a rate:

(i) Given that Iceland has 90.6 users of the internet for every 100 people, we can see that businesses in Iceland should ensure that they have good websites.

(ii) Given that the US imprisons 753 people for every 100,000 in the US population, it's clear that the US must spend a great deal of its national income on prisons. Denmark imprisons only 59 people for every 100,000 of its population, so expenditure on prisons in Denmark will be low. Thus, to reduce its public expenditure, the US should learn lessons from Denmark.

Weakness: distortions caused by average

Of course, like averages, rates can distort too. For example, the US has an imprisonment rate of 743 per 100,000. But the rate from state to state varies considerably: from 853 in Louisiana to 151 in Maine. Thus, when evaluating evidence with rates, do consider any possible distortions.

Exam tip

If evidence is presented as a rate (e.g. per 1,000), consider how useful this might be, taking into account any possible sources of distortion.

Index

Sometimes evidence is presented as an 'index'. This is designed to take into account differences from country to country and over time.

For example, we looked at house prices as an average and found significant problems in using this measure. A different way of looking at house prices is by using an index. This often takes a certain starting point (in this case a month of a year) and gives that point the value of 100. It has no significance beyond taking that figure as the starting point.

In the case of house prices, January 1995 is taken to be 100. House prices in May 2011 were 259.5. This gives us a useful guide to the degree of increase in house prices.

Another index is called 'the Big Mac Index'. This is used by *The Economist* to compare prices from country to country. It takes the cost of a Big Mac in different countries and converts it into a US dollar equivalent. On this basis, a Big Mac is cheapest in China ($1.83) and most expensive in Norway ($7.02). This index can then be used in all sorts of ways by economists.

What might Unit 2 questions in evaluating evidence look like?

Here are two for you to practise. You may remember the first paragraph from when you identified the principle in the previous chapter. Remember that Unit 2 builds on the skills learned in Unit 1, so you may be able to find additional points of weakness using skills such as representativeness and relevance.

Past paper practice 26

OCR Unit F502, January 2012

In the paragraph below, the author uses evidence from one London borough to support the claim that 'council ownership of parks is an inefficient use of taxpayers' money'.

Furthermore, council ownership of parks is an inefficient use of taxpayers' money. It simply costs too much. In one London borough, £5.4 million was spent on parks in one year, which was roughly £20 for each man, woman and child that lived in that area. If councils no longer had to look after parks, then the money would be spent on better things, like schools or hospitals. People should only have to pay tax for the things that they use or which benefit them.

Make two points of evaluation about the use of this evidence to support this claim. Your evaluations may be strengths and/or weaknesses. You must explain how effectively the use of this evidence supports this claim

Check your answer with the one given on page 343.

Past paper practice 27

OCR Unit F502, June 2009

In the following paragraph the author uses the evidence that 5% of the population have been diagnosed with SAD to support the argument that summer terms are better for schooling than winter terms.

Many children work less productively during the winter months. In the UK, approximately 5% of the population has Seasonal Affective Disorder (SAD). People with this condition work far more effectively during the summer months, when the days are longer and brighter. For both reasons, having schools open in the winter is not in children's best interests.

Explain one weakness in the use of this evidence.

Check your answer with the one given on page 344.

Summary

You have seen that you need to consider whether numerical evidence has any significance or, more accurately, whether it has the significance an author has given it. This is likely to involve you asking a number of questions:

➤ What explanation does an author require for their conclusion to be drawn?

➤ What other explanations would fit the evidence?

➤ What more do we need to know?

➤ Can useful comparisons be made between different groups even though numerical evidence has been given for each?

➤ Could extremes of low or high numbers have distorted the average?

➤ Could variations within a group have distorted the rate or index?

Chapter 23

Flaws in arguments

Learning objectives
By the end of this chapter, you will be able to:
➢ define flaws
➢ identify and explain specific flaws in their context

Defining flaws

The term 'flaw' is being used in an everyday sense. A flaw in anything is something that's wrong with it. A flawed argument has a weakness in it, such that the conclusion is overdrawn (in very flawed arguments, completely overdrawn).

These weaknesses come in many different forms, which are explained in this chapter. Flaws are known by technical names, and you should ensure that you know these. By knowing them, you can then both recognise and explain them accurately.

Exam tip

You need to:

➢ learn the names of the flaws

➢ be able to explain what they mean (in the context of the flawed reasoning on the examination paper).

If you were to look on the internet you would find that there are many flaws and that they are often known by different names. However, your learning is made easier by the fact that OCR Unit 2 has a limited number of flaws that can be examined and that these are listed in the specification. To help you gain an overview of what is expected, they are listed in the table below in the order in which they are explained in this textbook.

You will notice that some are grouped together, for example 'over generalisation' has two types of flaw: 'hasty' and 'sweeping'. In other cases, one flaw is a particular instance of another, for example 'false dichotomy' is a particular type of 'restricting the options' flaw.

Activity 22

To help you to gradually build up your understanding of the flaws you need to know for this exam, you may find it useful to fill in a copy of the following table as you are working through the chapter. Use the notes below to guide you.

Flaws in a nutshell

Flaw	Definition	Example	Assessment
Slippery slope			
Ad hominem			
Straw person/man			
Restricting the options			
False dichotomy			
Two wrongs don't make a right			
Tu quoque			
Confusing necessary and sufficient conditions			
Hasty generalisation			
Sweeping generalisation			
Confusing cause and effect (reverse causation)			
Confusing cause and correlation (e.g. *post hoc*)			
Simplifying causal relations			
Circular argument			
Begging the question			
Conflation			
Arguing from one thing to another/unrelated conclusion (*non sequitur*)			

Notes

➤ **Definition column:** you can find the definition of each flaw in the Key term boxes in this chapter.

➤ **Example column:** when you have used this chapter to work out what each flaw involves, try finding another example for each that you can easily remember. You can do this working in groups, using your own experience, or by using the internet. You might find the Mission Critical website helpful at:

www.sjsu.edu/depts/itl/

— but remember to use only the flaws used in the OCR specification which are listed here.

➤ **Assessment column:** once you have an example for each flaw, try writing an assessment of it in the same way you would be expected to do in the examination — that is, use the definition to explain why the example is weak in this particular way.

OCR AS Critical Thinking

In what follows we will be looking at clear-cut examples of each of the flaws to help you recognise the weakness in reasoning. In an exam situation, if you do not look at the whole of the reasoning concerned, you might be tempted to give an incorrect answer. It is therefore recommended that when you have attempted the past paper exercises, you look at the mark schemes and the reports to centres on the OCR website (www.ocr.org.uk) to find out about common errors and why these are incorrect answers. This might help you to avoid making these mistakes yourself.

Identifying and explaining specific flaws in their context

Slippery slope

This is one of the easiest flaws to spot, as an extreme conclusion is usually reached. The term '**slippery slope**' is nicely descriptive of this type of flawed argument.

Key terms

➢ **slippery slope argument:** the flaw in slippery slope arguments is that the author wrongly argues that a particular claim must lead to another, which must lead to others, such that an extreme or even absurd conclusion is drawn.

The flaw here is one of *inadequate* evidence, in that accepting the initial claim does not require the subsequent claim (and so on), such that the conclusion cannot be drawn.

An example with a short slope
This is part of a letter written to the newspaper *Metro*:

> As a mother of two, I was shocked to see the image accompanying your article 'Too raunchy to be scene'. It left little to the imagination. Please remember that children have access to your newspaper. We do not need any more of our youth getting hooked on pornography after viewing free, easily accessible images like these.

Note the spelling of 'scene': the original article had been about sex scenes in films. Here are the parts to this particular slippery slope spelled out.

➢ Children will see images like the one in *Metro*.
➢ They will then start looking at pornography after they have seen these.
➢ Then they will become 'hooked on pornography'.

This is a flaw of inadequate evidence because, literally, there is none at all. All we have are claims without anything to show why they are to be accepted. Is it really *Metro* today, addictive craving for pornography tomorrow?

Examples with longer slopes
The following exercise should help you to recognise the longer type of slippery slope arguments:

Exercise 30

Identify the point in each argument where the slippery slope starts, and explain why it is an example of this type of flawed argument.

1 Abortion is allowed under certain circumstances. One of these is when the foetus shows serious abnormalities. But, if we allow this, we'll end up killing all children with serious abnormalities. Then we'll feel able to kill all adults with abnormalities. In the end, the only people who will be allowed to live are those who are healthy. Therefore we shouldn't allow abortion.

2 The British Medical Association (BMA) voted overwhelmingly at its 2011 conference for a total ban on smoking in vehicles. However, if such a ban were to be introduced, then the next step would be to ban it outside all shops, then on all pavements. In the end, smoking would be banned in people's own homes. In consequence, the BMA's proposal should be rejected.

Should smoking be banned in vehicles?

Check your answers against those on page 344.

Exam tip

In identifying a slippery slope, you need to see that the author gives *no* (or *inadequate*) evidence to show that one thing leads to another (which leads to another ...).

Ad hominem

An example of an *ad hominem* flaw

Thousands of people protested at the G20 summit in March 2009. Most of them looked as if they didn't bother to work. So we should take no notice of their demands.

The conclusion 'We should take no notice of their demands' is supported by the second sentence. It's clear that this is an example of irrelevant evidence being used in an ***ad hominem*** way. The significance of not bothering to work is meant to devalue the importance of their demands. The author is attacking the people making the demands rather than dealing with the content of those demands.

> **Key term**
>
> ➤ **ad hominem**: this translates as 'at (or to) the man (or person)'. This type of flawed reasoning attacks the arguer, not their argument.
>
> The flaw here is one of *irrelevant* evidence, because the author directs the attack towards some (irrelevant) feature of their opponent as the reason against their opponent's case, rather than addressing the opponent's argument itself.

Using personal information in a relevant way

Some arguments that use information about a person will not be *ad hominem*, because this information is relevant, as in the next example:

> Lord Black (otherwise known as Conrad Black) was convicted of fraud by a Chicago court in 2007. His offence was to steal about £30 million from investors in a company he owned. So it would not be a good idea to invest in any company that he might manage in the future.

The conclusion in the last sentence is drawn from the information about Conrad Black's conviction for fraud. It does seem a reasonable conclusion, given the nature of the fraud he committed.

Exercise 31

Read these arguments to see if they are examples of *ad hominem* argument. If you think either or both is such an example, identify that part of the argument that is *ad hominem*.

1 David Irving is a historian who has questioned whether millions of Jewish people were murdered during the Holocaust in places like Auschwitz. For this, he has served a year in an Austrian prison. He also lost a libel case against a publisher and author who produced a book claiming that he denied the Holocaust. Although he still believes that he's right about the Holocaust, the evidence against him is overwhelming — from significant historians like Martin Gilbert and from the accounts of survivors. Thus we should not take seriously the views of David Irving on the subject of the Holocaust.

2 David Irving is a historian who in 2000 lost a libel case against a publisher who had published a book in which he was described as someone who denied that the Holocaust happened. As a result of not paying his legal costs for this case (an estimated £3 million), he was made bankrupt. In 2006, in Austria, he was

sentenced to three years in prison for denying that the Holocaust happened (though he was released on probation after serving just over a year). So he's both a bankrupt and an ex-prisoner. In consequence, we should not take him seriously as a historian of the Holocaust.

Check your answers against those on page 344.

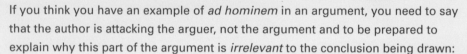

Exam tip

If you think you have an example of *ad hominem* in an argument, you need to say that the author is attacking the arguer, not the argument and to be prepared to explain why this part of the argument is *irrelevant* to the conclusion being drawn:

The author says that *X* has the quality of *Y* but this *Y* is not relevant to arguing that *Z* should be the case.

Straw person

Key terms

> **Straw person** (also known as **straw man**): a straw person/straw man flaw is found when an author deliberately misrepresents an opponent's position in order to attack it more easily. It should be clear why it's called a 'straw man' flaw: men made of straw are easy to knock down.

The flaw here is another flaw of *irrelevant* evidence. This flaw is when someone gives a version of a counter-position that is deliberately distorted in order to show it as weak. In this way, the 'evidence' of the counter-position is irrelevant because it does not provide anything like an accurate version of the real version.

An example of a straw person flaw
Here's a piece from the *Daily Mail* in 2008:

Asking teenagers who carry knives nicely to stop might be polite, but as any sane person knows by now, it is pointless pleading or making empty threats. We need to deal with knife crime by punishing those directly responsible. This will give a clear message which will deter others from falling into the teen-gang cycle of violence and retribution that so blights many inner-city areas.

This is part of an article which argues that punishments for knife crime should be much more severe than they are now. Can you spot the straw man in it?

It is right at the beginning. Those against the use of greater punishments for people who carry knives are characterised as suggesting that we should ask 'teenagers nicely to stop' carrying knives. It is a deliberately weak position, which the author sets up in order to knock it down.

In this way, a straw man is an example of the use of irrelevant evidence: the evidence of the opposing position is not given accurately, so what is given is irrelevant.

Past paper practice 28

OCR Unit F502, January 2011

With reference to the text explain the straw man in the following paragraph.

Actually it's organic farming that threatens our health. Mother Nature isn't our friend. Putting animal droppings on our food is clearly an unhealthy idea. Just look at the scare in 2006, when organically grown spinach was infected with E.coli *bacteria.*

Check your answer with the one given on page 344.

Exam tip

In a question asking you to explain why what you've identified as a straw person is a weakness in the argument, your answer needs to stress that the evidence is *irrelevant* because the author gives the counter-position in a *deliberately* weak way in order to more easily show the strength of his or her own argument.

Restricting the options

Key term

> **restricting the options:** this applies when an author has presented a number of options that do not exhaust the possibilities.

The flaw here is that restricting the options is a weakness in an argument if the options should not have been restricted. It is a case of *inadequate* evidence through presenting a *false position*.

An example of restricting the options to three

It needs to be remembered that **restricting the options** can be a problem even when more than two options have been given.

Binge-drinking among young people (especially among girls) is an increasing problem. The Government can do one of three things: increase the price of alcohol significantly, make it more difficult for young people to get alcohol by restricting the places that can sell it, or increase the fines for retailers who sell it to under-age people. The Government must therefore show it is serious about acting to reduce binge-drinking among the young by doing one of these things.

In this example, the options are restricted to three. But it's clear that there are many more: for example, the Government could have an advertising campaign highlighting various unpleasant consequences of binge-drinking, directed to young people. In addition, of course, the Government could do all three (or just two) of the listed options.

An example of restricting the options to one

Another version of an inappropriate restriction of options is when someone sees only one option available. Here is an example.

> The school's exam results have been declining over the past 2 years. It is obvious that the headteacher will need to recruit better teachers for the results to improve.

As you can see, this example restricts the option to just recruiting 'better teachers'. There will be other options (improving school discipline, changing the exams that are taken, organising the timetable differently and so on).

False dichotomy

Two examples of restricting the options to two

You may be familiar with a **false dichotomy** by thinking of the way in which Marmite advertises itself.

> Marmite — you either love it or hate it.

Some of you reading this might well fall into the 'love it' category and some of you into the 'hate it' category. But, very importantly, some of you might fall into a 'take it or leave it' category. Some of you might even fall into a 'never tasted it' category.

What we see, then, is that the claim is not correct. What it does is restrict the options available to only two, when there might be more.

Look at the next example:

> Playing poker is either a game of skill or it's a game of luck. If it's a game of luck, then it's no different to gambling games like roulette. However, if it's a game of skill, then it's closer to chess or darts. This distinction is important because, if it is a game of luck rather than skill, then it must be played only in licensed casinos. However, given that there are many professional poker players, this shows that it must be a game of skill. So it should be possible to play it anywhere.

Key term

➤ **false dichotomy** (also known as **false dilemma**): this is a specific form of restricting the options, where only two options are presented when a number of other options are possible. Often one of the options is presented as a more favourable choice in comparison to an extreme option.

Is poker a game of skill and luck?

This argument presents only two options: poker is a game of skill or it's a game of luck. What any poker player will tell you is that it is mostly skill with some luck. The skill will come from bluffing, reading the other players' body language, making predictions and so on. The luck comes from what cards are dealt. As a result, the argument ignores the third option that poker is a game involving both skill *and* luck.

You can see how, in this example, the weakness came from the evidence being inadequate (if we take 'evidence' to mean claims). It didn't present us with enough evidence.

An example of where two choices represent legitimate reasoning

This might sound obvious but it needs to be remembered that there are times when there *are* only a few options (perhaps only two).

> The body under the floorboards is either that of the wife of the accused or somebody else. Therefore it is very important that an early identification of the body is made.

Clearly the two options cover everything: it is either her or it isn't, so this isn't an example of this flaw.

Exam tip

In a question asking you to explain why what you've identified as restricting the options is a weakness in the argument, your answer needs to stress that the evidence is *inadequate* because the author has *deliberately* limited the options, often in order to make their position look stronger.

Reasoning from wrong actions

Two versions are given of the term 'reasoning from wrong actions'. These are '**two wrongs don't make a right**' and what is called *tu quoque*.

An example of two wrongs don't make a right

> Protestors at the G20 summit argued that smashing the property of the banks was acceptable because banks had smashed the lives of millions of ordinary people.

Here the negative impact of the banks on people is an irrelevant justification of the need to attack banks. What weakens the argument is that the wrongness of one action does not enable one to defend a different wrong action.

Key term

➤ **'two wrongs don't make a right':** this is a familiar response to an argument in which someone tries to defend one wrong action on the basis that a different wrong action was accepted.

The flaw here is one of *irrelevant* evidence as wrongness can never be a justification for right action.

Exam tip

In a question asking you to explain why what you've identified as two wrongs don't make a right is a weakness in the argument, your answer needs to stress that the evidence is *irrelevant* because another wrong action cannot be used as evidence to justify this wrong action.

An example of reasoning from wrong actions in the form of two wrongs don't make a right

In September 2007, the then Labour Prime Minister, Gordon Brown, said that he wouldn't attend the proposed Europe–Africa summit meeting if Robert Mugabe of Zimbabwe attended. This was because of what Mr Brown called 'the abhorrence' that people felt about what's happening in Zimbabwe.

In an interview with the BBC, Zimbabwe's UN ambassador, Boniface Chidyausiku, responded to the point made by the interviewer that there were 'particular problems with Mr Mugabe's regime' with a question: 'Are you telling me Zimbabwe is the only country in Africa that has problems?'

Is it right to criticise Zimbabwe?

This response can be interpreted as an argument:

Zimbabwe is seen as a country with problems. But there are other African countries that have problems. So it is not right to criticise Zimbabwe.

However, just because other African countries have problems, doesn't mean that we can't criticise Zimbabwe for its problems. It simply doesn't answer the point that Zimbabwe has got problems. This is a straightforward example of reasoning from wrong actions in the form of two wrongs don't make a right.

An example of *tu quoque*

An advert for a well-known supermarket company was recently criticised by one of their rivals as misleading customers. The company had advertised its pork as being free-range when, in fact, the pigs spent only part of their lives in free-range conditions. The first company responded by pointing out that their rival had similarly misled its customers when it had advertised its lettuces as 'organic' when, in fact, some of the farmers who supplied it were found to be using pesticides and artificial fertilisers. As a spokesperson for the first company argued, 'our rivals can hardly accuse us of misleading customers when they have done the same'.

The spokesperson's response is a straightforward example of **tu quoque**, in that it consists of no more than a rejection of their rival's accusation of misleading the public on the basis that their rival has similarly misled the public. As you can see, it might be right that the second company is guilty of hypocrisy but their accusation of misleading the public still stands.

> **Key term**
> ➤ **tu quoque:** this flaw is found when someone argues that something apparently unacceptable that they've done is actually acceptable on the basis that others have done this and it was accepted. The two Latin words translate straightforwardly as 'you too', indicating the opposing arguer is guilty of the same wrong actions. The meaning is often extended to include others also doing this.
>
> The flaw, again, is one of *irrelevant* evidence as wrongness can never be a justification for right action in one's defence.

Confusing necessary and sufficient conditions

> **Key term**
> ➤ **confusing necessary and sufficient conditions:** occurs when someone mistakes one for the other. A *necessary* condition is one that must be fulfilled alongside others for something to happen. A *sufficient* condition is one that is enough by itself to ensure that something will happen.
>
> The flaw here is one of *inadequate* evidence as the author has made a mistake in what counts as sufficient or necessary.

A simple way of understanding the distinction between necessary and sufficient conditions is to think of an order for fish and chips. Both are necessary for the order, but neither is sufficient for it.

We'll now look at an important part of a wedding day to further illustrate the terms necessary and sufficient conditions. In a marriage service, the person conducting the service is required to say early on in the service:

> If any person present knows of any lawful impediment to this marriage he or she should declare it now.

This is quite simply because, if there was a 'lawful impediment', then the wedding could not continue: the lawful impediment would be a necessary reason to stop it. ('There is a lawful impediment to you getting married, therefore the wedding cannot take place.')

But the lawful impediment would not only be a necessary reason to stop the wedding, it would also be a sufficient one. It would, on its own, be enough.

Looking at this issue in more detail, we can see how necessary and sufficient conditions would operate:

➤ To get married in the UK, a person has to not already be married. This is a necessary condition. But it is not a sufficient one.

➤ To get married in the UK, a person has to be aged 18 or over. This is also a necessary condition. But again it is not a sufficient one.

➤ To get married in the UK, a person has to be aged 18 or over and not already be married. These two necessary conditions together are close to being sufficient. Technically, we would have to add in that the person is conscious (not in a coma, for example). In addition, we would have to add that the person is willing to be married. For most situations, however, they are enough.

➤ We could also add that to get married in the UK, a person who is aged 16–17 needs parental consent (a necessary condition).

➤ It is a sufficient condition of not being able to be married to be younger than 16.

A problem in argument can arise when the author confuses necessary and sufficient conditions.

> The UK government has spent £2m to conduct a survey to find out how happy the nation is. The prime minister believes that the evidence from this survey will show what government policies make people happy. However, as many economists argue, the government has got this the wrong way round. Money makes us happy: the more we have, the happier we become (even if we have already got lots). Thus, if the government wants to increase happiness, all it needs to do is to adopt policies that will increase the amount of money that people have.

In this argument, the author has taken it that since 'money makes us happy', all the government has to do to increase happiness, is 'to adopt policies that will increase the amount of money that people have.' But this takes money to be a sufficient condition for happiness. It could, however, be no more than a necessary condition: money makes us happy, but it is not the only thing necessary for happiness. Good health could be another, safe streets could be another, or a good education system could be another.

Here's another example of confusing necessary and sufficient conditions.

The herbal pain-relief product Tiger Balm (made in Singapore) was investigated by the US Food and Drug Administration (FDA) in 2010. There was a problem with the labelling of the product. The FDA argued that, if it was a drug, then it had to satisfy the labelling conditions required for drugs before it could be imported into the US. However, the makers of Tiger Balm argued that **the product met all the labelling requirements which showed that it was a safe product.**

In this passage we have the argument by the makers of Tiger Balm that, having met the labelling requirements, it was therefore safe.

Approaching this argument from a necessary and sufficient conditions position, is accurate labelling a necessary condition of safety to have met the conditions and/or is it a sufficient condition?

We could say that it is necessary to have labelled the product accurately before it's considered safe, but it's not likely to be a sufficient condition. It could be, for example, that rigorous testing of a product is needed and that such testing would make it sufficient for safety. But accurate labelling does not.

In this example, then, there is a confusion between necessary and sufficient conditions.

Exam tip

In a question asking you to explain why what you've identified as confusing necessary and sufficient conditions is a weakness in the argument, your answer needs to stress that the evidence is *inadequate* because the author has taken 'what's necessary' to be sufficient or 'what's sufficient' to be necessary.

(Over) generalisation

This is an unwarranted generalisation, when a general claim is made from specific evidence. It is also known as over generalisation because the conclusion has reached out too far. Unit 2 focuses upon two types of over generalisation: hasty and sweeping generalisations.

Exam tip

When you're identifying an example of sweeping or hasty generalisation, you need to be able to explain why there is a problem in the way the author has generalised from one thing to another.

Hasty generalisation

An example of hasty generalisation

Research on personality traits and birth rates in Western countries typically showed that neurotic women had fewer children. However, we need to rethink this. There is recent evidence that

> suggests it's the other way round. A study of 65 families in four villages in the west African country of Senegal shows that neurotic women had more children than the non-neurotic women.

In this example, the **hasty generalisation** is that:

> The author generalises from a limited number of neurotic women in sixty-five families in four villages in Senegal to all neurotic women. Sixty-five families, four villages, one west African country is a very limited sample on which to base a judgement.

You will have seen that the weakness comes from hasty use of evidence to jump to a conclusion.

Key term

> ➤ **hasty generalisation:** this flaw involves reasoning in which the author seeks to make a far-reaching or over-generalised claim from very limited evidence that is specific to a particular instance. It is known as 'hasty' because the author is rushing to apply this specific case more generally, without considering any wider evidence.

The flaw here is when a general claim is drawn from what amounts to *insufficient* evidence.

Sweeping generalisation

An example of sweeping generalisation

This piece refers to research from the Institute for Fiscal Studies published in 2007:

> Research has shown that those born in August are significantly disadvantaged in education. This is because of the way the school year (and thus the exam system) is structured. Children whose birthdays are in August enter their school year up to almost one year behind their classmates. It used to be believed that children made up the difference as they got older, but this research suggests this is not necessarily so. For example, at the age of 16, August-born girls were 5.5 percentage points less likely than September-born girls to achieve 5 GCSEs (and August-born boys 6.1 percentage points less likely than those born in September). Exam boards should therefore take account of a student's birthday in giving out grades.

Are students born in August disadvantaged in exams?

FOTOLIA

As you can see, the conclusion is based on evidence on students with birthdays in August and September. This is not evidence based on a small survey. It is based on data supplied by the Government, looking at all students (so it is not an example of hasty generalisation). In this way, the conclusion does fit with the evidence.

It seems reasonable to look at ways of doing things differently, but a **sweeping generalisation** is going on. The argument is generalising from these August-born young people to all August-born young people.

We can't conclude that, if you were born in August, your GCSE results won't be as good as those of your September-born friend. You will obviously see that this is problematic, as at the individual level there's considerable room for differences.

Key term

➤ **sweeping generalisation:** this argues from one or a number of cases in a category to all cases in the category. It can be seen to create a stereotype where all instances within a category are seen as having the same characteristics.

The flaw here is one of *inadequate* evidence because it moves from some to all without considering the complexities that make cases within a category different.

Exam tip

In a question asking you to explain why what you've identified as sweeping generalisation is a weakness in the argument, your answer needs to stress that the evidence is *inadequate* because the author has made a leap from some to all without considering the impact of possible differences upon the group.

Confusing cause and effect

Confusing cause and effect is also known as reverse causation.

Key term

➤ **confusing cause and effect:** this where the actual effect is seen as the cause. It can be expressed simply as:

Where A has caused B, B is seen as having caused A.

The flaw here is one of a *mistaken* understanding of the causal relationship, where the author has interpreted the causal relationship the wrong way round, so it cannot be used to support the conclusion.

An example of confusing cause and effect

Young people must have less good hearing than older people. They always want to have the volume of the music they're listening to really loud.

In this example, the causal relationship is given as:

B Poor hearing causes **A** the choice of high volume.

But, of course, the causal relationship is just as likely (you might think more likely) to be the other way round:

A Listening to loud music caused **B** their poor hearing.

The flaw would then be that the author got the causal relationship between high volume and hearing loss the wrong way round.

Of course, it could be that there is no causal relationship at all. It could be that young people listen to loud music simply because they prefer their music loud.

> **Exam tip**
>
> In a question asking you to explain why what you've identified as confusing cause and effect is a weakness in the argument, your answer needs to stress that the evidence is *mistaken* because the author has made an error in the causal explanation, getting this the wrong way around.

Confusing correlation and cause

An example of confusing correlation and cause

The number of people joining the Royal Society for the Protection of Birds (RSPB) has increased significantly over the past 20 years. Unfortunately, the opposite has happened with the number of wild birds in the UK. In fact, the increase in the RSPB membership follows exactly the decline in wild birds. So trying to protect birds has had the opposite effect.

The number of wild birds has declined despite increased protection

So what's going on here?

The most likely explanation is that of coincidental correlation. They happen together but neither one causes the other. There are independent causes for each.

> ➤ Perhaps the RSPB has had a strong advertising campaign that has led to a continuing increase in membership.
> ➤ Perhaps farmers have removed habitat needed for wild birds, or fewer gardens now have grass and flowers, with the growth of decking and paving.

In other words, the two have happened independently. Rising membership has not caused the decline in wild birds. The flaw is that the author claimed a **false cause** — a causal connection when there was none.

Key term

> **false cause:** this is when an author takes a correlation (connection) to indicate causation, without there being a very good reason to believe that causation has happened or is happening. It can be expressed as:
>
> A and B have no causal relationship and are correlated coincidentally.
>
> The flaw, again, is one of a *mistaken* understanding of a causal relationship, but this time it is because there is no causal relationship at all.

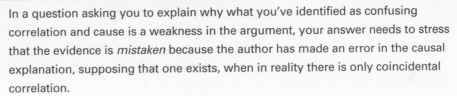

Exam tip

In a question asking you to explain why what you've identified as confusing correlation and cause is a weakness in the argument, your answer needs to stress that the evidence is *mistaken* because the author has made an error in the causal explanation, supposing that one exists, when in reality there is only coincidental correlation.

Post hoc

One of the most common examples of a confusing correlation and cause is what's called ***post hoc*** (which simply means 'after this'). The full version of this Latin term is *post hoc ergo propter hoc* ('after this, therefore because of this') and it's useful to think of this full version to focus attention on what's going on.

Key term

> ***post hoc:*** *post hoc* reasoning takes it that, because one thing *follows* another, the latter is caused by the former, when in fact this is a coincidence and a third factor is involved. Put simply:
>
> A is said to have caused B, when in fact it was C.

An example of *post hoc*

> Shortly after electrical cabling was updated in a village primary school to accommodate a new suite of computers, a fire broke out which was attributed to an electrical fault. In letters to the editor in the local paper one reader asked, 'Was it worth the risk to our children's lives?'

Here the 'it' was a reference to the installation of the computers and the updated cabling. The reader had made a causal connection between the installation and the fire. You might think that this was a reasonable explanation in that, all things remaining the same, this change was the most likely cause, especially as the cause was said to be an electrical fault. However, after investigation, the cause of the fire was found to be rodent damage to the wiring.

The flaw was that the reader had thought that:

A the electrical installation had caused **B** the fire

when in fact it had been caused by **C** rodent damage.

Cum hoc: this causal flaw is not examined in OCR Unit 2, but it is described here so that you can have a clearer picture about *post hoc* flaws.

Sometimes, of course, one thing does not *follow* another but *happens at the same time as* the other. This has a name of its own, very similar to *post hoc*. This is *cum hoc ergo propter hoc* (or simply, *cum hoc*). This means 'with this, therefore because of this'. It looks at two things that happen together and then sees a causal relationship between the two. This would fit with the RSPB/wild birds example. You'll also find it in the cosmetic surgery example, because the author might say that British vanity and high levels of spending on cosmetic surgery exist at the same time, so there is a causal relationship between the two.

An example of a legitimate causal connection

It needs to be stressed that both *post hoc* and *cum hoc* are flaws in an argument only when the causal relationship is an *inappropriate* one. There are obviously many examples when we could say, without any problem, that one thing followed another, therefore the latter caused the former.

The car skidded out of control into a tree; the driver of the car was injured.

In this example, we are not going to puzzle over the causal relationship between the car's accident and the driver's injury.

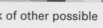

Exam tip

When evaluating correlation and causation material, think of other possible explanations for the material than that given by the author.

(Over) simplifying causal relationships

An example of oversimplifying causal relationships

You will remember that we looked at the following argument in Chapter 22:

Britain spends the highest amount on cosmetic surgery of any country in Europe. In 2006 this was £497m. The second highest was Italy with £158m. In fact, if we add up the total amount spent by the countries that were second, third (France), fourth (Germany), and fifth (Spain) in the league table of spending, this total is still less than the amount spent in Britain. This shows that British people are the vainest in Europe.

You saw how, in this argument, the author relied on only one explanation: the vanity of British people has caused the highest expenditure in cosmetic surgery. However, you will also remember that we could think of other explanations that fitted the same evidence.

The flaw is that:

A   the vanity of British people is said to have caused

B   the highest expenditure in cosmetic surgery

when in fact it may have been caused by a number of factors:

A   plus

X   the British definition of cosmetic surgery may be more inclusive

Y   people from abroad use British clinics because there are more of them

Z   people from abroad use British clinics because of high standards of practice.

> **Key term**
> ➤ **(over) simplifying causal relationships:** this is a case of giving an oversimplified explanation, when in fact the situation is complex where a number of causes are interrelated. Put simply:
>
> A is seen as causing B when in fact it is a case of A plus X, Y and Z.
>
> The flaw here is one of *inadequate* evidence, because only part of the causal explanation is given.

Exercise 32

Evaluate each of the following arguments, focusing on whether the correlation given can usefully be seen in terms of causation.

1   In January 2005, the *Daily Mirror* carried an advertising campaign by Cadbury's Dairy Milk chocolate. This included having a purple masthead (the same colour as the Dairy Milk wrapper and branding), having lots of advertisements for Dairy Milk, and special offers for the chocolate. In the two weeks following the campaign, sales of Dairy Milk went up by 37% above their normal expected level, and *Daily Mirror* readers increased their spending on the chocolate by 75%. This shows that dedicated advertising like this really boosts sales of a product.

2 In 2007, Ada Mason, the then oldest woman in Britain, died aged 111. Her granddaughter said that Ada attributed her long life to 'clean living' and a daily meal of bread and dripping with salt. We should follow Ada Mason's example.

3 Women's levels of self-reported happiness are lower than they were 30 years ago. This is even though they're more successful in education, healthier, and have relatively higher incomes than 30 years ago. Although we normally think of success in education, greater health and higher incomes as making us happier, it's clear that they have the opposite effect. If we are to be happier, we must look for other things to do this.

Check your answers against those on page 345.

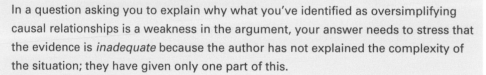

Exam tip

In a question asking you to explain why what you've identified as oversimplifying causal relationships is a weakness in the argument, your answer needs to stress that the evidence is *inadequate* because the author has not explained the complexity of the situation; they have given only one part of this.

Circular arguments

In **circular arguments**, the conclusion essentially repeats the reason. In other words, there is no process of drawing a conclusion. The author concludes what is already claimed.

Key term

➢ **circular argument:** in circular arguments, the conclusion is no more than a restatement of the reason(s) — that is, it says the same thing twice.

The flaw here is one of *inadequate* reasoning because no support is given for the conclusion.

Two examples of circular arguments

(i) People should spend less and put more money aside each month. Thus people ought to save more than they do.

As you can see, the conclusion is no more than a restatement of the reason given for it. Why should people save more? Because they should.

What about the next one?

(ii) Fish have the ability to feel pain in the same way as other animals. Therefore, when they are in pain, they feel like a dog, a cat or a person feels.

This, as you can see, has the same problem. 'Other animals' must include dogs, cats and people, so the conclusion has already been claimed in the reason.

The flaw is one of inadequate evidence — there is *no* evidence given to enable the conclusion to be drawn.

A test for circular arguments

You can test for a circular argument by simply reversing the sequence of reasoning.

People ought to save more than they do. Thus people should spend less and put more money aside each month.

As you can see, it doesn't change anything. The argument is circular.

> **Exam tip**
>
> In a question asking you to explain why what you've identified as a circular argument is a weakness in the argument, your answer needs to stress that the evidence is missing and therefore *inadequate* to support the conclusion.
>
> When you think you might have found a circular argument, test it to see if swapping the reason(s) for the conclusion makes any difference. If it doesn't, then you've found a circular argument.

Begging the question

This is a special type of circular argument where the author doesn't offer reasoning for the key point that they are putting forward.

> **Key term**
>
> ➤ **begging the question:** the author either makes a claim, such that they are asserting what they are trying to prove, or they assume this step in the reasoning.
>
> The flaw, again, is one of *inadequate* evidence as a key area of support is missing.

An example of begging the question:

There has been considerable pressure for shops to open on Sundays despite the Sunday trading hours, as for many people Sunday is their one day off work and the best time for them to shop without the pressure of having to squeeze this into lunch hours or the short time before shops close in the evening. However, the hard line is that shops should keep to the Sunday trading hours because that is the law and the law after all is the law.

Here the author is not giving any reason why the law is right; they are simply assuming that this is so.

The flaw is again one of *inadequate* evidence.

Conflation

Key term

➤ **conflation:** this is where the author takes at least two different terms and treats them as if they are the same.

The flaw here is one of *partly irrelevant* evidence, as some of the evidence is about something that is different.

An example where three terms are conflated
See if you can spot them:

> More than two-thirds of the UK's insect pollinators are in decline, including many species of butterfly, hoverfly, moth and bumblebee. This is thought to be related to the decline in open-headed flowers where the pollen is more accessible to these species. The BBC has recently launched a series of programmes which seek to inspire town and city councils, villages and gardeners everywhere to plant insect-friendly plants. The Royal Horticultural Society (RHS) has joined in the movement by labelling plants that attract insect pollinators, i.e. have accessible pollen, while seed merchants have even produced meadow flower grow-mats, so that all you have to do is to roll out the mat, cover it in soil and watch the flowers grow. This must surely help to reverse the downward trend in our insect pollinators.

This sounds convincing but the author has **conflated** 'plants that attract insect pollinators' with both 'insect-friendly plants' and 'meadow flowers'. Insects may be friendly to plants without being pollinators, for example predators to pests that would otherwise destroy leaves. Also, not all meadow flowers attract insect pollinators, as for some the wind does the pollinating.

The flaw is that the author here has used three terms as if they are the same. As they are not, this weakens the evidence for the author's claim about the reverse in the downward trend.

Exam tip

In a question asking you to explain why what you've identified as conflation is a weakness in the argument, your answer needs to stress that the evidence is *partly irrelevant* and therefore inadequate to support the conclusion. You need to identify the terms that are conflated and to explain how they are different.

Arguing from one thing to another/unrelated conclusion

An example of arguing from one thing to another

The general public has been very concerned about the environmental health issues arising from fly-tipping. Old sofas and washing machines are regularly left on road verges, in cul-de-sacs in housing estates, on wasteland by railway tracks and even in front of field gates, preventing farmers tending their crops and stock. There is a distinct need to look at the primary school curriculum to teach our children from an early age to have a much greater respect for the countryside.

Is fly-tipping related to the primary school curriculum?

So what have we here?

The author outlines the problem of fly-tipping and gives examples of where it occurs. The immediate problem is with some adults fly-tipping, whereas the conclusion deals with children and the primary school curriculum, without any indication of why this should be.

The flaw is that the conclusion about the primary school curriculum is not strongly related to the reasoning about fly-tipping.

Key term

> **arguing from one thing to another**: here the author draws a conclusion that is not related to the reasoning. This is also known as *non sequitur* which literally means 'It does not follow'.

The flaw here is one of *irrelevant* evidence, as the conclusion is unrelated to the reasoning.

Exam tip

In a question asking you to explain why what you've identified as arguing from one thing to another is a weakness in the argument, your answer needs to stress that the evidence is *irrelevant* because the conclusion is unrelated to the reasoning. You need to identify the conclusion and the reasoning and explain how they are unrelated.

Now try these examination questions to test out the skills that you have been learning in this chapter. Here are three types of question that have been asked in the past.

Past paper practice 29

OCR Unit F502, June 2011

The following argument contains a flaw in the reasoning.

The British Museum has a set of bronzes which were taken from the Kingdom of Benin, now part of Nigeria, in 1897. Nigeria now wants them back. But the British Museum has refused to return many other artefacts over the years; for instance, it has frequently refused to return the Parthenon marbles, which were taken from Athens in the 1800s and which Greece wants back. Since the British Museum has decided not to return other items, it must not return the Benin Bronzes either.

The flaw would be best described as:

(a) circular argument
(b) hasty generalisation
(c) *post hoc*
(d) reasoning from wrong actions.

Check your answer with that given on page 345.

Past paper practice 30

OCR Unit F502, January 2012

Which is the best statement of the flaw in the following argument?

In Denmark, children start school at six or seven years old. In comparison, children in the UK begin school at the age of five or earlier and endure assessments every two to three years, including SATs, controlled assessments and GCSEs. Denmark consistently scores highly on so-called 'happiness' scales, whereas the UK scores are significantly lower. It is obvious that starting education later will help to improve the happiness of the population of the UK.

(a) The author conflates education with GCSE examinations.
(b) The author confuses necessary and sufficient conditions: education is necessary for happiness, but not sufficient for it.
(c) The author implies a causal link between Denmark's happiness ratings and the later start to education.
(d) The author unreasonably generalises from Denmark to all countries.

Check your answers with those given on page 345.

OCR AS Critical Thinking

Past paper practice 31

OCR Unit F502, January 2012

Explain one flaw or weakness in this reasoning:

If councils no longer had to look after parks, then the money would be spent on better things.

Check your answer with that given on page 345.

Activity 23

Your completed 'Flaws in a nutshell' table from Activity 22 can be turned into a useful set of revision cards. These can help you to bring together the skills you need in order to identify and explain flaws in the Unit 2 examination.

To make the cards:
> Copy your completed table into a document file and edit your table so that each of the cells is the same size.
> Print your table and cut out the individual cells to make the cards.

Once you have produced the cards, you can:
> exchange sets of cards with another group and try a straightforward task of matching the cards into their rows
> practise the assessment task by matching the first three columns in a row and then writing your own assessment for the example and checking it against the missing assessment card
> use the cards to play flaws bingo, snap and dominoes

Summary
> A flaw is an error in the reasoning, such that it weakens the case for the conclusion to be drawn.
> You need to look for such things as irrelevance, and inadequate, mistaken and even missing reasoning.
> To be able to answer the examination questions effectively, you need to know the name of the appropriate flaw and its definition, and be able to apply this with reference to the text to explain the flawed reasoning.
> There are many interactive websites that allow you to test out your skills in recognising the flaws, but remember to refer to your list of flaws that can be tested in Unit 2.

Chapter 24

Appeals in reasoning

Learning objectives

By the end of this chapter, you will be able to:

➤ distinguish between flaws and appeals in reasoning

➤ identify and explain specific appeals in their context

Distinguishing between flaws and appeals in reasoning

In this chapter we look at a specific type of reasoning — the use of appeals.

Whereas a flaw was seen as a weakness or error in the reasoning, so that the conclusion is weakened, an appeal can be seen as giving minimal or no rational support to the conclusion. Instead it uses forms of persuasion, often emotion, to persuade the reader to accept a conclusion. This is done with reference to people and events. Although appeals can be examples of legitimate reasoning, it depends upon which appeal is used in specific circumstances. In Unit 2 the specification guides us that we *'should be able to explain why an appeal may not support a conclusion',* so we will be looking to identify where there is a weakness. However, to be able to do this you also need to recognise where an appeal would be legitimate, so that you can distinguish it from weakness.

Relevance turns out to be the central question you need to ask when judging the significance of an appeal. If the evidence in the appeal is not relevant, then you have a weakness.

We'll now look at different types of appeals and see how they are meant to work.

Exam tip

Although an appeal can strengthen reasoning, in Unit 2 the focus is on weakness in reasoning.

When you have identified an appeal that is a weakness, you'll need to:

➤ identify where the appeal has been used instead of relevant reasoning

> explain how the appeal is irrelevant to the point being made and how this is so

However, when an argument has reasoning *as well as* an appeal, then the strength or weakness of that argument cannot be judged simply on the basis of the significance of the appeal; you also need to look at the reasoning.

Identifying and explaining specific appeals in their context

If you were to look on the internet you would find that there are many appeals but, as with the flaws, OCR Unit 2 has a limited number of appeals that can be examined; these are listed in the specification. To help you have an overview, they are listed below in Activity 24 in the order in which they are explained in this textbook.

Exam tip

You need to learn the names of the appeals and be able to explain what they mean in the context of the reasoning on the examination paper.

In the exam, you might well be asked in the multiple-choice questions to see whether an appeal is used in an argument. For this, you will need to have learned the different terms and be able to identify the different appeals.

Activity 24

To help you to gradually build up your understanding of the appeals you need to know for this exam, you may find it useful to fill in the following table as you are working through the chapter. Use the notes below to guide you.

Appeals in a nutshell

Appeal	Definition	Example	Assessment
Appeal to popularity			
Appeal to authority			
Appeal to emotion			
Appeal to history			
Appeal to tradition			

Notes
> **Definition column:** you can find the definition of each appeal in the Key term boxes in this chapter.
> **Example column:** when you have used this chapter to work out what each appeal involves, try finding another example for each that you can easily remember. You can do this working in groups, using your own experience, or by using the internet. You might find the Mission Critical website helpful at **www.sjsu.edu/depts/itl/,** but remember to use only the appeals used in the OCR specification.
> **Assessment column:** once you have an example for each appeal, try writing an assessment of it in the same way you would be expected to do in the exam — that is, use the definition to explain why the example is weak in this particular way.

Appeal to popularity

Identifying the appeal

An **appeal to popularity** uses evidence about what people think or do (or have thought or done) in order to draw a conclusion on something seen as relevant to this. Typically, you'll find appeals to popularity expressed in terms of survey data.

Key term
> **appeal to popularity:** this uses the weight of numbers that demonstrate likes and dislikes or beliefs and attitudes amongst a particular group, in order to persuade the reader to accept a conclusion relevant to these.

In weak appeals to popularity, the weight of numbers will be irrelevant to the point being made.

For example:

The majority — 55% of people — in Britain believe in the existence of heaven and 70% believe that the human soul exists. This shows that science can't explain everything.

An example of an irrelevant appeal

In the example above, evidence of belief among the British population is used to draw a conclusion about science. The appeal is not relevant. Whether or not science can explain everything is not dependent on what the public believe. Science presumably can or can't explain this, regardless of what people believe.

An example of a relevant appeal

In 1998, 38% of people in Britain said that they believed in horoscopes. Ten years later, the figure was only 22%. This shows that British people have become more sceptical about the claims of people such as Russell Grant.

In this example, the appeal to popularity is relevant. The decline in belief in astrology is relevant to the claim that people have become more sceptical about astrology.

Judging the relevance of an appeal

It can be difficult to judge the appropriateness (the relevance) of an appeal to popularity. But normally you can follow these guidelines:

➤ Appeals to popularity are relevant when drawing a conclusion about what people think (or thought).
➤ Appeals to popularity are irrelevant when what people think (or thought) makes no difference to the conclusion being drawn.

This approach will work with any of the appeals. Working out the relevance of an appeal is a task that requires us to look at the nature of the conclusion drawn from it. So when you see any appeal in an argument, you need to consider whether it is a relevant one.

Exam tip

Normally, in the exam, appeals to popularity are going to be irrelevant ones, thereby making the appeal weak reasoning.

When assessing weakness in reasoning, and you have found an appeal to popularity, you need to show with reference to the text how the author has replaced relevant reasoning with evidence of people's likes or beliefs that is irrelevant to the conclusion, explaining why this so.

Exercise 33

Are the appeals to popularity relevant or irrelevant in these arguments?

1 Sixty-seven per cent of people in the UK believe that all bacteria are dangerous. Therefore there should be a campaign to show people that many bacteria are necessary for our health.
2 Sixty-three per cent of people in the UK believe that parents of young people involved in antisocial behaviour are 'a great deal to blame'. The Government should therefore introduce penalties for such parents, to encourage them to keep their children under better control.

Check your answers with those given on page 346.

Appeal to authority

Irrelevant appeals authority

Appeals to authority need to be assessed in terms of whether the authority is relevant or irrelevant to the conclusion drawn.

For example, an argument about the causes of the recession might well include a relevant appeal to the authority of an economist who has studied such causes. An irrelevant appeal to authority in this situation could include looking at what a popular entertainer has to say on the subject.

> **Key term**
>
> ➢ **appeal to authority:** this uses a recognised source to justify a conclusion that is drawn. It inevitably involves looking at the expertise of that source.

In weak appeals to authority, either the expertise of the recognised source will be unrelated to the point being made or the source will be used in place of any relevant reasoning to justify the point being made.

In order to know what happens to a beam of light when it has a close encounter with a massive object, you would probably be happy to read what Einstein has to say on the subject. This is because of his enormous expertise (and thus authority) in this area of knowledge. An argument that used what Einstein had to say about such things should provide reasonable conclusions if it used his writings accurately.

So, feeling impressed by what Einstein has to say, let's look at an argument that uses something he wrote:

> The greatest scientist of the twentieth century was Einstein. He argued that: 'Nothing will benefit human health as much as the evolution to a vegetarian diet.' So we should all become vegetarians as soon as possible.

So should we? There might be all sorts of good reasons for people to become vegetarian, but the fact that Einstein said that we should isn't necessarily a compelling reason to do so. Why? Because, for all his brilliance, he had no particular expertise in the fields of diet and health.

Was Einstein an expert on vegetarianism?

Weak appeals to authority

Appeals to authority also need to be assessed in terms of whether the experts' views are explained. Even if the expert is relevant to the issue, if only their name is used to support the conclusion, then this can be seen as a weak appeal to authority.

Look at the next example:

> Nobel Prize winners in physiology and medicine said that experiments on animals are crucial to the development of many medical treatments. Therefore the people who protest against medical experiments on animals should be ignored. They clearly have nothing useful to say.

This is obviously an appeal to authority. In this argument, is the evidence of Nobel Prize winners relevant? This is a difficult one. Clearly, these Nobel Prize winners would have been/are very significant scientists and it would be difficult to dismiss what they have to say as irrelevant. The conclusion that 'people who protest against medical experiments on animals should be ignored' is drawn from the conclusion that 'they clearly have nothing useful to say'. This conclusion is drawn only from the evidence on the Nobel Prize winners. As a result, we can see that, although the appeal to authority is certainly not irrelevant, it isn't enough for the author to draw the conclusion and can be considered to be a weak appeal to authority.

Exam tip

When evaluating an argument where you have found an appeal to authority, you need to consider whether the expertise of that authority is relevant to the argument. If not, you need to explain why.

If the authority is relevant, then you need to consider whether the author explains the authority's views or simply name-drops.

Exercise 34

Assess whether the authority of John Brenkus used in the following passage is relevant or irrelevant and whether it is weakened by lack of reasoning.

John Brenkus' predictions

Predictions about the future of athletic records have been made by John Brenkus of the US, the presenter of the award-winning programme on American TV called *Sports Science*. His predictions have included that

Should we take John Brenkus' predictions seriously?

a below nine-second 100 metres will not be run until 2909 (and that the new record of 8.99 seconds that will be set at that time will never be broken) and that a marathon time of 1 hour 58 minutes will be achieved very soon and will then never be broken. Brenkus studied 200 athletes at a special laboratory in California and has also completed the Iron Man challenge, an endurance event that involves swimming for 2.4 miles, cycling for 112 miles, and then running a marathon — in that order, and within 14 hours. Given the expertise of John Brenkus, we should take his predictions very seriously.

Check your answer with the one given on page 346.

Appeal to emotion

There is no reason why a good argument cannot include an emotional dimension, but if the *sole* means of persuasion is an emotional one then it becomes weak.

Key term

➢ **appeal to emotion:** this uses reasoning designed to provoke an emotional response (such as pity, disgust or pleasure) in those reading the argument, to persuade them to accept the conclusion.

It is weak where the appeal replaces any relevant reasoning.

An example of a purely rational argument

The appeal here is for a campaign to raise funds for a new children's hospice:

> There has been a campaign to raise funds for the new children's hospice. The improvements in the nursing care of very sick children will be considerable. This will mean that there will be fewer occasions when parents and other carers have to care for the children at home, with all the domestic and work disruptions this can cause. People should give generously to the campaign.

This argument largely avoided using the readers' emotions to persuade them to give generously.

An example with a relevant emotional element added

> There has been a campaign to raise funds for the new children's hospice. The improvements in the nursing care of very sick children will be considerable. In addition, both the children and their families will be able to experience some joy and pleasure, even though there will also be sadness and, at times, despair. People should give generously to the campaign.

Although the third sentence includes emotions, it does so in a context where this fits, alongside other reasoning.

An example of an irrelevant appeal to emotion

> Curdsworthy should have been awarded first prize for best village in bloom in this area as they had prepared for it all year and had a dedicated team of gardeners out there for weeks tending the hanging baskets and keeping their displays going. The winners only pulled off their attempts right at the last minute.

Here the persuasion lies *solely* in the appeal to pity. You are asked to pity the time, planning and dedication of the losing village as against that of the winning village. However, this is *irrelevant* if what is being judged is the quality of the displays, regardless of the relative lack of effort bringing this about. This is therefore a weak appeal to emotion.

Exam tip

When assessing weakness in reasoning, and you have found an appeal to emotion, you need to show with reference to the text how, to support the conclusion, the author has replaced relevant reasoning solely with language that appeals to the readers' emotions.

Exercise 35

Read the following argument.
> Does it rely on an appeal to emotion?
> If so, is the use of emotion here relevant to the conclusion?

Eric Lucas

In November 1938, a young German Jewish boy named Eric Lucas was put on a train by his parents. The train was going to take him from Germany to Belgium, from where he would go to Britain, where he would be safe from the persecutions that were taking place against Jewish people at the time. As the train drew away from the station, Eric could see his parents. 'There stood my father and my mother. An old man, leaning heavily on his stick and holding his wife's hand. It was the first and the last time in my life that I had seen them both weep… My father's eyes were gentle and soft, but filled with tears of loneliness and fear.' When he got to Britain, Eric tried to get a visa for his parents to come here too. He was not successful and he never saw them again. They were murdered by the Nazis in 1941. Although Britain saved more than 50,000 German Jews by giving them refuge, it should have opened its doors to many more of them.

Check your answers with those given on page 346.

Appeal to history

Here the author looks back in time to an event or series of events and argues that because it has happened before, we should use this knowledge to predict what will happen in the future. Depending on whether it was a good or bad event, the author will argue that we should do the same, or take action to prevent it happening again. They do not consider that times change so that people or events may not react in the same way in the future.

Key term

> **appeal to history:** this uses evidence of a past event or events to persuade the reader to accept a prediction about the future or a recommendation for a future action (and sometimes to accept a conclusion about the present).

It is weak where the appeal replaces any relevant reasoning (including where the events lack relevance to each other because different conditions apply).

Exam tip

As with other appeals, you need to consider whether an appeal to history is relevant in the argument.

We will look at a relevant appeal so that you know what to discount when you are looking for an irrelevant appeal to history.

An example of a relevant appeal to history

The rapidly growing countries that surround the Bay of Bengal (such as India and Bangladesh) need urgently to find ways to protect themselves from some of the world's most devastating storms. History shows the dangers of this area. For example, the 1737 Hooghly cyclone was once considered the worst disaster in human history, with 12-metre waves that almost wiped out Calcutta. More recent disasters have included the 1876 and 1970 cyclones, each of which killed 300,000 people in what is now Bangladesh. As recently as 1991, a

History has shown the Bay of Bengal to be vulnerable to devastating storms

storm surge killed more than 100,000 people in that country. If global warming does bring an increase in cyclonic activity, the heavily populated coastline of the Bay of Bengal will be among the most vulnerable regions in the world.

This argument uses various historical examples to support the conclusion in the first sentence that these countries need to prevent a re-occurrence. The appeal to history is a relevant one, because the events are likely to occur in exactly the same way, as a result of global warming.

Examples of irrelevant appeals to history

(i) Neville Chamberlain tried to avoid war with Germany in 1938 by giving in to Hitler's demands, the policy that came to be known as 'appeasement'. The policy did not work because dictators like Hitler are not going to be stopped by getting them to sign bits of paper. **We should learn from this in our dealings with present-day regimes that threaten us, and not allow them to have their way.**

In this example, the appeal to history is weak. Although we now know that appeasing Hitler was wrong, it does not necessarily follow that the act of appeasement will also be wrong if used in the future as future dictatorial regimes may behave differently.

The next example has the same problem:

(ii) In 1962 President Kennedy demanded that Russia (the old USSR) remove its missiles from Cuba. It led the world to the brink of war, but President Kennedy calculated correctly. The Russian missiles were removed, and the threat of war receded. **This episode shows us that the best way to deal with threatening regimes is to confront them**.

Again, the appeal to history is weak as present political conditions differ from the 1960s. Perhaps present-day threatening regimes (such as North Korea and Iran) would not act like the Russians in 1962, so the appeal to history is not relevant.

Here's another example of a weak appeal to history.

(iii) The chef Heston Blumenthal complained that serving 12,000 people at a big event for the Diamond Jubilee in April 2012 would mean that the food would have to be served cold. However, at the Installation of the Archbishop of York in 1465, 104 cows, 1,000 sheep, 304 pigs, 2,000 pigeons and 4,000 rabbits (as well as lots of other meats) were served to the guests. Thus, if food on that scale could be served almost 550 years ago, Heston Blumenthal should have been able to serve hot food in 2012.

This appeal to history is weak because the similarities between the two events are likely to be very different. For one thing, we don't know how many people were invited to the archbishop's feast. For another, we don't know if all the guests had their food hot. In addition, we don't know how many people were employed in cooking the food in 1465 (were there hundreds?) and over what timescale the feast was provided (1 day, 2 days, more?)

Exam tip

When assessing weakness in reasoning, and you have found an appeal to history, you need to show with reference to the text how the author has replaced relevant reasoning with evidence from the past that is irrelevant to the conclusion as conditions today are likely to be different, explaining why this so.

Appeal to tradition

It is not surprising that this type of reasoning goes by the name of an **appeal to tradition**. It is an appeal to accept a belief because it has a long history of acceptance.

Key term

➤ **appeal to tradition:** this argues that because something (a ceremony, practice, belief, custom and so on) is very old and/or well established, it is a good reason for this to continue today.

It is weak where present conditions mean that the practice or belief is no longer relevant.

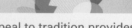

As with other appeals, you need to consider whether an appeal to tradition provides a relevant reason to persuade you to accept the conclusion.

The author uses nothing more than the fact that because we have always done things this way, it should continue. It does not take on board that circumstances might have changed so that the tradition may no longer be relevant.

Examples of irrelevant appeals to tradition

Let's look at an example that uses the tradition of capital punishment to try to persuade the reader that it should be reintroduced:

> **(i)** The belief that capital punishment deters people from committing serious crime is a very old one. For thousands of years, the fear of death — especially a humiliating and possibly very painful one — has been seen as the thing that would stop most people from breaking laws. This strong and persistent belief in the deterrent effect **must therefore make any proposal to reintroduce capital punishment worth supporting.**

The conclusion of this argument is drawn from one claim — the first sentence — that, because the belief that capital punishment acts as a deterrent to crime is a very old one, it is worth supporting today.

Is it relevant to this argument? No. The conclusion about the strength of the deterrent effect of capital punishment cannot be drawn from the fact that a belief in this effect has a long history, as its acceptance may have been wrong, or conditions now may make it wrong to accept today.

Here's another example:

> **(ii)** 'God Save the Queen (or King)' was first performed in 1745. It became the British National Anthem at the beginning of the nineteenth century. Although there is much criticism of it as a national anthem, it's the one we've sung for 200 years, **so we should keep it.**

You will have noticed that the argument is no more than the second half of the last sentence: '… it's the one we've sung for 200 years, so we should keep it'. It is specifically appealing to a tradition that has been in place for some time and gives no other reason to keep the national anthem. It assumes that it is still relevant, whereas some might

When assessing weakness in reasoning, and you have found an appeal to tradition, you need to show with reference to the text how the author has replaced relevant reasoning with evidence of a well-established custom or belief that is irrelevant to the conclusion as beliefs today are likely to be different, explaining why this so.

want to argue that a decline in the belief in God, and the changing level of support for the Royal Family may mean that it is time for a change.

Now use the following exam questions to test out your skills. Identifying 'appeals' can be tested both through multiple-choice questions and short-response questions that ask you to identify the appeal and explain it with reference to the text.

Past paper practice 32

OCR Unit F502, January 2012

Which of the following is an appeal made in response to the following argument?

Many people love the violent aspect of American football. This is shown in the many sponsored video games and TV coverage which focus on brutal tackles. The proposal to suspend or fine players who use their helmets to injure their opponents should be ignored.

(a) Appeal to emotion

(b) Appeal to history

(c) Appeal to popularity

(d) Appeal to tradition

Check your answers with those given on page 347.

Past paper practice 33

OCR Unit F502, January 2012

In response to a proposed ban on ball games in parks, a park user commented, 'Cricket has been played in most parks for over 150 years, so it must be allowed to continue'.

(a) Name the appeal in the above comment.

(b) Explain why using this appeal may not give strong support to the park user's conclusion that 'it must be allowed to continue'.

Check your answers with those given on page 347.

Past paper practice 34

OCR Unit F502, June 2011

The problem seems to be that zookeepers are reluctant to intervene when baby animals are neglected by their parents. A good example is Gana, a female gorilla, and her baby. Gana had a history of neglecting her children and was not feeding her baby. Despite this, the heartless zookeepers decided not to intervene. Gana's baby died — a tragic, unnecessary death. At least this zoo is now starting to re-think its policies because it has received some highly negative publicity.

(a) Name the appeal in the above comment.

(b) Explain why the use of this appeal may not give strong support to the argument that zookeepers must be required to do everything within their power to save the lives of baby animals.

Check your answers with those given on page 347.

Activity 25

Your completed 'Appeals in a nutshell' table from Activity 24 can be turned into a useful set of revision cards. These can help you to bring together the skills you need to identify and explain appeals in the Unit 2 examination.

To make the cards:
➢ Copy your completed table into a document file and edit your table so that each of the cells is the same size.
➢ Print your table and cut out the individual cells to make the cards.

Once you have produced the cards, you can:
➢ exchange sets of cards with another group and try a straightforward task of matching the cards into their rows
➢ practise the assessment task by matching the first three columns in a row and then writing your own assessment for the example and checking it against the missing assessment card
➢ use the cards to play appeals bingo, snap and dominoes

Summary
➢ Appeals give minimal or no rational support to the conclusion.
➢ Reasoning consists of (or includes) an irrelevant reference to beliefs, events or people.
➢ When identifying weakness in reasoning, you need to explain why the appeal is irrelevant to the conclusion, referring to the text.

Chapter 25

Assessing the use of analogies in arguments

Learning objectives

By the end of this chapter, you will be able to:

➤ assess the analogy itself

➤ assess the support the analogy gives to the conclusion

Assessing the analogy by finding both strengths and weaknesses

In Chapter 20, you looked at how we can identify analogies. You will remember that you need to look for both a change in scenario and for specific types of language.

We'll focus now on how to evaluate the analogy. You will remember the point that analogies cannot be judged against the yardstick of: 'are the two things/situations the same?' Of course they're not the same or there wouldn't be an analogy. The author takes the two things or situations to be *sufficiently similar* such that they see the analogy as supporting the reasoning.

> ### Exam tip
>
> ➤ Identifying a strength means looking for similarity between the two scenarios.
>
> ➤ Identifying a weakness means looking for difference between the two scenarios.
>
> There are often language clues in finding an analogy, with the author saying 'this is like', 'similarly', 'the same thing can be seen with...', and so on.

Illegal downloads analogy

When you looked at identifying analogies, you read the following passage on illegal downloads:

> A recent study has shown that the average teenager's iPod or digital music player contains almost 850 illegally copied songs. Each one of these illegally copied songs represents a loss of income for a large number of people (artist, company, producer, etc.). This is no less than theft. *It's just like stealing a CD from a shop, so it's about time that young people started to realise that they're nothing but common thieves every time they download a track without paying for it.*

You will remember that we identified the analogy as the following:

> The author sees the act of illegally downloading a song as just like stealing a CD from a shop.

Exam tip

If a question asks you to evaluate an analogy, it might be that it asks you to make one point of evaluation, in which case you could look for either a strength or a weakness.

Identifying the similarities — strength

In August 2008, Kid Rock posted a video on YouTube attacking illegal downloading, which included a message very much emphasising that such downloading was theft:

> ... I'm not going to miss the money. While you're about it, you need a new iPod, or a laptop? Steal it. Trust me, they won't notice it's gone. Want a new car? Just hot-wire a Toyota and drive it off the lot. They're foreign, so who cares?
>
> This is Kid Rock saying, 'It's okay to steal music and anything else you want to.'

Kid Rock's sarcasm very much supports the author's analogy. Illegal downloading for him is straightforwardly theft, like any other theft (of iPods, laptops, cars, and anything else).

So here is a crucial similarity that would give a strength in the analogy:

> We can see that, by definition, *illegal* downloading is the same as other types of theft. The person who does it gets something without paying for it (and without ever intending to pay for it), and without any intention of returning it.

Identifying the differences — weakness

Here are three differences that could be pointed out. These would be weaknesses in the analogy:

1   Downloading is presumably common practice with thousands of people

    whereas

    stealing CDs from shops is presumably not common practice.

2   People who download tracks might well not know that it is illegal to do this

    whereas

    it would be difficult to find someone who doesn't know that stealing CDs is wrong.

3   Stealing CDs is a criminal offence, no question

    whereas

    illegal downloading might well be dealt with as a civil law offence.

So we have found both strength and weakness in this analogy. Now let's apply the same skills to a new analogy.

Bear-baiting analogy

In September 2007, a judge condemned *The Jeremy Kyle Show* as a 'human form of bear-baiting'. This was because he had to deal with the case of David Stainforth, who had head-butted Larry Mahoney during the show. Mahoney had had an affair with David Stainforth's wife.

Because bear-baiting involves deliberate cruelty and pain for public entertainment, the parallel with *The Jeremy Kyle Show* is obvious. *Bear-baiting was banned in this country in 1835 because it was seen as so cruel. It's clear then that shows like Jeremy Kyle's should no longer be broadcast.*

What we have here is an analogy between banning bear-baiting and no longer broadcasting *The Jeremy Kyle Show*. The conclusion is drawn from the stated similarity between bear-baiting and *The Jeremy Kyle Show*.

Let's look at the characteristics of the two things being compared before we try to find strengths and weakness in the analogy.

Jeremy Kyle claims that he is trying to help people

➤ **Bear-baiting:** bears have their teeth and claws pulled out before they are used in bear-baiting events. They are chained in some way (either with a collar or by the legs). Specially trained dogs are used. Massive injuries to either dogs or bears or both are common. Young bears will often lie on the ground and cover their heads with their paws as they are being attacked by the dogs.

➤ **The Jeremy Kyle Show:** people request to be on the show in order to deal with some problem (such as 'Is he the father of my child?' or 'Is she sleeping with my boyfriend?'). Jeremy Kyle claims that, although being on the show might be a difficult experience, there is 'a dedicated team of people who provide an aftercare service, whether that is rehab or motivational counselling'. Kyle claims that he 'is trying to help people rather than titillate audiences'. Some people on the show are insulted and humiliated by Kyle (and by the studio audience).

So how similar are they? How different (or dissimilar) are they?

Identifying the similarities

> Bear-baiting always involves some psychological distress, and *The Jeremy Kyle Show* can involve similar distress to participants.
>
> Both bear-baiting and *The Jeremy Kyle Show* are played out in front of an audience, are a form of entertainment, and are profitable for the organisers.
>
> Both bear-baiting and *The Jeremy Kyle Show* change the lives of the participants in some way (further pain and injury to the animals; psychological insights/revenge/etc. for the participants on *The Jeremy Kyle Show*).

Identifying the differences

The two things are very different in that:

> Bear-baiting involves a captive animal
>
> *whereas*
>
> *The Jeremy Kyle Show* involves volunteers.
>
> Bear-baiting involves much physical pain and serious physical injuries to the animals
>
> *whereas*
>
> *The Jeremy Kyle Show* normally involves no physical pain or physical injuries.
>
> There is no after-performance care for the animals in bear-baiting
>
> *whereas*
>
> *The Jeremy Kyle Show* offers considerable after-performance care to the participants.
>
> The animals are never better off as a result of the activity

whereas

those on *The Jeremy Kyle Show* might be better off as a result of getting information ('he is the father of your child', 'the lie detector test shows she did sleep with your boyfriend').

This was a very straightforward task. We simply looked for key similarities leading to strength and key differences leading to weakness. In doing this we were assessing the strength and weakness of the *analogy itself.*

We now need to look at another skill that can be tested, which is assessing the *use of the analogy.*

Assessing the support the analogy gives to the conclusion

So in its context, is the analogy a good one? If the analogy is a reason, does it provide effective support for the conclusion?

That's the crucial question. The analogy might be striking, imaginative, colourful and thought-provoking, but does it provide a good reason?

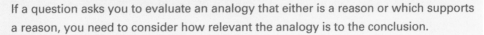

Exam tip

If a question asks you to evaluate an analogy that either is a reason or which supports a reason, you need to consider how relevant the analogy is to the conclusion.

Illegal download analogy

Numerically we identified far more differences than similarities in the illegal download analogy. However, the similarity was such a powerful one that we would probably decide that the analogy is a good one.

We could therefore say this:

Given that theft is wrong, and given that illegal downloading is theft in the way that stealing a CD from a shop is theft, the author is right to conclude that 'it's about time that young people started to realise that they're nothing but common thieves every time they download a track without paying for it'.

Bear-baiting analogy

Because the bear-baiting analogy was the *only* reason for the conclusion, this argument stood or fell by the quality of its analogy. Given that the analogy is not a good one, we have to say that:

The conclusion that *The Jeremy Kyle Show* should no longer be broadcast is very much overdrawn, because the reasoning/analogy to support this is weak, in that the cruelty to the animals justifies a ban, whereas any negative outcomes of the show on the participants are far fewer and are agreed to by the participants.

Exercise 36

Evaluate the analogies in the following arguments. In doing so, be clear what the analogy is, what its role is in the argument, and how effective it is in the argument.

1 There have been all sorts of problems raised about parents putting photographs of their children on social networking sites like Facebook and Flickr. These problems have included parents finding these photographs being used on pornographic sites. However, it is difficult to accept that the solution is to prevent parents from using these sites to share pictures of their children. There are lots of dangers that children might face, but having their photos on social networking sites isn't a serious one, even though strangers could possibly identify from the photos where they lived.

As a blogger from Massachusetts in the US put it, 'hundreds of children die in swimming pools every year, but we don't shut down all the pools. We teach kids how to swim.' We must do the same with the photos issue: just teach children to be careful.

2 The organisation SETI (the Search for Extraterrestrial Intelligence) has been using radio telescopes since 1959 to try to detect intelligent life on other planets. Apart from a strange signal picked up in 1977 that has yet to be explained, no evidence of extraterrestrial intelligent life has yet been found. But not finding any evidence so far should not be seen as meaning that there is no such intelligent life 'out there'.

The amount of evidence that has been collected so far is tiny compared with all that is out there to be analysed. As Jill Tarter at SETI has explained, 'It's like dipping a small glass into the ocean and, on discovering it empty, concluding that there are no fish in the sea.'

Check your answers with those given on page 347.

Now let's look at what an examination question would look like. Try answering the following two questions.

Past paper practice 35

OCR Unit F502, June 2011

Young people have not got the same control as adults. No sensible parent would allow their son or daughter to spend hours in a sweet shop with no control. To do so would be madness. Similarly, parents who allow their children to have PCs with internet access in their bedrooms are putting them in harm's way.

The reasoning in the above paragraph uses an analogy.

(a) State precisely what is being compared in this analogy.

(b) Make one point of evaluation about this analogy. You must explain how effectively it supports the author's reasoning.

Check your answers with those given on page 349.

Past paper practice 36

OCR Unit F502, January 2012

You will recognise this passage from Chapter 20 on identifying analogies when you answered question (a) (see Past paper practice 23 on page 204). Now you are ready to take the next step in assessing the analogy in questions (b) and (c).

Under council ownership, parks are not being used to their full capacity. They should be a facility for all sectors of the community to enjoy. However, young people are often not provided for. Much more could be done with that amount of space. Just as muscles become wasted without exercise, so too with parks; they are under-used and have become unpleasant, neglected and worthless.

In the above paragraph there is an analogy.

(a) Identify precisely the situations being compared.

(b) Explain one strength or weakness in the analogy by commenting on a relevant similarity or difference between the situations being compared.

(c) Assess the support that it gives to the conclusion.

Check your answers against those on page 349.

Section D: Evaluating arguments

Summary

➤ If a question asks you to make one point of evaluation, you could look for either a strength or a weakness.

➤ Identifying a *strength* means looking for similarity between the two scenarios.

➤ Identifying a *weakness* means looking for difference between the two scenarios.

➤ You could also be asked to consider the strength the analogy gives to the conclusion.

Chapter 26

Assessing the use of principles in arguments

Learning objectives

By the end of this chapter, you will be able to:

➤ assess whether the principle applies in an argument

➤ assess the wider application of a principle

Assessing whether the principle applies

When assessing whether the principle applies we need to ask:

➤ Is the principle relevant to the reasoning?

➤ Does it support the author's conclusion?

➤ Is it consistent with the reasoning?

Assessing relevance and support for the conclusion

You'll remember the principle that we found in the following argument:

> A recent study has shown that the average teenager's iPod or digital music player contains almost 850 illegally copied songs. Each one of these illegally copied songs represents a loss of income for a large number of people (artist, company, producer etc.). So it is good that internet providers are now going to start taking tougher action against this illegal downloading. It's no less than theft. Since **theft is always wrong**, these illegal downloaders should be made to pay.

The principle is 'theft is always wrong'. How is the author using the word 'theft' in this argument? It is being used to mean 'taking someone's property (in this example, income from songs) by illegal means'. This is a straightforward use of the term. The principle is therefore relevant to the reasoning, because both are talking about theft.

Does it support the conclusion?

If we analyse the reasoning, we can see that the principle acts as a reason for the conclusion:

> **R**   It's (illegally copied songs) no less than theft
>
> **R**   **theft is always wrong,**
>
> **C**   these illegal downloaders should be made to pay.

We can see then that the principle applies to this argument, as it provides both relevance to the reasoning and direct support to the conclusion.

If, however, we could argue that there are exceptions where theft is legitimate, this would weaken both the principle and also its support for the conclusion.

Are these legitimate exceptions?

> Theft of a mad axeman's axe?
>
> Theft of a Nazi code machine in the war?
>
> Theft of an alcoholic's wallet?
>
> Theft of some money from someone who owes you money?
>
> Theft by a Polish man of secrets of the Enigma coding machine from the Nazis that was given to people in the UK during the war?

If these are legitimate exceptions of theft, then the principle and the argument would both be weakened.

Exam tip

When evaluating whether principles apply in arguments you can ask:

➤ if the principle and the reasoning are linked by relevance

➤ whether the principle gives support to the conclusion

Assessing consistency

Another way of evaluating whether principles apply in arguments is to look to see if the author is consistent in how the principle is regarded.

Look at the next example:

A national ID card system makes sense only if it enables the government to know what everybody's doing at any one time. Otherwise why have such a system? But for them to have this knowledge requires that we agree to constant monitoring. Clearly, the introduction of CCTV cameras in public places is a good thing both to deter crime and to help catch those who commit it. But the idea of further monitoring is unacceptable. **Privacy cannot be sacrificed for security.**

Can privacy be sacrificed for security?

You will have spotted the author's principle at the end of the argument. And you will probably also have spotted that the author is not consistent in applying this principle. The author commends the use of CCTV cameras on the ground that they help to reduce crime. But, if privacy cannot be sacrificed for security, then CCTV cameras cannot also be justified.

The author simply cannot hold both that 'the introduction of CCTV cameras in public places is a good thing both to deter crime and to help catch those who commit it' and that 'Privacy cannot be sacrificed for security'.

> **Exam tip**
>
> When evaluating whether principles apply in arguments, look at issues of consistency such as whether the author is consistent in how they regard the principle.

Assessing the wider application of a principle

In the earlier section on analysis, when we looked at how we can identify principles, we described them as general guides to action or belief. Because they are general guides, they can be used (indeed, have to be able to be used) to apply to a range of specific situations.

The way to assess the wider application of a principle is to ask about its range — where it would and would not apply and whether this range of application strengthens or weakens it.

We'll take one principle and see how it works:

(i) Causing unnecessary pain to animals can never be justified.

This principle has huge scope. It would have to be applied to a very wide range of situations, including experimentation on animals (for medical and other purposes), the killing of animals for food, the use of animals for entertainment (such as in circuses), and so on.

However, the key word here is 'unnecessary', as many things could be regarded as 'necessary', such as animal experimentation to develop treatments to save human lives. So although the principle could apply to many situations, its guidance is limited, because it is not clear what is necessary and unnecessary pain.

Let's look at another principle.

(ii) Whaling can never be justified.

This principle is more specific, so its range is more limited. It could be applied to any proposal, agreement, or argument on whaling. It would apply, for example, to any agreements made by the International Whaling Commission (IWC), the organisation that deals with the regulation of whaling.

Here's a small part of what was agreed in the International Convention for the Regulation of Whaling in 1946:

'... whaling operations should be confined to those species best able to sustain exploitation in order to give an interval for recovery to certain species of whales now depleted in numbers.'

However, as you can see, the principle is inconsistent with this position. This is because, although it lays down restrictions on whaling, it specifies the situations in which it can be carried out.

Can whaling ever be justified?

Principles are really like very little else in arguments in the power that they have. If whaling can *never* be justified, then there cannot be a useful argument in favour of whaling, whether to catch thousands or to catch one.

The application of a principle can therefore vary considerably.

Here is another:

(iii) The interests of future generations must always be considered.

As with the first principle about animals, the application of this principle is huge. It requires that, whatever is proposed or done (or not proposed or not done), the interests of future generations have to be considered.

Although the range (and thus effect) of this principle is huge, both the range and the effect are difficult to pin down.

Having always to consider the interests of future generations means that the scope is enormous (not just this future generation, but this one, and this one ...). And it's not just interests in terms of education, but also the environment, spending plans, space travel, use of oil and so on. So is this a very useful general guide to action? Probably not.

Is this wide ranging principle any more useful?

> **(iv)** Cheating is always wrong.

This can be applied to taking exams, competing in sport, being faithful in marriage, and many other situations. Although it is wide ranging, it gives clearer guidance than the previous principle because it can be pinned down to a specific area — cheating.

Exam tip

When assessing the wider application of a principle you can ask:

➤ whether it can be used in a wide range of situations

➤ whether it can be pinned down to act as guidance

Use the following examination questions to help you to identify principles that would apply to a particular argument.

Past paper practice 37

OCR Unit F502, January 2009

People who make hoax calls to the fire service should face serious punishment, because calls about false emergencies such as fires, car crashes and terrorist attacks have serious consequences. Hoax calls waste taxpayers' money. Worse, each hoax call draws life-saving services away from people in real need.

Which of the following is a principle which should support the argument?

(a) It is tasteless to play practical jokes.

(b) It is wrong to take actions which could lead to loss of life.

(c) Loss of life is the most serious consequence which could occur.

(d) Punishment is rarely effective as a means of preventing crime.

Check your answers against those given on page 349.

Past paper practice 38

OCR Unit F502, June 2011

The majority of women who have had a fracture are not getting treatment to prevent future breaks. A Cambridge University study shows that of 1,600 women going to a fracture clinic, a third have had a previous break but only a small number have been put on bone-strengthening drugs. The health service should increase the number of women that join bone-strengthening drug programmes. Doctors must make more effort to advertise these drugs to women with repeated breaks.

Which of the following is a principle which would best support the above argument?

(a) Doctors should try to avoid unnecessarily prescribing drugs.

(b) Medicine should aim to prevent future harm.

(c) Patients should be given a range of treatment choices.

(d) Women are more likely than men to break their bones.

Check your answers against those given on page 349.

Summary

When assessing whether or not a principle applies to a particular situation you should:

➢ assess the relevance of the principle to the reasoning

➢ assess the support the principle gives to the conclusion

You can also assess the range of the principle, that is:

➢ identify in which other situations it would apply

➢ identify where it would not apply

Chapter 27

Assessing the use of hypothetical reasoning in an argument

Learning objectives

By the end of this chapter, you will be able to:

➢ assess the hypothetical reasoning itself

➢ assess the support that the hypothetical reasoning gives to the conclusion

In Chapter 3 you learned about hypothetical arguments: hypothetical reasons and hypothetical conclusions. In this chapter, we look at what you need to do to evaluate such hypothetical reasoning. You can do this in two crucial ways:

➢ You can assess the reasoning *internally* by looking at its condition and consequence.

➢ You can assess it *externally* by looking at the support it gives to the conclusion.

Assessing the hypothetical reasoning itself

You will remember that when we looked at hypothetical reasoning in Chapter 3 we saw that it has two clauses, an 'if 'and a 'then' — that is, a condition and a consequence. We are arguing ... if this were to be the case, then that will follow.

If *X* is the case, then *Y* follows.

Let's look at the following example:

Condition	If the government ends modular A-levels and introduces linear A-level examinations,
Consequence	this will reduce the cost of examination entry fees for schools.

To assess this reasoning we need to use plausibility and ask:

➤ How likely is the condition to occur?
➤ If it did occur, is the consequence likely to follow?

Is the condition likely?

In this instance, 'Yes', the condition is highly likely. We can say this, as there have been several discussions where this possibility has been the preferred option of both the education minister and of Ofqual. As these have a great input into such decisions, then we can say that it is likely that their wishes will have a great influence on what will happen.

Is the consequence likely to follow?

'Yes': if the entry fees stay the same and if there are fewer exams, this will mean a lower cost in exam entry fees.

However, you will notice that we answered the question with our own hypothetical reasoning. We needed to do this as we don't know whether or not the linear exams will simply be the same length as the modular exams sat in one session — that is, a January 1½ hr module and a June 1½ hr module becoming a 3 hr module sat in June. If this were to be case, then the answer would be 'No', as the consequence of a lower cost would not be likely to follow. It would be more likely to be the same.

You will have seen, then, that to assess the hypothetical reasoning itself we need to consider what might be the case from several different angles.

Assessing the support that the hypothetical reasoning gives to the conclusion

To do this we need to identify what is being concluded from what.

Drawing a non-hypothetical conclusion from purely hypothetical reasoning

Here is a hypothetical argument:

HR	If herbal remedies (like ginseng, peppermint and dandelion) work, then they're medicines.
HR	If herbal remedies are medicines, then they will have side-effects.

HR   If they have side-effects, people who take them need to be warned about these.

C   Therefore companies and shops that sell herbal remedies need to warn their customers about the side-effects of using herbal remedies.

Do herbal remedies work?

You can see that there is a problem with the conclusion of this argument because it is a non-hypothetical one: an argument like this with no more than hypothetical reasons *must* have a hypothetical conclusion. In this example, the hypothetical reasons were all of the type 'if this is the case' which meant that the conclusion could not be 'this is the case'. Putting it precisely, it is of the following flawed form:

If *X* is the case, then *Y* follows. Therefore *X* is the case.

Drawing a non-hypothetical conclusion from reasons that include a hypothetical reason

In the next example, the hypothetical reason does lead to a non-hypothetical conclusion without being flawed because the author adds a further crucial reason:

HR   If there was evidence that polar bear populations were stable or increasing, then they couldn't be seen as in danger of extinction.

R   Fortunately, there is such evidence from Canada,

C   so we shouldn't worry that they could be extinct soon.

In this example, we have this:

If *X* is the case, then *Y* follows.

X is the case, therefore *Y* follows.

As you can see, in this argument the author supplies the necessary information to show that the hypothetical reason is no longer hypothetical.

Exam tip

In evaluating hypothetical reasoning, you need to check if a non-hypothetical conclusion can be adequately supported by any hypothetical reasoning.

We could do the same with our earlier argument about herbal remedies, to make it no longer flawed:

> **HR** If herbal remedies (like ginseng, peppermint and dandelion) work, then they're medicines.
>
> **HR** If herbal remedies are medicines, then they will have side-effects.
>
> **HR**   If they have side-effects, people who take them need to be warned about these.
>
> **R** *Herbal remedies do work.*
>
> **C**   Therefore companies and shops that sell herbal remedies need to warn their customers about the side-effects of using herbal remedies.

As you can see, the claim in italics supplies the necessary information to enable the conclusion to be drawn legitimately. The reasoning that before was not adequate now is.

> **Exam tip**
>
> In evaluating hypothetical reasoning, you need to see if the author has given the relevant information required for a hypothetical reason to support a non-hypothetical conclusion.

Hypothetical reasoning in slippery slope arguments

Hypothetical reasoning is frequently found in the flawed argument category of slippery slopes. This is because, as you saw, in such arguments the author sees a whole series of steps following from the first. For example, 'if you allow this, then you'll have to allow this, which means you'll have to allow that, which means you end up with…'. The crucial error is normally that first step. It does not necessarily follow that something *must* follow from that first position.

You will remember the following slippery slope argument from working on it in the Chapter 23, on flaws:

> Abortion is allowed under certain circumstances. One of these is when the foetus shows serious abnormalities. But,
>
> **HR**   if we allow this, we'll end up killing all children with serious abnormalities.
>
>   Then we'll feel able to kill all adults with abnormalities.
>
>   In the end, the only people who will be allowed to live are those who are healthy.
>
> **C**   Therefore we shouldn't allow abortion.

You can see that there is no other reasoning that would support the conclusion, making it weak.

Exam tip

When asked to assess hypothetical reasoning, you can do this in two ways:

➤ You can assess the reasoning internally by looking at the condition and consequence.

➤ You can assess it externally by looking at the support it gives to the conclusion.

Exercise 37

Assess whether the conclusion in the following passage can be drawn from the reasoning.

Jamie Oliver recipe

Jamie Oliver has written a recipe for a home-made granola with berry compote. It is described as a quick, easy, delicious and healthy pudding. It certainly sounds healthy enough with all its nuts, seeds, oats and yoghurt. But, if you were to eat the granola, you'd eat 912 calories per serving. (That's about half a woman's daily calorific needs just for one portion!) Alternatively, if you were to eat a sticky toffee pudding followed by a piece of cheesecake, then you've consumed only 750 calories. So people who think that Jamie Oliver is a good cook are going to put on a lot of weight.

Check your answer against that on page 349.

Past paper practice 39

Council ownership of parks is an inefficient use of taxpayers' money. It simply costs too much. In one London borough, £5.4 million was spent on parks in one year, which was roughly £20 for each man, woman and child that lived in that area. If councils no longer had to look after parks, then the money would be spent on better things, like schools or hospitals. People should only have to pay tax for the things that they use or which benefit them.

Overall, councils are doing a poor job of running parks and therefore parks should no longer be owned by councils.

(a) State the hypothetical reason used by the author in the passage above.

(b) Explain why this is a hypothetical reason.

(c) Explain one weakness in this hypothetical reason.

Check your answers against those given on page 350.

Summary

➢ Hypothetical reasoning can be assessed by using plausibility to see how likely the condition would be to occur and how likely the consequence would be to follow from the condition.

➢ It can also be assessed by looking at the structure of the argument, to see if a non-hypothetical conclusion is drawn from purely hypothetical reasoning.

OCR AS Critical Thinking

Chapter 28

Individual argument elements

Learning objective
By the end of this chapter, you will be able to:
➢ produce a range of individual argument elements

We can now turn our attention to Section C on the examination paper 'Developing your own arguments'. This is where you can bring your knowledge both of the definition of argument elements and of what makes them strong or weak within an argument into a new arena: that of producing reasoning of your own.

Within this section there are usually two shorter questions which focus on producing individual argument elements that would give support to claims made either in the passage or on a related issue.

Which argument elements could you be asked to produce?

Here is a useful list of argument elements, taken from the specification, that you could be asked to produce:
➢ reason
➢ hypothetical reason
➢ explanation
➢ evidence and example
➢ intermediate conclusion
➢ principles
➢ counter-assertion and counter-argument

Reason

When asked to produce a reason to support a claim, you need to remember the following:

➤ Use the argument indicator word 'because' to help you to produce a reason.

➤ Make sure the reason is specific to the claim. Look for the specific terms within the given claim to help you.

➤ Give only one argument element, i.e. the reason without any embellishments of examples, or explanation, or even a conclusion.

Exam tip

Use the argument indicator word 'because' to help you.

Now let's see if we can apply this. Suppose you were given the following claim and asked to support it with one reason:

> The government should put a tax on children's drinks that have a large amount of added sugars or sweeteners.

Looking at the tips above we need to look at the specifics of children's drinks, added sugars or sweeteners and the government's responsibility, and weave some of this into a single reason. We will need to mention: higher price, deter, healthier options, better for children.

We could answer:

> Because the increase in price would discourage families from buying them for their children.
>
> Because the higher price might deter childhood obesity.
>
> Because the higher price might force families to buy cheaper, healthier options for children.

All three contain no extra argument elements. What would a less focused answer look like? It might be too simplistic:

> Because then people won't buy them.

Or include other argument elements:

> Because the increase in price would discourage families from buying them for their children and this would help to reduce childhood obesity.

Should the government tax children's drinks?

Try out your skills with the following examination question.

OCR Unit F502, June 2011

Give two reasons which would support the following claim.

'Teachers should not set homework that involves the use of the internet.'

Check your answer with the one given on page 350.

Hypothetical reason

This is similar to the task above in that you are producing a reason, but of a particular kind. You need to remember that there will be two parts to your reason:

➤ condition — if something were to be the case
➤ a consequence — what would then happen

Give only one argument element — that is, the reason without any embellishments of examples or explanation or an additional conclusion.

Exam tip

Make sure that you include a condition and a consequence in your answer. Remember 'If ... then'.

Let's look at a previous claim and see if we can give a hypothetical reason to support it.

The government should put a tax on children's drinks that have a large amount of added sugars or sweeteners.

We could develop one of the reasons that we identified:

Because *if* the price of children's drinks with added sugars were higher, *then* this might force families to buy cheaper, healthier options for their children.

Let's look at the claim given in Past paper practice 40 above.

Teachers should not set homework that involves the use of the internet.

Again we could turn one of the answers given into a hypothetical reason. We gave the answer: 'Students unable to access the internet at home will be at a disadvantage.' This would become:

If students were unable to access the internet at home, *then* they would be at a disadvantage.

You could of course reverse the two parts and it would still be correct. You would be giving the consequence that would happen, if something were to be the case:

> Students would be at a disadvantage, *if* they were unable to access the internet at home.

What would a weaker answer look like? Look at this answer. It has the essence of being conditional but there is no consequence:

> Because students might not be able to access the internet.

To avoid this you should remember to use 'if … then'.

Past paper practice 41

OCR Unit F502, January 2012

Give one hypothetical reason which would give support to the following claim.

'It is important to have free leisure facilities.'

Check your answer with the one given on page 350.

Explanation

If you are asked for an explanation, in your answer you won't be seeking to persuade anyone, merely giving a plausible account of why this is the case. The question could give you a statistical claim and ask you for an explanation.

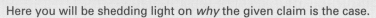

Exam tip

Here you will be shedding light on *why* the given claim is the case.

Here's an example. It's some evidence published in *The Economist* of 30 March 2009 about the rising trend in young females who binge-drink:

> **(i)** Thirty-three per cent of British girls aged 15–16 said that they had been drunk in the past 30 days.

This would seem to be an extremely high percentage of girls. You are not being asked to assess the evidence, merely to explain why it is so. Here are some plausible explanations:

> Many girls aged 15–16 see a good night out as drinking lots and letting their hair down.
>
> Many girls aged 15–16 like to act older than they are, but can't handle the effects of alcohol.

You will notice that explanations do not have to be long. If, however, you are asked for a developed or detailed explanation, you would need to say more.

Let's look at a second statistical claim:

(ii) Twenty-eight per cent of teachers report often being bored by their work.

Why might this be so? Here are some plausible explanations:

Teachers have to make careful records of what they teach, which takes time away from the creative side of preparing the actual lessons, which is a much more stimulating thought process.

Teachers often have to teach exactly the same lesson to several different groups several years in a row, which could limit the creative side of their teaching.

A weaker answer would be less plausible or too simplistic, as follows:

These teachers are easily bored.

These teachers are the ones who have been teaching for a long time.

Evidence and example

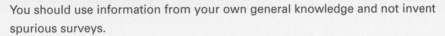

Exam tip

You should use information from your own general knowledge and not invent spurious surveys.

The specification is very clear when it says *'In choosing evidence or examples, candidates should use their own general knowledge.'* So you shouldn't try to make up spurious surveys or guess at the percentage of people who believe particular things. For example, if you were asked for an example to support the claim:

Health and safety regulations can often do more harm than good.

you would not be expected to give statistical information. It would be sufficient to say:

One example of this is where the Christmas spirit is ruined by health and safety regulations about Christmas trees, which have led some communities and shopping centres to stop putting these up, in case anyone accidently collides with the tree and it causes them harm.

One example of this is where school outdoor pursuits trips have been stopped because schools have to fill in so much risk assessment paperwork that is too time consuming or too complicated, that teachers choose more straightforward activities.

You can see that no statistical information was necessary here.

Past paper practice 42

OCR Unit F502, June 2011

Dr-Net claims:

'It is more dangerous to take risks away from children than to expose them to risks.'

Give one example other than internet use that would support this claim.

Check your answer with the one given on page 350.

Intermediate conclusion

When asked to produce an intermediate conclusion to support a claim, you need to remember to:

➤ produce a conclusion that follows from the reason(s) and in turn supports the main conclusion

➤ give only one argument element — that is, the reason without any embellishments of examples or explanation or even an additional conclusion.

Here you need to bear in mind that an IC is drawn from the reasons and that it also has to support the conclusion. So you need to see it as filling a gap between the reason given and the main conclusion given.

Let's try slotting an IC into the following argument:

> **R** Much of the country is suffering drought conditions.
>
> **C** Therefore the government ought to bring in hosepipe bans.

We could slot in:

> So we need to conserve water.

This would fill the gap, with the hosepipe ban being a further conclusion. If the question were to be presented like this, you can see that you are actually presenting an assumption.

The question could of course be phrased differently, where you are asked to produce a reason and an intermediate conclusion. Let's look again at the claim:

> The government should put a tax on children's drinks that have a large amount of added sugars or sweeteners.

You could give the reason we identified previously and add an IC as follows:

> **R**   Because the higher price might force families to buy cheaper, healthier options for their children.
>
> **IC** As a result, childhood obesity could be lessened.

Principle

When you are asked to suggest a principle that would support an argument:

➢ make sure that it acts as a general guide to action, rather than being something specific that applies to a particular case

➢ look for one that would be consistent with the argument. In this case, a principle comes in as an additional reason to support the conclusion.

➢ make sure that you don't add other argument elements such as examples, explanations or conclusions

Let's look at the following argument:

> In major sporting events, all sorts of strategies are put in place to deal with the problem of cheating in sport. These strategies might seem excessive and intrusive but they are increasingly necessary to deal with the many, often very sophisticated, ways that sportspeople and their trainers can seek to gain unfair advantages over their competitors. We should ensure that sufficient resources are always made available for this system to work.

The obvious principle that supports this argument is:

> It is right to ensure that in sport the rules are obeyed.

It might be seen that this is not just a principle that supports the argument, but is required by the argument as an assumed reason.

Exercise 38

The following provides information on what are called either the 'Elgin marbles' or the 'Parthenon sculptures'. Read it and then answer the questions on principles that follow.

The Elgin marbles

There has been a long controversy over what are called the 'Elgin marbles' or, as the British Museum (BM) prefers to call them, the 'Parthenon sculptures'. These once formed part of the Parthenon, the famous temple on the Acropolis in Athens. The Parthenon was built between 447 and 432 BC and was decorated with hundreds

The Elgin marbles in the British Museum

of sculptures of gods and people. The Parthenon survived for about 2,000 years with its essential structure intact. It then suffered massive damage in 1687 when Athens was under siege by the Venetians. Unfortunately the building was used as a gunpowder store and a huge explosion blew off the roof, destroying many of the sculptures. The Venetians took much of the material back to Venice. Lord Elgin, who was ambassador to the Ottoman Empire (which included Greece), arranged for other parts of the sculpture to be shipped to Britain at the beginning of the nineteenth century, having been given permission to do so by the authorities of the time.

The Greek Government has, for many years, requested/demanded that the sculptures be returned to Greece. The BM continues to refuse to return them, stressing that they were legally obtained in the first place.

The majority of the sculptures are divided roughly equally between Athens and London. The rest are found in important European museums such as the Louvre in Paris and the Vatican in Rome. Very few of the sculptures are in the Parthenon itself, with those in Athens being housed in a special museum.

1 Suggest at least one principle that could be used to support the Greek Government's request/demand for the return of the sculptures.
2 Suggest at least one principle that could be used to support the BM's refusal to return the sculptures.

You can check your answers against those on page 350.

Past paper practice 43

OCR Unit F502, January 2012

Suggest one principle which would support the following argument:

Parks allow a wide range of different activities, for example playing bowls, picnics and dog walking. This makes parks appeal to a huge range of people, showing that parks are an effective use of council money.

Check your answer with the one given on page 351.

Counter-assertion and counter-argument
When you are asked to suggest a counter-assertion or counter-argument that would challenge an argument, remember that a counter-assertion is a claim and a counter-argument is at least one reason supporting a conclusion.

Exam tip
Use the argument indicator word 'however' to help start you off.

This is a very straightforward task. Let's look again at the following claim to see if we can produce a counter-argument to challenge it:

> It is more dangerous to take risks away from children than to expose them to risks.

We would need to be saying the opposite:

> **CR** However, if you expose children to risks, then there is always the possibility that they will get seriously hurt,

> **CC** so it is better to leave actions that pose risks until they have the knowledge and physical ability to avoid harm.

You will notice that the counter-reason is a hypothetical one.

Now that you have practised producing individual argument elements, let's see if you can put them together into an argument of your choice, before we go on to look at producing an argument in response to a given claim.

Activity 26

Room 101
You may have seen the TV programme *Room 101* where several celebrities bring to the show something they think should be 'binned' and consigned to Room 101. It may be something like:
➢ family reunions at the seaside
➢ embarrassing Facebook photos
➢ dunking biscuits in tea

Each celebrity gives an argument as to why their pet hate should be binned. The host of the show decides which is the best argument and hence which pet hate should be consigned to Room 101.

Task

➢ Working in small groups, choose something which you think should also be binned and consigned to Room 101. Write a convincing argument with at least three reasons supported by evidence, and/or an example, and an intermediate conclusion.
➢ Hand your argument to another group and ask them to write a counter-argument challenging either one of your reasons or the whole concept of removing your chosen thing.
➢ When the counter-argument is handed back to your group, add an effective response to this challenge, so that your argument isn't weakened.

> Read out your argument to the other groups who can score it according to the score sheet below. The group with the highest score wins.

Element	Score	Justification
Room 101 score card *Award up to 4 marks for each element 1–5. Give a justification for each mark.*		
1 How far do the reasons support the conclusion?	__/4	
2 How far does the intermediate conclusion follow from the reasons and support the MC?	__/4	
3 How far are the evidence and example relevant?	__/4	
4 How far does the argument respond to the counter-argument?	__/4	
5 How persuasive is the argument? Should this item be consigned to Room 101?	__/4	
	TOTAL = __/20	

Summary

> Read the claim that is given carefully so that you provide a relevant argument element to support it.

> Take care to provide only the required argument element — that is, without the embellishment of added elements such as example, evidence or explanation.

> Use your general knowledge and avoid inventing spurious evidence or examples.

Chapter 29

A developed argument

Learning objectives

By the end of this chapter, you will be able to:

➢ use relevant reasons to give sound support

➢ use a progressive intermediate conclusion

➢ use a counter-argument and respond effectively to it

➢ use additional argument elements

➢ avoid common weaknesses that limit your marks

Before we look at how to make a developed argument, we need to know what these questions are likely to involve.

Writing your own arguments

The length of your argument

Section C has the two longest answer questions in Unit 2 and these carry the largest number of marks, so you need to make sure that you spend time developing these skills and allow sufficient time in the exam to answer these questions adequately. However, you need to concentrate on quality of argument rather than quantity. You should be guided by the space available for this question in the examination answer booklet.

Your conclusion

You are likely to be asked to develop two arguments, both of which have some relation to the topic in the passage. One may have a direct relationship to the conclusion.

Exam tip

Check the question to see whether you are directed to support **or** to challenge the given claim, **or** whether you have an open choice.

You could be asked to:

➤ write a **further argument** (technically further reasoning) for the conclusion of the passage you were given
➤ write a counter-argument in response to the conclusion of the passage you were given
➤ produce reasoning for or against a new conclusion that you will be given
➤ argue for or against a given principle

Key term

➤ **further argument:** an argument in support of a given conclusion, that uses different reasons from those already used in an existing argument.

So this is not a case of you just writing an argument of your choice. It needs to be in direct response to a claim that is given to you in the question. Thus your conclusion will bear a direct relation to the question on the examination paper. This will be your starting point.

Exam tip

Check the question to see that you are using the precise wording of the claim that you have been given.

Your argument elements

It is important to remember that this is an argument and not an essay. It should have a clear structure where the conclusion is drawn from the reasoning. You will be directed in the question as to which argument elements you are expected to include and these may be different for the two questions. One may ask you to include an intermediate conclusion, whereas the other may ask for you to include counter-reasoning. So you need to read the question carefully. Usually the question allows you to include any other argument elements.

Exam tip

Check the question to see which argument elements you must include and which additional arguments are optional.

Now that you know what the question involves, we need to work out how to make a start in developing an argument in response to a given claim.

Using relevant reasons to give sound support

Here we're working backwards. Here's a conclusion: what reasoning can support it or can oppose it?

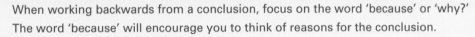
We'll start with a conclusion and see what we can do with it:

Conclusion: We should not allow children to be educated at home.

Producing reasons: ask the question 'why?' (or 'why not?')

Asking this question takes us straight to the heart of the task. If something has been concluded, what reasons might lead us there (for a further argument) or lead us away from there (for a counter-argument)?

Let's think of relevant reasons that would give strong support to why children should not be allowed to be educated at home. We'll just fire them off and then think what we're going to do with them. In an important way, although we've described them as 'reasons', they're not actually anything yet. They're just claims, claims that could be worked into reasons, or other argument elements.

➤ Children need to be able to learn a wide range of subjects.

➤ Children benefit from learning in the company of others.

➤ Most parents do not have the expertise to teach their children.

➤ Children need access to a range of facilities (such as laboratories) that cannot be available at home.

➤ Part of a child's education is to learn how to function with peers.

➤ Children benefit from interacting with many different adults, rather than just with parents.

Why shouldn't children be educated at home?

And that's just by asking the question 'Why?' In answering this question, don't get caught up with the structure of the argument you will need to write. For now, just come up with material you can use in creating it. So don't think 'I need to think of an intermediate conclusion now' or 'I need to think of the counter-argument now'. They will emerge out of the products of your 'Why?' answers.

Avoid producing trivial or irrelevant reasons

Trivial reasons are not very persuasive. They have little significance and can be easily answered. The mark schemes indicate that your reasons should not only be relevant to the conclusion, but also provide *sound* support for it.

Consider the following reasons and compare them with our first list. Hopefully you will see that they have far less significance.

> Children will get bored if they stay at home.
>
> Children might not get on with their brothers or sisters.

Children could just as easily be bored in school. Whether or not they are bored at home will depend — in the same way as at school — on whether they can become engaged in their learning. Similarly children might not get on with their classmates, and even be bullied.

The reasons that we came up with first were more significant, because we started with accepted aims in education, such as learning a wide range of subjects, and looked at whether schools or homes could fulfil these aims.

Exam tip

Make sure that your reasons look at important concerns that are directly relevant to the conclusion.

Using a progressive intermediate conclusion

Producing an IC — look for links using 'so'

Now you can look through your list and see if there are any that sit together to create lines of reasoning that will give you at least one intermediate conclusion. Try linking them together using the argument indicator word 'so'.

Exam tip

See different claims not just as different reasons but also as intermediate conclusions that can be drawn from other reasons.

What about these?

Children need to be able to learn a wide range of subjects.

so

So children need access to a range of facilities (such as laboratories) that cannot be available at home.

Already you can see that you have a reason for an IC (a mini argument), so a structure can start emerging without your having fretted about creating one. Let's add what we've done so far to the conclusion that we started with.

R Children need to be able to learn a wide range of subjects.

IC So children need access to a range of facilities (such as laboratories) that cannot be available at home.

C Therefore we should not allow children to be educated at home.

We need to keep going, as the question usually asks you to use at least three reasons and we have only used one.

Producing another line of reasoning

You'll see that, if you look at the ones that are left, we have three that will fit together somehow, in that they're dealing with the same sort of issue. These are:

➤ Children benefit from learning in the company of others.
➤ Part of a child's education is to learn how to function with peers.
➤ Children benefit from interacting with many different adults, rather than just with parents.

The first of these fits nicely as an IC from the other two:

R Part of a child's education is to learn how to function with peers.

R Children benefit from interacting with many different adults, rather than just with parents.

IC So children benefit from learning in the company of others.

And what can we do with the one we have left?

Most parents do not have the expertise to teach their children.

This gives us yet another, fourth, line of reasoning. So let's add this mini argument and the fourth reason to the one we've already created:

> **R** Children need to be able to learn a wide range of subjects.
>
> **IC1** So children need access to a range of facilities (such as laboratories) that cannot be available at home.
>
> **R2** Part of a child's education is to learn how to function with peers.
>
> **R3** Children benefit from interacting with many different adults, rather than just with parents.
>
> **IC2** Children benefit from learning in the company of others.
>
> **R4** Most parents do not have the expertise to teach their children.
>
> **C** Therefore we should not allow children to be educated at home.

Here's the structure of the argument:

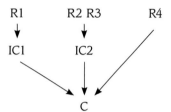

And all this from just firing off answers to the 'why?' question!

Before we move on to do more, let's slot in some connecting words and phrases, so that the argument flows and thus reads well:

> It's clear that children need to be able to learn a wide range of subjects. Consequently, children need access to a range of facilities, such as laboratories, that cannot be available at home.
>
> Furthermore, part of a child's education is to learn how to function with peers. In addition, children benefit from interacting with many different adults, rather than just with parents. So we can see that children benefit from learning in the company of others.
>
> There's also the point that most parents do not have the expertise to teach their children. Therefore we should not allow children to be educated at home.

It's looking good now. But let's check our ICs.

Producing a *progressive* intermediate conclusion

By 'progressive' we mean an IC that moves the reasoning on another step. It develops the reasoning further. Other types of IC will gain you fewer marks.

A simplistic IC

Let's look at the following IC:

> So there are many reasons why we should not allow children to be educated at home.

Technically this is an IC as it follows from the reasons, but it does not take the reasoning on a further step. It is very *simplistic*.

A summative IC

What about this IC?

> So there are negative consequences to educating children at home.

This is saying a little more, but again not moving on the reasoning. It is summing up what has gone before. It could be called a *summative* IC. It is not moving on the reasoning any further.

A summative IC can be more subtle than this, by summarising in a more significant way a key feature.

Look at our second IC.

R2 Part of a child's education is to learn how to function with peers.

R3 Children benefit from interacting with many different adults, rather than just with parents.

IC2 Children benefit from learning in the company of others.

This is bringing together the interacting with peers and different adults to draw a key feature of learning in the context of other people.

A progressive IC

How about our first IC?

R Children need to be able to learn a wide range of subjects.

IC So children need access to a range of facilities (such as laboratories) that cannot be available at home.

Here you can see that the IC is *progressive* because it is drawing something new from the reason. This is that facilities will be needed that you will not find at home. So it is moving the reasoning on a further step.

Exam tip

When linking together your reasons to form ICs, try to take the reasoning a step further by asking, 'So now what?'

Using a counter-argument and responding effectively to it

In some questions the counter-argument and responding to it effectively will be the main aim of the question. In others it will be one of the optional argument elements that you can use or leave out. You need to check which is the case.

However, in either case, it is weak reasoning if you have a counter-argument and you leave it hanging there and do not respond to it.

Thinking of a counter-argument

What about thinking of a counter-argument? We know the counter-position has to be 'we should allow children to be educated at home'. So all we need is at least one reason why this could be concluded.

> Some children have special talents that make it difficult for them to follow a normal school regime.

Let's do something with this one:

> **Counter-argument**
>
> **CR** It is the case that some children have special talents that make it difficult for them to follow a normal school regime.
>
> **CC** Thus, it is argued, we should allow children to be educated at home.
>
> **R** However, children need to be able to learn a wide range of subjects.
>
> **C** Therefore we should not allow children to be educated at home.

As you can see, we've given only part of the argument, but this is to highlight the counter-argument we've created.

> **Exam tip**
>
> Thinking of a counter-position should not be too difficult. You just need to think of how you'd go about writing the opposite argument — that is, what the other side would say.

Responding effectively to the counter-argument

When responding to the counter-argument you need to do more than just say 'but here is a different important point to support my argument'. It would be almost like the politician when asked a question about the high financial cost of a measure that they want to put through, who goes on to say, 'but what I want to say to you is that this will give huge social benefits'. They have ignored the challenge posed to them and gone on to look at the benefits.

Did we respond effectively to the challenge of the case of talented children? Let's look at it again:

CR It is the case that some children have special talents that make it difficult for them to follow a normal school regime.

CC Thus, it is argued, we should allow children to be educated at home.

R However, children need to be able to learn a wide range of subjects.

C Therefore we should not allow children to be educated at home.

We made the point that they need a wide range of subjects (as well as following their particular talent) but we did not get to the nub of the issue. We would need to put in another line of reasoning to deal with this more effectively. For example:

R However, there are Gifted and Talented co-ordinators within schools who can negotiate timetables to allow talented children to pursue these skills as well as gaining a breadth of skills in other subject areas.

This reason would address the counter-argument more directly.

Exam tip

You need to respond effectively to the counter-argument that you include, otherwise there will be a weakness in your argument.

Using additional argument elements

Additional argument elements can help to make your argument more convincing if they are relevant and used effectively. Amongst these are evidence, example and principle.

Adding evidence and example

Exam tip

You shouldn't invent evidence or example. These can rather be taken from everyday experience.

We could look at adding some examples or evidence to both the counter-argument and the main argument. These appear below in italics.

It is the case that some children have special talents that make it difficult for them to follow a normal school regime. ***Examples are top junior tennis players and young actors***. Thus, it is argued, we should allow children to be educated at home. However, children need to be able to learn a wide range of subjects. So children need access to a range of facilities ***such as laboratories*** that cannot be available at home. Furthermore, part of a child's education is to learn how to function with peers. If ***children learn at home, then they may find it very***

Schools provide a wide range of facilities, such as laboratories

difficult to cope when they go to university. In addition, children benefit from interacting with many different adults, rather than just with parents. So we can see that children benefit from learning in the company of others. There's also the point that most parents do not have the expertise to teach their children. Therefore we should not allow children to be educated at home.

Here evidence has been used in a hypothetical form, as we shouldn't add spurious surveys of invented statistical information.

Adding a principle

So we now have a counter-argument, four reasons, two intermediate conclusions, some examples, some evidence, and a clearly stated main conclusion. We don't need any more, but we're on a roll so let's add in a principle. Can you think of any that might fit this argument?

> ➤ Parents should not be able to choose to act against the interests of their children.
> ➤ All children should learn how to interact with their peers.
> ➤ Education of children is the responsibility of the state rather than the private citizen.

You could have used any of these, but here's the second one put into a relevant place. You can see that it becomes a fifth reason:

… Furthermore, part of a child's education is to learn how to function with peers. (If children learn at home, then they may find it very difficult to cope when they go to university.) It needs to be stressed that *all children should learn how to interact with their peers* …

Avoiding limiting your marks with common weaknesses

What you have seen is that, in writing arguments, you need to produce those that are well organised, well focused, and complex (with different levels of reasoning). Here are some tips to get you there.

Plan a coherent argument

Plan a structure with a journey to an end to avoid rambling

Read the next passage:

> Children should aim to get qualifications because they'll need them for going to college or university or getting a job. Getting qualifications can give children lots of satisfaction, just as when they open the envelope with the results in and find they've done really well. This feels like a good reward for all the hard work during the exams because sometimes exams can be really stressful, what with not knowing the answers and time pressure, and just feeling tired …

As you can see, this person is just rambling on with a stream of thoughts loosely connected to the point of the value of getting qualifications. It is not obviously heading anywhere. There is no organised reasoning, moving us step by step towards a conclusion.

Writing arguments requires you to focus on structure and organisation.

Keep the reasons tight and relevant to avoid going off on a tangent

Tangential reasoning is often interesting, but it is wandering away from the journey towards the conclusion.

Read the next passage:

> Children need to be able to learn a wide range of subjects. This should include at least one modern foreign language, like French or Spanish. Learning a language can be really useful if the young person wants to travel (or even work) abroad. Spain has many things going for it — lots of sunshine, and lots of good entertainment in its resorts. France is well known for its food and wine. Being able to ask questions in a shop would be a big advantage …

Although this has an air of organisation to it, in that it details the advantages of learning languages, much of it is of limited relevance. The information on Spain and France is barely relevant to the conclusion that 'Children need to be able to learn a wide range of subjects', in that it merely details why children should learn French and/or Spanish.

Consider how the parts of the argument link together to avoid big gaps in the reasoning

You need always to be thinking of how the bit you're writing fits with what's come before (if it's not the start) and with what's coming next (if it's not the end).

You need to think carefully, so that there are no big jumps in the reasoning. Keep any gaps in the reasoning small and straightforward. In the next example (from our previous argument), you can see that an assumption is being made, but it is not a problem:

> In addition, children benefit from interacting with many different adults, rather than just with parents.
>
> Assumption: *The range of adults that children interact with at school is sufficiently large to be beneficial.*

> So we can see that children benefit from learning in the company of others.

Use the correct conclusion

Supporting argument — use the exact given conclusion

In the Unit 2 paper, you are given the conclusion that you have to work with.

Look at the next passage:

> Children benefit from interacting with many different adults, rather than just with parents. So we can see that children benefit from learning in the company of others. There's also the point that most parents do not have the expertise to teach their children. *Therefore parents who want to educate their children at home should have to be able to provide evidence that their children won't suffer as a result.*

Although this conclusion might fit reasonably well with what's come before, it isn't the conclusion that was required. That was: *'we should not allow children to be educated at home'.*

Writing a well-organised argument with the wrong conclusion can limit the level of marks that you can be awarded. (There are usually four levels.) Make sure you check (and check again) that your conclusion has the wording you are told to give it.

An argument that challenges — use the exact opposite of the given conclusion

If you're writing a counter-argument to the conclusion, then it would be *'we should allow children to be educated at home'*, not a variation of your choice such as *'we should allow parents to keep children at home rather than send them to school'*. Thinking of different wording takes up your time and loses you marks.

Write a complex argument

You gain marks by writing an argument that has complex reasoning.

Include at least one intermediate conclusion

This means you need to have at least one intermediate conclusion to show that you can work with more than one level of conclusion, rather than just the simple R → C.

Avoid over-simple arguments

Read the next version:

> **R** Children need to get many qualifications.
>
> **R** Part of a child's education is to learn how to function with peers.
>
> **R** Children benefit from interacting with many different adults, rather than just with parents.
>
> **C** Therefore we should not allow children to be educated at home.

Concise — certainly. Simple — certainly. But it reads more like a shopping list than a well-organised piece of argument. It lacks the power that our original version had, with its different levels of reasoning. It would therefore only get your answer into one of the lower levels of marks.

Write a persuasive (cogent) argument

This is a difficult one. You are expected to write arguments that are persuasive. But what might persuade one person won't necessarily persuade another. So you need to make sure that your reasoning at least requires the reader to take the argument seriously.

Avoid using trivial reasons

Here's a version of a counter-argument to the one we've been working with:

> Children can find classrooms a bit dirty sometimes. Some children in a class might not have very good hygiene habits. Getting up early for school can be a bit much on a cold winter morning. Therefore we should allow children to be educated at home.

As you can see, apart from its shopping-list approach, the argument is not very persuasive. Each of the reasons given could be answered very robustly as being matters of very small significance, compared to the advantages of schools over home education.

Make sure that your reasoning could stand up to reasonable objections and that it is not trivial.

Avoid using flawed reasoning

Make sure that your reasoning is not flawed (no slippery slopes, circular arguments, inappropriate appeals and so on).

Exercise 39

Use each of the following as the starting point of an argument. These will be your main conclusion. You can either support or challenge the claim.

You should produce arguments with at least three reasons and an intermediate conclusion. In addition, try to add either a counter-assertion or a counter-argument. So that you can make you arguments realistic, one piece of evidence has been given for you to include.

1 Households that own more than one car should pay more tax for the second vehicle.
  More British households own two cars (27%) than have no car (23%).

2 The government should invest money into public awareness of how important it is for people to clean their homes thoroughly.

Eighty-five per cent of public toilets are cleaner than the average kitchen worktop in a British home.

3 We should re-think employers' responsibility towards the childcare of their employees.

It is predicted that, by 2030, women will be the main earners in one in four households in Britain.

4 Shake and wake programmes in primary schools need to be widely developed to extend even more physical exercise at the start to the day.

In 1970, 80% of primary school children walked to school on their own. Today this figure is 9%.

Most public toilets are cleaner than the average kitchen worktop

No specific answers are given here as a variety could be acceptable.

The two following past paper practice questions ask for different argument elements, so you need to make sure that you take notice of the requirements when you begin to answer each.

Past paper practice 44

OCR Unit F502, January 2012

Write an argument to support or challenge the claim:

'The government should provide a greater number of activities for young people.'

Marks will be given for a well-structured and developed argument. You should include:

➢ at least **two** reasons

➢ a counter-argument and response

➢ a main conclusion

Your argument may also contain other argument elements. You may use information and ideas from the passage (if you have read the Document in the Resource Booklet), but you must use them to form a new argument. No credit will be given for repeating the arguments in the passage.

Check your answer against the guidance on page 351.

Past paper practice 45

OCR Unit F502, January 2012

Write your own argument to support or challenge the claim:

'Ball games should be banned in parks.'

Marks will be given for a well-structured and developed argument. You should include:

> at least three reasons

> a well-supported intermediate conclusion

> a main conclusion

Your argument may also contain other argument elements. You may use information and ideas from the passage (if you have read the Document in the Resource Booklet), but you must use them to form a new argument. No credit will be given for repeating the arguments in the passage.

Check your answer against the guidance on page 351.

Summary

> Start with the given conclusion and make sure that you use the precise wording from the question.

> Then think of relevant reasons that are significant points to support the conclusion.

> Look at the links between these to produce a progressive intermediate conclusion that takes the argument forward.

> Add a counter-argument and make sure that you respond to it so that your argument is strengthened.

> Add relevant examples and/or evidence from your own experience.

Chapter 30

Maximising your performance on Unit 2

Learning objectives

By the end of this chapter, you will have:

➢ identified strategies for answering multiple-choice questions

➢ understood how to write effective answers for Sections B and C

➢ tackled an exam-style Unit 2 question paper

➢ checked your answers against the guidance

In this chapter we'll work with the critical thinking skills that you have learned, illustrating how you need to apply them to the questions in the Unit 2 examination.

The question paper

Let's remind ourselves of what appears where on the paper. For a fuller explanation look back to the introduction to Unit 2 on page 180.

Section A	Multiple choice	15 marks
Section B	Analysing and evaluating argument	30 marks
Section C	Developing your own argument	30 marks

Exam materials

You will be given:

➢ An **OMR sheet** on which to record your multiple-choice answers. You will need a pencil to fill this in and an eraser if you need to alter your choices.

➢ A **resource document** which will contain the passage(s) required for Sections B and C.

➢ A **question and answer booklet** in which you record your answers for Sections B and C. This will be scanned for electronic marking. You should only write on the dotted lines in the spaces provided and use the continuation sheets if you run out of space. Anything written elsewhere may not be able to be viewed.

Strategies for answering the multiple-choice questions

How much time to spend on them

You are advised to spend no more than *20 minutes* on this part of the paper. There are usually five short passages with three questions on each (although this can change from year to year). This would give you 4 minutes to read each passage and answer the three related questions.

If you spend more than the 20 minutes advised, you will be cutting into the time needed for the other two sections. If you find that you are running out of time in Section A, you can always go back to it if you have spare time at the end, as you don't have to hand in the OMR sheet until the end of the exam. It will be collected with your answer booklet.

When to answer them

The multiple-choice questions are an entirely separate part of the paper. There is no link between them and the questions in the other two sections. So you could in theory answer them when you like.

However, you are obviously expected to do Section A first. The question paper tells you 'on completion of Section A move directly on to Sections B and C'. This is because the passages need intense concentration if you are to decide between very near options in choosing each answer. This type of thinking sets you in the right frame of mind for the rest of the paper.

Knowing what types of question can be asked

You can be asked any question on the skills already covered in Unit 2. Think of multiple-choice questions as mini arguments. You can be asked to use your skills to identify a number of things, with four options to choose from each time.

Activity 27

Working in groups, each take a different Unit 2 past paper and write down the different types of question asked and then compare lists. You will be able to see which types of question are regularly asked in each paper and the ones that are asked less frequently.

Here are some examples that you should have found:
- Identify an argument element, e.g. MC, IC, R, HR, evidence, example, counter-argument, counter-assertion, principle, analogy, explanation.

➢ Identify assumption, flaws, appeals.
➢ Identify which statement if true/would most weaken (or strengthen) the argument.
➢ Identify a principle that would best support the conclusion.
➢ Identify from a claim the name of the argument element.
➢ Identify how a claim, if true, affects the argument.
➢ Identify the definition of a word in context.

How to tackle the questions

Here are some useful strategies for you to consider:

➢ Read the *question* first.
➢ Then read the *passage*.
➢ *Underline the conclusion* (unless it is attached to a question 'Which of the following is a conclusion that can be drawn ...?' in which the conclusion has not been reached).
➢ Then look at the *options* available.

Although the question is laid out by giving you the passage first, there is little point reading the passage without knowing why you're doing so. When you *do* know, you then read it with a purpose. Sometimes a passage will support two or even three questions. In these cases, you should certainly read the passage with (at least) the first question in mind.

Having read the passage with the question in mind, you will very often have seen the answer before you even read the responses. For example, if asked to find the main conclusion, then you will probably have already seen which bit of the passage it is as you read through it. It is a good idea to underline the conclusion as you are reading through, as many of the questions need you to have an understanding of what has been concluded.

One type of question needs special care. This is one that has a negative in it:

Which of the following is **not** ...?

The reason these questions are more difficult is that you have to slot out of one way of thinking and into another one. You've been looking for what is assumed, inferred and so on, and then you're looking at something that is not assumed, inferred and so on. The brain has to change gear from forward to backward, from yes to no. You need to take time to do this carefully.

How to eliminate the distracters

If you have already tried some of the critical thinking multiple-choice questions, you will know that you can often eliminate two choices without too much difficulty and then you are left with the two others to choose between. The wrong answers are often referred to as distracters, because they distract your attention away from the right answer. When you get it down to two choices you have eliminated the weakest distracters.

Recognising what the wrong options are can help you to see the correct answer more clearly. When you are first working through multiple-choice questions you can use these to help you identify what options are being offered.

Here are some examples of what *might* be included.

Finding the main conclusion
There might be:
➢ an IC
➢ or wording that has the look of a conclusion, e.g. 'should'
➢ or a conclusion that could have been drawn but wasn't

Choosing a conclusion that could be drawn
There might be:
➢ a reason in the passage that looks like a conclusion
➢ a conclusion that would cover part but not all of the reasoning
➢ further relevant information

Choosing the principle
There might be:
➢ a rule that is too specific to be a principle
➢ a principle that is so broad it is not directly relevant
➢ a statement that is relevant but descriptive
➢ a principle that goes in the opposite direction to the argument.

From the above, you will recognise that each of the options that you are given is closely related to the correct answer.

Activity 28

Working in groups, choose a multiple-choice option (a), (b), (c) or (d). Go through five multiple-choice questions looking only at that option and explain what that option is doing in each of the questions. This will help you to understand how the multiple-choice questions work and what you need to look out for when you are eliminating the incorrect options.

You can check your findings against the OCR mark scheme, as this explains why each option is either correct or incorrect.

Practice exam-style paper

Unit 2 practice exam-style paper

Section A – Multiple choice
Question 1

People buy bottled water when they are out and about. If they are discouraged from buying bottled water when they're out and about, then they'll buy cans of drink instead. There are many problems with such drinks (high sugar levels, additives, and so on). This shows that people ought to be encouraged to buy bottled water.

1 Which of the following is the **main conclusion** of the above argument?

   (a) If people are discouraged from buying bottled water, they'll buy cans of drink instead.

   (b) People buy bottled water when they're out.

   (c) People ought to be encouraged to buy bottled water.

   (d) There are many problems with cans of drink.

Question 2

Plastic bottles used for water are a massive problem. They are a big source of litter, and when they're not sent for recycling, they end up swelling landfill sites. In this country we are very lucky to have a supply of good clean water at the turn of a tap. Much of the world is not so lucky. So we should drink tap water rather than bottled water.

2 What is the following **argument element** in the above argument?

   'Plastic bottles used for water are a massive problem.'

   (a) Conclusion

   (b) Evidence

   (c) Intermediate conclusion

   (d) Reason

Questions 3 and 4

The famous Nobel Prizes, awarded since 1901, remain the measure of scientific achievement. Of the 500 awards for science, 74 (15%) have gone to the UK. Given our population size, it's an impressive achievement that so many have been won. But since 1970 the percentage has declined. During the same time, the US has dominated the awards. (They won about 60% of all science awards and in 2006 won all the awards for academic work.) Today it spends over twice the proportion of its national wealth on universities as we do. Since scientific discovery is heavily reliant on university spending, we need to spend more on our universities.

3 Which of the following is the **main conclusion** of the above argument?

    (a) It's an impressive achievement that so many Nobel Prizes have been won by the UK.

    (b) Nobel Prizes remain the measure of scientific achievement.

    (c) Scientific discovery is heavily reliant on university spending.

    (d) We need to spend more on our universities.

4 What is the following **argument element** in the above argument?

  'in 2006 won all the awards for academic work.'

    (a) Evidence

    (b) Example

    (c) Intermediate conclusion

    (d) Reason

Questions 5 and 6

UK births have risen since 2000 by about 10%. Despite the availability of screening for Down's syndrome, the number of Down's syndrome births has risen at a much greater rate during the same period, in fact by as much as 25%. This shows that more people are deciding not to abort Down's foetuses. This must then show that we have become a more caring society.

5 Which one of the following is **NOT assumed** in the above argument?

    (a) Before 2000, most foetuses with Down's syndrome were aborted.

    (b) Not aborting Down's syndrome foetuses is a sign of a caring society.

    (c) The effectiveness of screening for Down's syndrome has not declined since 2000.

    (d) The explanation for the increase in Down's syndrome babies is not due to something other than choice.

6 Which one of the following is the **best statement** of the flaw in the above argument?

    (a) The author fails to consider an alternative explanation for the increase in Down's syndrome babies.

    (b) The author fails to define what is meant by a 'caring society'.

    (c) The author gives insufficient evidence on the percentage of Down's syndrome births as part of the birth rate.

    (d) The rate of increase in births and that of the number of Down's syndrome babies cannot be compared.

Question 7

Caffeine is found naturally in both tea and coffee plants. It is often pointed out that tea has more caffeine in it than coffee, so that, some say, drinking tea is more likely than drinking coffee to give you that caffeine 'lift'. However, though tea naturally has more caffeine in it, there is less tea than coffee per cubic centimetre in a cup, leading to a lower caffeine level. Thus, if you need a lift, always choose coffee.

7 Which one of the following is an **explanation** used in support of the conclusion?

   (a) Caffeine is found naturally in both tea and coffee plants.

   (b) Drinking tea is more likely than drinking coffee to give you that caffeine 'lift'.

   (c) Tea has more caffeine in it than coffee.

   (d) There is less tea than coffee per cubic centimetre in a cup.

Question 8

Though the English army was outnumbered by the French army by possibly twenty to one at the Battle of Agincourt in 1415, Henry V's English army was victorious. The French knights would have been wearing armour weighing between 30–50kg and they got bogged down in mud as they advanced. This would have exhausted them. Furthermore, wearing constricting steel armour would have made it impossible for knights to breathe deeply, as they struggled to make progress. The same sort of armour would have been worn by the English knights, but they didn't have to cover the same amount of ground before the battle. About 8,000 Frenchmen died at Agincourt; only a few hundred Englishmen died. This shows that military victory is not necessarily a matter of numbers.

8 Which one of the following is **NOT an explanation** used in support of the conclusion?

   (a) The English knights didn't have to cover the same ground as the French.

   (b) The English knights would have worn the same type of armour as the French.

   (c) The French knights were exhausted by being bogged down in mud.

   (d) The French knights would have found it difficult to breathe deeply.

Question 9

Nintendo, the maker of active-play games such as Wii Sports and Wii Fit Plus (in which players can play various sports or perform dances using their computer), hope that 'the games encourage users to be more physically active'. However, researchers who looked at how families used these games over 3 months found no evidence that the games had this effect. In the first 6 weeks of use, the games were used an average of 22 minutes a day by everyone in the family; in the second 6 weeks, this usage fell to only 4 minutes a day. At the end of the study, health-related fitness measures were unchanged. It is clear that active-play games should not be seen as encouraging people to be more physically active.

9 Which one of the following **most strengthens** the above argument?

   (a) Fitness levels have fallen over the past 30 years.

   (b) People who play active-play games often believe that doing so will increase their fitness level.

   (c) Some active-play games (such as Extreme Challenge) are more physically demanding than others.

(d) When people are expected to increase their physical activity, they normally reduce other physical activity to compensate.

Question 10 and 11

Millions of pounds are spent each week on the National Lottery, with many charities benefiting from this. The jackpot prizes each week can be anything from about £4m to sometimes over £150m. These amounts are too big. There have been plenty of cases of people's lives being changed for the worse by becoming multi-millionaires overnight. The prize money should be distributed differently, such that, instead of there being one really big prize, there should be lots of smaller prizes (of, say, £50,000) to be won. As a result, charities would still get their money and the overall levels of happiness would increase.

10 Which one of the following **most weakens** the above argument?

(a) A lot of charities don't get any money from the National Lottery.

(b) Many people would not play the National Lottery if prizes were not big.

(c) Some millionaires have very high levels of happiness.

(d) The jackpot prizes are sometimes split between lottery players.

11 What **argument element** is the following sentence in the above argument?

'These amounts are too big.'

(a) Conclusion

(b) Explanation

(c) Intermediate conclusion

(d) Reason

Question 12

Computer security is always under threat from hackers, keen to access people's personal details. This is because the main method of preventing this access is through computer passwords. Unfortunately, people prefer to use simple passwords they can remember, such as birthdays or pets' names. (Young people are especially guilty of this.) In addition, people are complacent about the problem of security, thinking that websites will protect them from hackers. It needs to be made much more difficult for hackers. The simplicity of passwords needs to be replaced by the greater complexity of 'passphrases'. With these, hackers will have to guess far more letters, especially if the phrase is unpredictable (1056 murders of 94 iguanas).

12 Which one of the following is an **intermediate conclusion** of the above argument?

(a) Computer security is always under threat from hackers, keen to access people's personal details.

(b) It needs to be made much more difficult for hackers.

(c) The simplicity of passwords needs to be replaced by the greater complexity of 'passphrases'.

(d) With passphrases, hackers will to have to guess far more letters.

Question 13

Most people in the UK reject the use of torture in all situations, but, in doing so, they have to face real and serious issues. An example from Australia shows this well. A car had been stolen which had a baby inside. The police arrested the suspect not long afterwards but he refused to say where he had left the car. It was a very hot day. Unless the police could find the car quickly, the baby would die. So the police literally beat the information out of the suspect, resulting in the baby being found just in time. This example shows that we have to accept that sometimes things have to be done that we would normally reject as morally wrong.

13 Which one of the following is a **principle** that would best support the above argument?

   (a) Torture is justified if it leads to the saving of life.

   (b) Torture is justified if someone refuses to co-operate in a lawful investigation.

   (c) Torture is never justified with innocent people.

   (d) Torture is justified only if useful information can be obtained by using it.

Section B — Analysing and evaluating argument

Read the passage 'Fishing to extinction' and answer questions 14 to 18.

You should use the exact words of the author in your answers to 14(a), (b) and (c).

Fishing to extinction

There has been a very serious decline in the numbers of shallow-water fish (such as cod) as a result of over-fishing. People still want to eat fish, so the fishing industry must look at

other sources, especially the deep waters of the Atlantic. Unfortunately, this has resulted in a catastrophic decline in the numbers of many of the species caught.

Conservation measures will have to be put in place if these deep-sea fish are to survive. Research on five of such species shows that numbers have declined by between 87% and 98%. This puts them in the category of 'critically endangered'. Many species could well disappear completely, if the present trend continues. These are species that have been swimming in our oceans for hundreds of millions of years.

The problem is emphasised by the fact that the decline in numbers happened in less than 20 years. We can't simply take whatever we want from the seas, as if we are robbers with a key to a bank. Deep-sea fish take a long time to reproduce and normally live for many years. Unfortunately their reproduction rate is very low. The average size of such fish also declined, with one species showing a 57% decline in average size. This is of particular concern as large fish tend to produce more offspring than small ones.

None of these facts has been taken into account by the fishing industry, which has fished the deep-sea species as if they were the fast-breeding sardine and herring. It is like culling elephants as if they reproduced at the same rate as rabbits.

14 (a) State the **main conclusion** of the argument presented in the document 'Fishing to extinction'.

(b) State the **intermediate conclusion** of the argument presented in the document 'Fishing to extinction'.

(c) State the **principle** used in the argument presented in the document 'Fishing to extinction'.

15 In paragraph 2 of 'Fishing to extinction', the author states:

'Many species could well disappear completely, if the present trend continues.'

(a) Name the argument element used.

(b) Justify your answer with reference to the text.

16 The author argues that 'conservation measures' for deep-sea fish are necessary for the survival of deep-sea fish. State what the author must assume in order to argue this.

17 In paragraph 3, the author uses the analogy that we can't just take what we want from the sea 'as if we are robbers with a key to a bank'.

(a) State what is being compared in this analogy.

(b) Make two points of evaluation about this analogy. You need to show how effectively it supports the author's argument.

18 In paragraph 2, the author uses evidence of research on five deep-sea species of fish which 'shows that numbers have declined by between 87% and 98%'.

(a) Explain one strength in the use of this evidence.

(b) Explain one weakness in the use of this evidence.

Now read the response 'Going, going gone' and answer questions 19 and 20.

Going, going gone

The entire eco-system of the world's seas could collapse by 2050. There is no other future for the world's coral reefs except in huge artificial aquaria or their complete destruction. Only urgent action taken very soon can prevent this collapse from happening. One of the major causes of the problem for the eco-system of the seas is over-fishing. The Black Sea has shown what happens. Large fish disappeared from this sea by the 1970s. Twenty years later, the smaller ones had gone. This is the fate that will soon await all the world's seas, unless large-scale action is taken. We must remember that fish are a crucial part of the eco-system of the seas and therefore of the world. We must stop thinking of fish as a food product that can simply be collected for our plates.

19 The reasoning about coral reefs in the passage 'Going, going, gone' contains a flaw. Name the **flaw** and explain the weakness in this reasoning.

20 Evaluate the reasoning in 'Going, Going, Gone'. You should refer to at least two strengths or weaknesses.

Section C — Developing your own argument

21 The author of 'Going, going, gone' argues that the eco-systems of the world's seas could collapse by 2050 'unless large-scale action is taken'.

Give one detailed example of problems that there could be in getting this 'large-scale action' to be taken.

22 'Dolphins should never be kept in captivity.'

Give two **reasons** that would support this claim.

23 'People should ensure that what they eat doesn't contribute to damaging the planet.'

Write your own argument to support or challenge this claim.

Section A answers and discussion

What follows are the answers to the multiple-choice questions with a detailed explanation of the correct answers (and why the incorrect ones are so).

Question 1

> People buy bottled water when they are out and about. If they are discouraged from buying bottled water when they're out and about, then they'll buy cans of drink instead. There are many problems with such drinks (high sugar levels, additives, and so on). This shows that people ought to be encouraged to buy bottled water.

1 Which of the following is the **main conclusion** of the above argument?

(a) If people are discouraged from buying bottled water, they'll buy cans of drink instead.

(b) People buy bottled water when they're out.

(c) People ought to be encouraged to buy bottled water.

(d) There are many problems with cans of drink.

The correct answer is (c).

The structure of the argument is as follows.

R1 People buy bottled water when they are out and about.

IC If they are discouraged from buying bottled water when they're out and about, then they'll buy cans of drink instead.

R2 There are many problems with such drinks (high sugar levels, additives and so on).

C This shows that people ought to be encouraged to buy bottled water.

Question 2

> Plastic bottles used for water are a massive problem. They are a big source of litter, and when they're not sent for recycling, they end up swelling landfill sites. In this country we are very lucky to have a supply of good clean water at the turn of a tap. Much of the world is not so lucky. So we should drink tap water rather than bottled water.

2 What is the following **argument element** in the above argument?

'Plastic bottles used for water are a massive problem.'

(a) Conclusion

(b) Evidence

(c) Intermediate conclusion

(d) Reason

The correct answer is (c).

The structure of the argument is as follows.

IC Plastic bottles used for water are a massive problem.

R1 They are a big source of litter, and

R2 when they're not sent for recycling, they end up swelling landfill sites.

R3 In this country we are very lucky to have a supply of good clean water at the turn of a tap.

R4 Much of the world is not so lucky.

C So we should drink tap water rather than bottled water.

Questions 3 and 4

> The famous Nobel Prizes, awarded since 1901, remain the measure of scientific achievement. Of the 500 awards for science, 74 (15%) have gone to the UK. Given our population size, it's an impressive achievement that so many have been won. But since 1970 the percentage has declined. During the same time, the US has dominated the awards. (They won about 60% of all science awards and in 2006 won all the awards for academic work.) Today it spends over twice the proportion of its national wealth on universities as we do. Since scientific discovery is heavily reliant on university spending, we need to spend more on our universities.

3 Which of the following is the **main conclusion** of the above argument?

(a) It's an impressive achievement that so many Nobel Prizes have been won by the UK.

(b) Nobel Prizes remain the measure of scientific achievement.

(c) Scientific discovery is heavily reliant on university spending.

(d) We need to spend more on our universities.

The correct answer is (d).

> **4** What is the following **argument element** in the above argument?
>
> 'in 2006 won all the awards for academic work'
>
> **(a)** Evidence
>
> **(b)** Example
>
> **(c)** Intermediate conclusion
>
> **(d)** Reason

The correct answer is (b).

The structure of the argument is as follows.

Ev The famous Nobel Prizes, awarded since 1901, remain the measure of scientific achievement.

Ev Of the 500 awards for science, 74 (15%) have gone to the UK. (Inference from evidence) Given our population size, it's an impressive achievement that so many have been won. But

R1 since 1970 the percentage has declined.

R2 During the same time, the US has dominated the awards.

Ev (They won about 60% of all science awards and

Ex in 2006 won all the awards for academic work.)

R3 Today it spends over twice the proportion of its national wealth on universities as we do.

R4 Since scientific discovery is heavily reliant on university spending,

C we need to spend more on our universities.

In question 3, you should have had no trouble finding the conclusion of this argument. It is working out which bits are reasons and which no more than evidence or examples that requires careful thought.

In question 4, the correct answer is example as this is one instance of dominating the awards.

Questions 5 and 6

> UK births have risen since 2000 by about 10%. Despite the availability of screening for Down's syndrome, the number of Down's syndrome births has risen at a much greater rate during the same period, in fact by as much as 25%. This shows that more people are deciding not to abort Down's foetuses. This must then show that we have become a more caring society.

> **5** Which one of the following is **NOT assumed** in the above argument?
>
> **(a)** Before 2000, most foetuses with Down's syndrome were aborted.
>
> **(b)** Not aborting Down's syndrome foetuses is a sign of a caring society.

(c) The effectiveness of screening for Down's syndrome has not declined since 2000.

(d) The explanation for the increase in Down's syndrome babies is not due to something other than choice.

The correct answer is (a).

The argument moves from the evidence on the relative increase in the number of Down's syndrome births to the conclusion that 'this shows that more people are deciding not to abort Down's babies'. This then serves as an intermediate conclusion from which the conclusion 'This must then show that we have become a more caring society' is drawn.

We need to work out what the author does *not* have to assume in this argument:

➢ **(a) is *not* assumed.** Although the author argues that fewer Down's syndrome foetuses are now aborted, they do not have to believe that 'most' were before 2000. The author can be silent on this.

➢ **(b) is assumed.** This is needed to connect the intermediate conclusion with the main conclusion. Without it, the author could not draw the main conclusion.

➢ **(c) is assumed.** If the effectiveness of screening had declined, then this would provide an alternative explanation for the increase in Down's syndrome births. In that the author rules out any other explanation by drawing the intermediate conclusion, the author has to assume (a).

➢ **(d) is assumed.** This is central to the argument. The author must rule out any explanation other than people *choosing* not to abort Down's syndrome foetuses.

6 Which one of the following is the **best statement** of the flaw in the above argument?

(a) The author fails to consider an alternative explanation for the increase in Down's syndrome babies.

(b) The author fails to define what is meant by a 'caring society'.

(c) The author gives insufficient evidence on the percentage of Down's syndrome births as part of the birth rate.

(d) The rate of increase in births and that of the number of Down's syndrome babies cannot be compared.

The correct answer is (a).

From doing question 5, you can see how the argument is weakened by the author's having to rule out any explanation other than the one about choice. This is captured in (a).

➢ **(b) is incorrect.** Although the author does not define exactly what is meant by a 'caring society', he or she must include in the definition a concern for the existence of Down's syndrome babies. Not to have given it in specific terms is not in itself a flaw.

➢ **(c) is incorrect.** Although the author gives no evidence on this percentage, it is not necessary to in that this isn't the point. The author is concerned only with explaining why there has been a relatively greater increase in the number of Down's syndrome births.

> **(d) is incorrect.** There is no reason why the two cannot be compared. It is the conclusion that the author draws from this comparison that is the problem.

Question 7

Caffeine is found naturally in both tea and coffee plants. It is often pointed out that tea has more caffeine in it than coffee, so that, some say, drinking tea is more likely than drinking coffee to give you that caffeine 'lift'. However, though tea naturally has more caffeine in it, there is less tea than coffee per cubic centimetre in a cup, leading to a lower caffeine level. Thus, if you need a lift, always choose coffee.

7 Which one of the following is an **explanation** used in support of the conclusion?

(a) Caffeine is found naturally in both tea and coffee plants.

(b) Drinking tea is more likely than drinking coffee to give you that caffeine 'lift'.

(c) Tea has more caffeine in it than coffee.

(d) There is less tea than coffee per cubic centimetre in a cup.

The correct answer is (d).

The information that there is less tea than coffee per cubic centimetre is used as the explanation for why, though tea plants have more caffeine than coffee, we should drink coffee if we want a caffeine 'lift'.

> **(a) is incorrect.** This is no more than a claim that introduces the subject of the argument. It is not used to support the argument.

> **(c) is incorrect.** Though this is an explanation, it is one that is used to show why some people say that 'drinking tea is more likely than drinking coffee to give you that caffeine "lift"'. Thus it is not used to support the argument (but rather provides an explanation for the counter-position).

> **(d) is incorrect.** This is the position that the author argues against.

Question 8

Though the English army was outnumbered by the French army by possibly twenty to one at the Battle of Agincourt in 1415, Henry V's English army was victorious. The French knights would have been wearing armour weighing between 30–50kg and they got bogged down in mud as they advanced. This would have exhausted them. Furthermore, wearing constricting steel armour would have made it impossible for knights to breathe deeply, as they struggled to make progress. The same sort of armour would have been worn by the English knights, but they didn't have to cover the same amount of ground before the battle. About 8,000 Frenchmen died at Agincourt; only a few hundred Englishmen died. This shows that military victory is not necessarily a matter of numbers.

8 Which one of the following is **NOT an explanation** used in support of the conclusion?

(a) The English knights didn't have to cover the same ground as the French.

(b) The English knights would have worn the same type of armour as the French.

(c) The French knights were exhausted by being bogged down in mud.

(d) The French knights would have found it difficult to breathe deeply.

The correct answer is (b).

This claim does not contribute to the explanation of why the English defeated the French at Agincourt. Without the extra piece of information that the English knights did not have to advance so much as the French knights, this claim would sit oddly in the passage.

➤ **(a) is incorrect.** This is used to explain why the English knights, though wearing the same sort of armour as the French, would have been better able to fight.

➤ **(c) is incorrect.** This provides a significant part of the explanation of why the French knights were unable to make a big contribution to the battle.

➤ **(d) is incorrect.** This is used as part of the explanation for why the French knights were limited in the contribution they could make to the battle.

Question 9

Nintendo, the maker of active-play games such as Wii Sports and Wii Fit Plus (in which players can play various sports or perform dances using their own computer), hope that 'the games encourage users to be more physically active'. However, researchers who looked at how families used these games over 3 months found no evidence that the games had this effect. In the first 6 weeks of use, the games were used an average of 22 minutes a day by everyone in the family; in the second 6 weeks, this usage fell to only 4 minutes a day. At the end of the study, health-related fitness measures were unchanged. It is clear that active-play games should not be seen as encouraging people to be more physically active.

9 Which one of the following **most strengthens** the above argument?

(a) Fitness levels have fallen over the past 30 years.

(b) People who play active-play games often believe that doing so will increase their fitness level.

(c) Some active-play games (such as Extreme Challenge) are more physically demanding than others.

(d) When people are expected to increase their physical activity, they normally reduce other physical activity to compensate.

The correct answer is (d).

This gives us a possible explanation of why people's fitness levels did not increase following their playing of the games. As such, it supports the conclusion that 'active-play games should not be seen as increasing people's fitness levels'.

➤ **(a) is incorrect.** Though this might emphasise the significance of the conclusion for fitness programmes, it does not strengthen the argument that active-play games do not increase fitness levels.

➤ **(b) is incorrect.** This has a neutral effect on the argument. Whether or not people believe that active-play games increase their fitness level, the conclusion is that they don't.

➤ **(c) is incorrect.** Though this claim might be significant for showing that some games might affect levels of physical activity more than others, it does not support the argument that active-play games do not increase people's fitness levels.

Question 10 and 11

Millions of pounds are spent each week on the National Lottery, with many charities benefiting from this. The jackpot prizes each week can be anything from about £4m to sometimes over £150m. These amounts are too big. There have been plenty of cases of people's lives being changed for the worse by becoming multi-millionaires overnight. The prize money should be distributed differently, such that, instead of there being one really big prize, there should be lots of smaller prizes (of, say, £50,000) to be won. As a result, charities would still get their money and the overall levels of happiness would increase.

10 Which one of the following **most weakens** the above argument?

(a) A lot of charities don't get any money from the National Lottery.

(b) Many people would not play the National Lottery if prizes were not big.

(c) Some millionaires have very high levels of happiness.

(d) The jackpot prizes are sometimes split between lottery players.

The **correct answer is (b).**

The author argues that eliminating very big lottery prizes and having an increased number of smaller ones can be supported in two ways: 'charities would still get their money and the overall levels of happiness would increase'. However, if many people would not play if the big prizes were no longer available, then at the very least, charities would not still get the same amount of money (and overall levels of happiness might not increase).

➤ **(a) is incorrect.** Though the author refers to 'many charities' benefiting from the National Lottery, it is not inconsistent that 'a lot of charities' don't.

➤ **(c) is incorrect.** This has a neutral effect on the argument. Though this seems to counter the author's claim that 'people's lives' have been 'changed for the worse by becoming multi-millionaires overnight', it does not directly counter this. Some millionaires could still be very happy; most millionaires do not have their money from winning the lottery.

> **(d) is incorrect.** Though this would seem to weaken the author's point about the problem of the big prizes, it is not sufficiently a problem. The word 'sometimes' is pretty weak and we are not given information on the degree to which prizes are split when they are (between two, three, or what?)

---

11 What **argument element** is the following sentence in the above argument?

'These amounts are too big.'

(a) Conclusion

(b) Explanation

(c) Intermediate conclusion

(d) Reason

The correct answer is (c).

The structure of the argument is as follows.

R1 There have been plenty of cases of people's lives being changed for the worse by becoming multi-millionaires overnight.

IC These amounts are too big.

C The prize money should be distributed differently, such that, instead of there being one really big prize, there should be lots of smaller prizes (of, say, £50,000) to be won. (If there were lots of smaller prizes instead of there being one big prize)

R2 charities would still get their money and

R3 the overall levels of happiness would increase.

Question 12

Computer security is always under threat from hackers, keen to access people's personal details. This is because the main method of preventing this access is through computer passwords. Unfortunately, people prefer to use simple passwords they can remember, such as birthdays or pets' names. (Young people are especially guilty of this.) In addition, people are complacent about the problem of security, thinking that websites will protect them from hackers. It needs to be made much more difficult for hackers. The simplicity of passwords needs to be replaced by the greater complexity of 'passphrases'. With these, hackers will have to guess far more letters, especially if the phrase is unpredictable (1056 murders of 94 iguanas).

12 Which one of the following is an **intermediate conclusion** of the above argument?

(a) Computer security is always under threat from hackers, keen to access people's personal details.

(b) It needs to be made much more difficult for hackers.

> **(c)** The simplicity of passwords needs to be replaced by the greater complexity of 'passphrases'.

> **(d)** With passphrases, hackers will to have to guess far more letters.

The correct answer is (b).

This is drawn from three reasons.

R1 Computer security is always under threat from hackers, keen to access people's personal details.

R2 People prefer to use simple passwords they can remember.

R3 People are complacent about the problem of security, thinking that websites will protect them from hackers.

IC It needs to be made much more difficult for hackers.

C The simplicity of passwords needs to be replaced by the greater complexity of 'passphrases'.

In turn, this IC is used to draw the main conclusion 'The simplicity of passwords needs to be replaced by the greater complexity of 'passphrases'.'

➤ **(a) is incorrect.** It is the first reason of the argument.

➤ **(c) is incorrect.** This is the main conclusion of the argument.

➤ **(d) is incorrect.** This is an explanation for why passphrases will increase the complexity for hackers.

Question 13

Most people in the UK reject the use of torture in all situations, but, in doing so, they have to face real and serious issues. An example from Australia shows this well. A car had been stolen which had a baby inside. The police arrested the suspect not long afterwards but he refused to say where he had left the car. It was a very hot day. Unless the police could find the car quickly, the baby would die. So the police literally beat the information out of the suspect, resulting in the baby being found just in time. This example shows that we have to accept that sometimes things have to be done that we would normally reject as morally wrong.

13 Which one of the following is a **principle** that would best support the above argument?

(a) Torture is justified if it leads to the saving of life.

(b) Torture is justified if someone refuses to co-operate in a lawful investigation.

(c) Torture is never justified with innocent people.

(d) Torture is justified only if useful information can be obtained by using it.

The correct answer is (a).

In the example used in the argument, the outcome of the beating of the suspect was the saving of the baby's life. This outcome is used to draw the conclusion that 'we have to accept that sometimes things have to be done that we would normally reject as morally wrong'. The principle that would best support this conclusion is the one that refers to the saving of life.

> **(b) is incorrect.** This is much too broad, in that it would justify torture in every police investigation in which the suspect refused to co-operate, regardless of the seriousness of the outcome.

> **(c) is incorrect.** The limitation of this principle for the argument is that it doesn't deal with the issue of the guilty (as in the Australian example).

> **(d) is incorrect.** This is, like (c), much too broad. Though the argument justified the use of torture to get essential information, it does not follow that it would support using torture in order to get no more than 'useful' information.

Section B answers and discussion

In the examples below, the correct student answers are flagged blue and the incorrect student answers are flagged red.

The first few questions are all concerned with the analysis of the argument in a passage.

Question 14

> **14 (a)** State the **main conclusion** of the argument presented in the document 'Fishing to extinction'.

In longer passages, you'd normally expect to find this near the beginning or near the end.

So what's the answer?

 Conservation measures will have to be put in place if these deep-sea fish are to survive.

This answer accurately reproduces the main conclusion of the argument. You can see that it gives the conclusion exactly as it appears in the text.

What is a less accurate answer?

 Conservation measures are needed for the survival of deep-sea fish.

In this version there is a paraphrasing of the conclusion that doesn't take it too far from the original, but is still not quite accurate. The question will ask you to 'state' the main conclusion, intermediate conclusion and so on. So state it rather than paraphrase it. Indeed, in stating the conclusion, etc. you are told to 'use the exact words of the author'.

> ### Exam tip
>
> It cannot be stressed too strongly that, in giving the main conclusion, intermediate conclusion, reasons and so on, you need to use the exact words of the author. This does not mean you have to include words like 'but', 'however' and so on but you are not penalised if you do.

One other word of warning. Don't think that you can use the conventional way of quoting something by shortening it through the use of ellipsis (...).

Student	Conservation measures ... these deep-sea fish are to survive.

The examiner is instructed to credit only the actual words that are used.

14 (b) State the **intermediate conclusion** of the argument presented in the document 'Fishing to extinction'.

Student	Unless something is done very soon, the problem will get worse.

This is entirely accurate: it reproduces the intermediate conclusion, using the exact words of the author.

Any variation involves paraphrasing, and thus a move away from stating the intermediate conclusion.

Student	➢ We must act soon to stop the problem getting worse. ➢ Unless we act soon, things will get worse.

14 (c) State the **principle** used in the argument presented in the document 'Fishing to extinction'.

Student	We can't simply take whatever we want from the seas.

Again we just need to find what's being asked for and then to *state* it. This answer does exactly that.

What about the next answer?

Student	We can't simply take whatever we want from the seas, as if we are robbers with a key to the bank.

This second answer is less accurate because it adds in something that is not part of the principle. The analogy that follows the principle is not part of it, so it should not be included.

An even weaker answer is one that loses the accuracy of the original:

 Student We shouldn't allow fishing in the sea.

Question 15

> **15** In paragraph 2 of 'Fishing to extinction', the author states:
>
> 'Many species could well disappear completely, if the present trend continues.'
>
> **(a)** Name the argument element used.
>
> **(b)** Justify your answer with reference to the text.

In this type of question, you need to write very little. All that's needed is the term used for the specific argument component, e.g. explanation, example, evidence, reason, counter-argument.

The answer to this specific question is:

 Student Hypothetical reason

These questions that ask you to name part of an argument are accompanied by a further question asking you to explain or justify your answer. In the case of hypothetical reasoning, you'll remember from Chapter 27 what's going on with them.

 Student It is a reason that includes a consequence, 'many species could well disappear', that requires the condition, 'if the present trend continues', to happen.

Exam tip

The question asks you to justify your answer with reference to the text, so you must be sure to do this and not just give a definition as your answer.

Question 16

> **16** The author argues that 'conservation measures' for deep-sea fish are necessary for the survival of deep-sea fish. State what the author must assume in order to argue this.

Here are two possible answers:

 Student
➤ Conservation measures for deep-sea fish haven't already been put in place.
➤ Conservation measures for deep-sea fish would work.

Here's an example of an inaccurate version.

 Student Conservation measures for fish haven't already been put in place.

Small as it might be, the omission of the words 'deep-sea' is crucial because that's what the author's argument is about.

The further you move away from accuracy, the more straightforwardly wrong your answer will be.

Student | People shouldn't eat fish.

Apart from the fact that this conflicts with the author's counter-argument (about which we don't know the author's position), the author does not have to assume it in order to argue for the need for conservation measures for deep-sea fish.

Question 17

> 17 In paragraph 3, the author uses the analogy that we can't just take what we want from the sea 'as if we are robbers with a key to a bank'.
>
> (a) State what is being compared in this analogy.
>
> (b) Make two points of evaluation about this analogy. You need to show how effectively it supports the author's argument.

So what is being compared in this analogy?

Us taking however much fish we want from the sea is seen as the same as robbers taking whatever they want from a bank using a key to the bank.

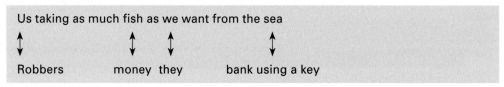

When it comes to evaluating the analogy, your task, as you can see from spelling it out clearly, is to consider how similar the two scenarios are.

It is likely that you will be asked to provide just one point of evaluation, but we have looked at quite a few. Remember that, when answering this question, you need to make reference to both sides of the analogy.

What follows are possible answers to this question.

Student | **Strengths**

The analogy captures the idea of deep-sea fishing taking something that doesn't belong to those who take the fish, just as bank robbers take something that doesn't belong to them.

The analogy has the idea of an unacceptable consequence: the deep-sea fishing industry takes something that causes others to suffer. These others might include people who care about this issue. Similarly, bank robbers cause suffering by their actions.

People who are taking the deep-sea fish are being irresponsible and not caring about others. Bank robbers do not care about those who are affected by their actions.

In both scenarios, there is short-term benefit at the expense of others, fish, other marine species, caring people, scientific researchers and so on; bank customers, bank employees and so on.

Weaknesses

There is the point about legality. Even if robbers have a key to a bank, what they're doing is straightforwardly illegal. What the deep-sea fishing industry is doing is, presumably, not illegal.

Robbers in a bank are stealing other people's property; deep-sea fishing people are not, in the same sense, stealing others' property, in that deep-sea fish don't belong to anybody as such.

It might be argued that there is a wider benefit from deep-sea fish being caught, in the sense that people eat the fish that are caught. Although one could argue that robbers will spend the stolen money on various things, thus benefiting the suppliers of these things, the money would have been used in some way by those from whom it was stolen. On the other hand, fishing the deep-sea fish adds to the stock of things that can be used.

Less well-focused answers might not show this double relationship.

Student People who take deep-sea fish are just taking the fish without any regard for the consequences.

This has a heavy hint of 'just like bank robbers', but this isn't developed.

Student Robbers in a bank are doing something illegal even though they've got a key.

Again, the possible connection with fishing has not been made, thus weakening the evaluation.

Of course, there is also the answer that identifies a difference but the difference isn't relevant to an evaluation of the analogy.

Student People who go fishing for deep-sea fish do it as a job and so get paid. Bank robbers don't rob banks as their job.

Question 18

18 In paragraph 2, the author uses evidence of research on five deep-sea species of fish which 'shows that numbers have declined by between 87% and 98%.'

(a) Explain one strength in the use of this evidence.

(b) Explain one weakness in the use of this evidence.

Student (a) The very high percentage in each case is significant because it's unlikely that other deep-sea fish are not also suffering decline, in that they're unlikely to be able to escape the nets used by the fishing boats.

(b) We don't know how typical the five species are: it could be that they are the ones most likely to be caught.

An answer that provides no development would attract less credit.

Student Some species might not have declined so much.

As we saw earlier, you might have a passage and a response to this used for the questions. Here then is a response to the passage 'Going, going, gone'.

Question 19

19 The reasoning about coral reefs in the passage 'Going, going, gone' contains a flaw. Name the **flaw** and explain the weakness in this reasoning.

Student **Flaw:** Restricting the options

We get credit for correctly naming the flaw. We could have put 'false dilemma' or 'false dichotomy' instead.

Student **Weakness:** The author gives only two options for the future of coral reefs, which is a problem given that he or she argues that complete destruction could be prevented if we take urgent action. Presumably, if we take this urgent action, there could be other scenarios, like marine reserves to protect the reefs.

We also get credit for explaining why this is an example of restriction of options. A less useful answer gives much less detail:

Student The author gives only two things that could happen to coral reefs, but there could be more.

Question 20

20 Evaluate the reasoning in 'Going, going, gone'. You should refer to at least two strengths or weaknesses.

The way to get marks in questions set out like this is to make sure that you do all the following:
➢ state what is a strength or weakness
➢ explain why it is
➢ develop this explanation by referring especially to the passage

We give two answers:

> The author argues that 'over-fishing' is 'one of the major causes of the problem for the eco-system of the seas'. The rest of the argument focuses entirely on fishing as a problem. However, we need to know about these other causes (such as pollution, presumably). Because the author doesn't say anything about these other causes, the conclusion addresses only part of the problem. Even if we changed our attitude to fish, it is likely that there will still be problems for the seas.
> If the Black Sea is somehow typical of other seas and of the world's oceans, then this example can be used to show what will soon happen. The short timescale in which the Black Sea collapsed emphasises the problem that over-fishing cannot be sustained.

An alternative treatment of the Black Sea example could show it as a weakness:

It could be that the Black Sea is not typical of the world's seas and oceans. Perhaps it is more polluted than the global oceans; perhaps it has been particularly over-fished, to a level much greater than other seas and oceans. In this way, we could see this example as not being very relevant to the wider problem.

You can see that we have identified a strength or weakness in the text, explained why it was so, and developed this explanation sufficiently.

Weaker answers would not provide so much development:

We're told about only one of the causes of the problem. Perhaps over-fishing isn't the biggest problem.

Section C answers and discussion

The questions in this section fall into two categories:

> The first is a short question — that of asking you to develop a position that's given or to indicate problems that a position might create.
> The second, and by far the bigger of the two in terms of marks – that of asking you to produce developed arguments.

Question 21

21 The author of 'Going, going, gone' argues that the eco-systems of the world's seas could collapse by 2050 'unless large-scale action is taken'.

Give one detailed example of problems that there could be in getting this 'large-scale action' to be taken.

We give two answers:

> ➤ The author doesn't explain what this large-scale action should be and how it could be achieved. Presumably it will involve lots of, if not all, countries agreeing to significantly reduce their levels of fishing. Perhaps there will have to be no fishing at all in some parts of the world. It is difficult to see this agreement being reached.
> ➤ There would be huge problems in getting agreement on large-scale action, as there is with climate change policies, but even if it was agreed, it would be very difficult to get it controlled. The world's oceans are so big that we couldn't patrol them all to ensure that the restrictions were being kept to.

How do these answers fit the requirement for a 'detailed examination of problems'?

They explain clearly what the problem is (getting agreement and policing it) and give plenty of details to show why it is a problem.

Less useful answers would therefore be less clear and/or less developed.

> ➤ It would be a problem getting countries to agree because there are lots of them.
> ➤ It would be a problem working out how to stop people still fishing.

There could be a further question in this section. This asks you to come up with reasons for a given claim. In other words, you are coming up with reasons such that the claim becomes a conclusion that can be usefully drawn from them.

The following is an example.

Question 22

22 'Dolphins should never be kept in captivity.'

Give two **reasons** that would support this claim.

Here's one reason.

Dolphins are social animals, needing to be part of a large group.

This answer provides useful support for the claim that 'Dolphins should never be kept in captivity'. It supports it by focusing on the need for dolphins to live with many other dolphins, something that is highly unlikely to be the case in captivity.

Dolphins need to be able to cover large areas of open sea in order to use their powerful brains.

This is a very good answer, with a well-developed reason for not keeping dolphins in captivity. The contrast between 'captivity' and 'large areas of open sea' is well made. The reference to 'their large brains' gives a very relevant focus to this contrast.

Here's another answer.

Dolphins are very intelligent animals.

This answer provides much more limited support for the claim. The claim has the specific focus of 'captivity' and, though the intelligence of dolphins might be a very good reason not to keep them in this way, the point needs developing much more.

The same point would apply to the next answer.

Student **Dolphins can get easily distressed.**

With this answer, we need further development because it could be that, in the wild, they can also get easily distressed. The point could have been usefully developed by referring to the state of captivity being a cause of their distress.

Here's an answer that doesn't do anything useful.

Student **Dolphins look as if they're smiling but they're probably not.**

Indeed, but what's this got to do with the claim?

Question 23

23 'People should ensure that what they eat doesn't contribute to damaging the planet.'

Write your own argument to support or challenge this claim.

Now we need to look at what are likely to be the final two questions.

Exam tip

Each of these would carry a substantial number of marks so you need to make sure that you have enough time to do them as well as possible.

The most likely task that you'll be given in these two questions will be to write a further and/or a counter-argument.

As you know from Chapter 29, a further argument is an additional one in support of an existing argument, using additional reasons to the ones already used.

A counter-argument, as you also already know from Chapter 29, is an argument against an existing one. However, you could find yourself being presented with a claim that has the look of a conclusion and be asked to write an argument that either supports or challenges the claim. This will be a claim in the general area of the material you will have been looking at.

Let's have a look at how the marks are going to be awarded for the questions on writing arguments.

The mark scheme will probably be based on four levels of performance.

It will be useful to remind ourselves what the instructions on the paper tell you to do:

> Marks will be given for a well-structured and developed argument. You should include at least *three* reasons, *a well-supported intermediate conclusion* and a main conclusion. Your argument may also contain other argument elements.

Alternatively it may say:

> Marks will be given for a well-structured and developed argument. You should include at least *two* reasons, a *counter-argument and response* and a main conclusion. Your argument may also contain other argument elements.

In addition, you're likely to find this:

> You may use information and ideas from the passage, but you must use them to form a new argument. No credit will be given for repeating the arguments in the passage.

Depending on the specific question, here is what may be needed for a high level of marks. However, questions vary over time and may focus upon only some of these:

> A well-structured/clearly-structured argument. This is one with **signposting** throughout , i.e. uses appropriate argument element indicator words and paragraphing.
> One that has what we can call **'coherence'**: it fits together well; things follow from each other; and the structure helps the reader to follow the direction and content of the argument.
> At least three **relevant reasons**. The reasons need to fit with the specifics of the conclusion, such that the conclusion can be seen as usefully following from the reasons.
> A well-supported/**properly supported intermediate conclusion**. You need to have at least one of these, preferably supported by two of the reasons. The intermediate conclusion(s) should *follow from* reasons rather than merely summarise them. In this way, the intermediate conclusion(s) move the argument on a further stage.

And/or — depending on the question:

> A **counter-argument and response.** You saw this in Chapter 29 when we constructed the argument against home education.
> A **main conclusion**, which is correctly stated.

There are two other things that are worth noting:

> The argument may also contain relevant argument elements, which are used effectively.
> Grammar, spelling and punctuation are very good: errors are few, if any.

The first of these invites you to use other argument elements, such as evidence (and/ or examples), hypothetical reasoning, or principle.

There is also the point about the need for good 'grammar, spelling and punctuation'. The essential point here is to ensure that any possible deficiencies in these don't get in the way of the examiner understanding what you've written.

We can now apply all of this to a question based on the general area of the material we've been using for the earlier questions.

'People should ensure that what they eat doesn't contribute to damaging the planet.'

Here's a possible answer. It's one to **support** the claim.

CA Some people might say that what's on their plate couldn't possibly make any difference to the health of the planet. Individuals can't make any difference to what's sold for food, they will say.

R1 However, nobody would go out and catch fish if individuals weren't asking them to do it by buying the fish they bring back.

IC1 So everyone who eats fish contributes to the catching of fish.

HR2 If fish disappeared from the world's seas and oceans by 2050, the seas and oceans would no longer work as an eco-system.

R3 The majority of the planet is water.

IC2 So the decline of marine life is very disturbing.

IC3 It's not just fish that's a problem, it's also meat

R4 *because* the huge energy bills that are required to produce meat are a big contributor to global warming.

R5 (Including evidence/example) And the methane gas that comes in large volumes from animals farmed for meat, especially cattle and sheep, is a big contributor to the problem of what are called greenhouse gases.

C Therefore people should ensure that what they eat doesn't contribute to damaging the planet.

You might think that this is little over the top with its five reasons and three intermediate conclusions. But it should show you that writing an argument with complex reasoning, including a number of intermediate conclusions, is not that amazing.

So what does an argument that attracts few marks look like?

Too many people are eating too much fish, which is going to leave the world's oceans and seas without fish. They don't seem to realise that this will be bad for the planet. Some deep-sea fish take a very long time to breed and they're being caught before they can do this. People just seem to eat what they like without caring. They should care. If they don't, they'll make the problem worse. People shouldn't damage the planet when they eat.

This is clearly an argument related to the claim. But it suffers from a lack of development and careful organisation.

The first sentence starts things off well, by giving a reason. But then things get somewhat less clear. There is no intermediate conclusion. The conclusion follows but is not expressed as it should have been, given the claim in the question.

Summary

You have now worked through the Unit 2 skills and applied them to an exam-style question paper. You should be able to see that success on this paper requires you to:

➢ **Read the questions carefully and underline key words** to remind you about how many points you need to make; what should be included; whether strengths or weaknesses or both should be given; whether you should support or challenge a claim.

➢ When asked to evaluate, **use key terms to focus your answers**, such as relevance, significance, representativeness and selectivity; also the precise names of flaws and appeals.

➢ When developing your own arguments, **refer back to the claim given** to make sure that your response is directly relevant.

What you need to do now is to keep practising these skills. You can do this by working through the past papers and mark schemes which you can find online at:

www.ocr.org.uk/qualifications/type/gce/hss/critical_thinking/documents/

Unit 2 answers

Activities 19–28

Classroom and revision activities.

The Unit 2 examination

Past paper practice 19

Here are some inferences that could be drawn:

- The council was wrong.
- The council made a mistake.
- (The author thinks that) if ball games were allowed, then childhood obesity could be reduced.
- The author thinks that childhood obesity will be even higher without ball games.

Chapter 18

Exercise 21

1 This passage provides an explanation for why women preferred dancers who made large moves in all three planes. This is that 'such moves showed both strength and suppleness'.

Interestingly, this explanation is then further explained as 'therefore indicating a genetically fit male'. There is no argument that uses the explanation(s).

2 This passage provides explanations — why cases of lead poisoning in children have declined, and why old buildings are still a cause of lead poisoning. There is also a third, to show why there is a problem during redecorating. At the end, the author draws a conclusion ('People need to take great care...') based on the last explanation. In this way, you can see that the passage provides an argument based on explanations.

3 This provides an argument based on two possible explanations. The conclusion that 'it is very important that young children get enough sleep' is drawn from the reason 'sleep plays an important role in weight regulation'. This reason is explained in two possible ways.

4 This passage is no more than an explanation for why some people in Finland are violent. The explanation is a combination of an abnormal gene and 'various environmental factors'. No argument is given.

5 This provides an argument only. The conclusion in the first sentence is supported by reasoning in the rest of the passage. There might be seen to be a hint of an explanation in what follows — how the loss of trees would bring light to the forest floor — but the focus is on using this point to support the argument. If the author had gone on to show how this increased light would have increased the growth of other plants, then an explanation would indeed have appeared.

Past paper practice 20

The explanation is: 'eating too quickly reduces the ability of the body to respond to the "feeling of fullness"'. This explains why fast-eating people are more likely to become obese.

Past paper practice 21

It is an argument because it wants to persuade you that things should be changed. This is the conclusion which is based on two reasons: that parks cost a lot to maintain and that anti-social behaviour discourages people from using them.

Chapter 19

Exercise 22

1 The first three sentences are scene-setting (and include, as you will have seen, an example — the village of Firhall). The argument then proceeds as follows:

R1 This anti-child attitude might discourage people from having children.

R2 Children are, in a very real sense, our future.

IC This (people not having children) would be a big problem for our society.

C We need to change this anti-child attitude.

As you can see, the IC is drawn from two reasons, both of which it needs. The main conclusion then follows from the IC.

2 The evidence in the first sentence provides some scene-setting detail to give emphasis to the words 'the significantly increasing birth rate' in the second. The argument then proceeds as follows:

R1 The significantly increasing birth rate will be the major cause of these huge increases that, in turn, will lead to massive pressure on schools, universities, employment and housing.

IC Having more than two children should be seen as being antisocial (like being a benefits cheat).

C The Government should introduce a law to make people pay heavily for their third or further children (just as in China, where couples pay the 'family planning fine' for their second).

As you can see, this argument has a simple structure, with the main conclusion being drawn directly from (and only from) the IC.

Exercise 23

1 This argument has a lot going on in it. You will, hopefully, have found a number of intermediate conclusions in it.

The structure is as follows:

R The pay gap between men and women has been narrowing, but very slowly.

Example Recent pay increases for female managers have been only half a percentage point higher than those for male managers.

IC1 If the present trends continue, the pay gap will not close until 2067.

IC2 Companies must be ignoring the law requiring that women's pay is equal to that of men.

IC3 The existing law must not be strong enough.

C New stronger laws must be introduced as soon as possible.

2 In this version, a sentence was added. What is its function? It turns out to be an additional reason.

R1 The pay gap between men and women has been narrowing, but very slowly.

Example Recent pay increases for female managers have been only half a percentage point higher than those for male managers.

IC1 If the present trends continue, the pay gap will not close until 2067.

IC2 Companies must be ignoring the law requiring that women's pay is equal to that of men.

IC3 The existing law must not be strong enough.

R2 It is wrong that women are still treated unfairly with regard to their levels of pay compared to those of men.

C New stronger laws must be introduced as soon as possible.

As you can see, R2 opened up a new line of reasoning, with this reason supporting the main conclusion directly, rather than through a further intermediate conclusion.

Past paper practice 22

The answer is (a). Here is the structure of the argument:

R Bioethanol made by fermenting sugar crops or maize can be added to petrol.

R Replacing some of the petrol with bioethanol would cause less pollution,

IC ... so insisting that bioethanol is added to petrol would be good for the environment.

C The Government should insist that all petrol contains at least 15% bioethanol.

Chapter 20

Exercise 24

1 The two things being compared are growing cannabis and growing tomatoes, neither of which is a nuisance to neighbours.

So, to be consistent, they should both be treated in the same way.

2 The two things being compared are not eating bread to save wheat, and recycling paper to save trees, both of which are pointless actions.

So, to be consistent, we should do neither.

3 The two things being compared are car manufacturers making fast motor cars and telling people not to drive at this speed, and information technologists creating the facilities for texting and e-mailing and then pointing out the problems of 24/7 communication. Both are being hypocritical in that they have created the problems that they abhor.

So, to be consistent, we should listen to neither of them.

Past paper practice 23

The two things being compared are:

- muscles becoming wasted when they are not exercised
- parks becoming unpleasant, neglected and worthless when they are not used

So, if we avoid the situation with muscles, then for consistency we should avoid the situation with parks and use both, so that they can function at their best.

Chapter 21

Exercise 25

1 *Not a principle.* This is certainly a recommendation for the UN to act in a certain way, but it is not a general guide to action. There's only one Zimbabwe and only one Robert Mugabe. So the recommendation can't be used to justify intervening in Iran, Syria, and so on.

2 *Principle.* Unlike (1), this is a general guide to action. It could be used to justify intervention in Zimbabwe and other countries where the government is corrupt.

3 *Principle.* This is a straightforward principle. It gives a general guide to action such that there are no exceptions to allow child trafficking.

4 *Not a principle.* This provides a general description of a feature of sheep, but does not provide a general guide to action or belief. If this statement were used to lead to 'sheep should be treated with respect', then we would produce a principle about sheep.

5 *Not a principle.* This is a statement that certainly takes a general position — that the veal trade is very cruel — but it doesn't provide a general guide to action. It would, of course, be relevant to a principle: 'deliberate cruelty to animals can never be justified'.

6 *Not a principle.* This is a statement of a general position but falls short of being a principle in that it doesn't recommend action. The principle that could be generated from this statement could be: 'Animals should not be used for medical therapy.'

Exercise 26

1 You will have spotted the principle 'theft is always wrong'. It had the language clue of 'always'. (The author could have said 'theft is never justified/right/acceptable'.)

You might have been tempted by 'these illegal downloaders should be made to pay'. It has a look of a principle to it, with its use of the word 'should'. But this claim restricts itself to the specific case being discussed, without having a relevance to other scenarios or situations.

2 The principle is the last sentence ('people whose own behaviour results in their being ill must be made to pay for their own healthcare'). You can see that it is a general guide to what should be done: it's a guide to all situations in which

someone's behaviour results in their being ill (and needing medical care). Thus it would apply to all smokers whose illness is caused by their smoking, and all drinkers whose illness is caused by their drinking.

Exercise 27

1 *This is not assumed.* This is too weak for the argument. Although the argument is entirely consistent with this as a principle, the argument requires a stronger version. This is because the Government could 'help' the sick without doing what the argument concludes: to ensure that the needs of everyone with medical needs are met.

2 *This is not assumed.* Although this looks as if the author must assume this as a principle, it is too broad a principle for this argument. The argument is concerned only with meeting people's medical needs. Although increasing taxation to do this is how the author concludes, it is to ensure the meeting of only these needs, not needs in general.

3 *This is assumed.* The author argues 'that the Government can't allow' people with medical needs not to have them met. This position requires the principle (which is assumed rather than stated) that people's medical needs should always be met.

4 *This is not assumed.* This is too strong a principle for this argument. It does not require that sick people should always be given priority over others, just that their medical needs should be met. It could, for example, be consistent with the argument that a public building programme would give priority to schools rather than hospitals, as long as the cost isn't at the expense of medical treatment for all who need it.

Past paper practice 24

The principle is in the last sentence, 'People should only have to pay tax for the things that they use or which benefit them.'

It is a general rule that can be used to give guidance in several different specific situations, such as people without children not having to fund maternity benefits or school budgets.

Past paper practice 25

1 This is stated and is not a principle.

2 This goes against the conclusion, so cannot be assumed.

3 This is the assumed principle. It supports the conclusion that players who use their helmets to injure others should be fined. It can be generalised to many other situations.

4 This is stated and is not a general principle.

Chapter 22

Exercise 28

This evidence has many instances of incompleteness. Here are some other questions that you might want to ask.

• Did the other 56% of children feel safe when their mother was driving? Did only some of them feel safe, with the others saying they felt neither safe nor unsafe?

• How unsafe did the 44% feel? Very, somewhat, a bit?

• How safe or unsafe did the children feel when their father was driving?

• How safe or unsafe did the children feel when other people were driving?

• Did 10-year-olds give different answers to 16-year-olds? (The same question can be asked about the other age groups.)

• Do we need to know about when mothers were likely to be driving? (The school run, shopping, taking children at busy times, etc.)

Exercise 29

1 Although the average figure is £161,823, none of the regions has this figure or anything very close to it, so the average figure does not give us a good indication of the cost of houses across the regions.

The closest to the average figure is the East, with its average of £171,531.

2 You can see that the huge range of variation in average house prices between regions (and, if London is typical, within regions) shows that *fixing public service salaries at a national level fails to take into account what the salaries can buy*. For example, you could buy about nine averagely priced houses in the North East for what it will cost you to buy one averagely priced house in Kensington and Chelsea. Even taking London out of the equation, the doubling of the average price between the North East and the South East is significant.

Past paper practice 26

• *Significance of the rate.* The amount of money needed for the parks is large, as not every person is a taxpayer, so it supports the idea that the cost is too much.

• *Alternative explanation.* Although the amount of money needed for the parks is large, it doesn't necessarily mean that this is because the councils are using this inefficiently. It could be large because there are a large number of large parks that require a lot of maintenance.

• *Representativeness (Unit 1 skill).* It cannot be said that the cost in general is too high as the cost of parks in the London borough may not be representative of elsewhere where there are fewer parks of smaller size.

Past paper practice 27

- *Relevance.* The 5% is for the whole population. We are not told the figure for how many school children have SAD, so this weakens the support that the evidence gives to the conclusion about not having schools open in winter for children.

- *Significance.* The percentage is only very small, so it doesn't justify such a big change to the system.

- *Significance.* There may be other groups of children who work better in the winter than the summer months, for example, because they are less distracted by outside activities. This would reduce the significance of those children suffering from the SAD phenomenon.

Chapter 23

Exercise 30

1 The slippery slope starts with the following sentence:

But, if we allow this, we'll end up killing all children with serious abnormalities.

The author starts on the slippery slope by moving from a description of what already happens to a prediction of what will happen as a result. There is nothing in the argument to explain why this move will take place (especially in that it hasn't). Given that this move in the argument is a big problem, so is everything that follows it.

2 The slippery slope starts with the first step of banning smoking in vehicles.

It sees this as leading to the next step of banning smoking 'outside all shops'. Although this might happen, the move from vehicles to outside shops to pavements to homes is not argued for, being just claimed.

Exercise 31

1 The conclusion that 'we should not take seriously the views of David Irving on the subject of the Holocaust' is drawn from the reason that 'the evidence against him is overwhelming...'. This reason is not an attack upon Irving himself, but an attack on his position.

This is therefore not an example of *ad hominem* reasoning.

2 The conclusion that 'we should not take [David Irving] seriously as a historian' is drawn only from the reason that 'he's both a bankrupt and an ex-prisoner'. Although the reason for his being a bankrupt and an ex-prisoner are to do with his denying the Holocaust, the author does not present it like that. It could be that bankrupts and ex-prisoners could be very good historians of the Holocaust.

This is therefore an example of *ad hominem* reasoning.

Past paper practice 28

This is a straw person flaw because it unfairly represents the organic farming position as putting animal droppings on our food, when in fact it is a much more complex process using non-chemical fertilisers and pest controls.

Exercise 32

1 *Legitimate cause and effect.* This offers a straightforwardly acceptable causal link between the advertising of Dairy Milk and subsequent increases in sales. The two pieces of evidence (overall sales of Dairy Milk and spending by *Daily Mirror* readers) are both sufficiently strong (37% and 75%) to enable the author to draw the conclusion that sales were boosted by the dedicated advertising. You might, of course, want to argue that this specific example is not enough to support the general conclusion, but you are likely still to be prepared to accept that, in this case, dedicated advertising did boost sales.

2 *Post hoc flaw.* Here you have a *post hoc* (or indeed *cum hoc*) argument: Ada Mason eats a daily meal of bread and dripping with salt and is 'clean living': therefore she lives until she is 111.

It should be quite simple for you to explain the problem. With due respect to Ada Mason and her granddaughter, we can question the claimed causal relationship between long life and bread and dripping (with salt). Remember the health warnings about fat and salt. It is more likely that genetics is the cause.

3 *Oversimplifying cause and effect flaw.* In this argument, the author sees a causal relationship between improvements in female education, health and income, and reduction in happiness. There are two main issues here:

There's the point about 'self-reported happiness'. It hasn't been taken into account that women might be more honest about reporting their happiness levels than they were 30 years ago.

There are problems in using this evidence to argue that improvements in female education, health and income lead to reductions in happiness. Although there is a correlation here, it cannot be taken that there is a causal relationship. It could be that improvements in female education, health and income have actually increased happiness, but that other things have had the effect of reducing it (such as aspects of women's private lives — relationship with partners, expectations of them as mothers, and so on).

We have here an example of what can be called 'oversimplifying cause and effect'. The author takes a big area (changes in levels of education, health, income and self-reported levels of

happiness) and sees the relationship between them as a simple causal one. Almost certainly, the reality is much more complex than this.

Past paper practice 29

The answer is **(d)**.

It is possible that it was wrong not to return the Parthenon marbles and the other artefacts. If so, then the argument is claiming that it is now acceptable not to return the bronzes on the basis of having done other things that are wrong.

(a) The conclusion is different from the reason so it cannot be a circular argument.

(b) It is not generalising from one to all of a type.

(c) It is not saying that one thing has caused another.

Past paper practice 30

The answer is **(c)**.

The author does imply the causal link between Denmark's happiness ratings and the later start to education. These may not be related let alone the cause of one another.

(a) GCSEs are just given as an example of assessments. There is no conflation.

(b) Happiness and education are linked, but one is not seen as the condition for the other.

(d) Denmark is used as evidence, but not to relate to all countries.

Past paper practice 31

Two flaws were possible as answers to this question:

- *Confusing necessary and sufficient conditions.* The author confuses necessary and sufficient conditions because transferring ownership of parks may be sufficient to save money, but it is not necessary for money to be saved — the council could raise taxes.

- *False dichotomy.* It does not give strong support to the conclusion because it provides a false dichotomy, as the money may not be used for other things, so it does not prove that the council shouldn't own the parks.

Chapter 24

Exercise 33

1 *This is a relevant appeal to popularity.* The evidence on what people believe about bacteria shows that they don't understand that many bacteria are not only good for us but necessary for our health. Since it would be useful for people to know this, the conclusion is not therefore an irrelevant appeal to popularity.

2 *This is an irrelevant appeal to popularity.* The conclusion that the Government should introduce penalties for the parents of antisocial children is based on no more than the evidence that 63% of people believe that such parents are largely to blame for the problem. It could be that people's belief is wrong, making the conclusion, therefore, also wrong.

Exercise 34

The author concludes that, given the expertise of Brenkus, 'we should take his predictions very seriously'. The question you were looking at was how relevant this appeal to his authority was in the argument.

You will have seen that his expertise can be seen in three ways:

- He is the presenter of the award-winning TV programme *Sports Science*.

- He studied 200 athletes at a special laboratory.

- He has completed the Iron Man challenge.

Which of these would be a strong source of his authority?

His studies of 200 athletes would seem to be the strongest, given the fact that this is a large number of athletes and that 'a special laboratory' sounds as if it has been designed for research.

Being the presenter of the TV programme would also indicate some expertise (especially given that it is an 'award-winning' programme). Presumably, in a programme on sports science, the presenter has to be able to talk usefully about the material being presented.

Completing the Iron Man challenge would give Brenkus a great deal of insight into competing in an endurance event, but not much into running 100 metres and other events.

However, despite the proviso about the relevance of the Iron Man challenge, we can see *this appeal to authority as a relevant one*, such that it supports the conclusion being drawn.

Exercise 35

The answer to the first question is that the argument *does* rely on an appeal to emotion (and no more).

The argument is built on only the example of Eric Lucas. There is a reference to Britain saving 'more than 50,000 German Jews', but this is given as a piece of evidence to suggest that this was not enough. So is the example of Eric Lucas sufficient for the conclusion that Britain should have saved more?

It would only be a relevant appeal if you could argue that that reducing the unhappiness of Jews on a big scale should have determined the British immigration policy. If not, it is an irrelevant appeal to emotion.

Past paper practice 32

The answer is **(c)** Appeal to popularity.

Just because many people love it does not mean that it is right, or that the conclusion should be accepted.

Past paper practice 33

(a) It is an appeal to tradition.

(b) Although cricket may have been played for a long time, this does not mean that the same conditions apply today.

Past paper practice 34

(a) Appeal to emotion, e.g. pity, sympathy.

(b) The author uses emotive language — 'a tragic and unnecessary death' — to make the readers feel sorry for Gana's baby. It appeals to their emotions, rather than giving reasons why the zookeepers should intervene.

Chapter 25

Exercise 36

1 The analogy is that solving the problem of the possible danger to children from having their photos on social networking sites is like eliminating the possible danger to children from swimming pools: the answer in both cases is to teach children how to deal with the possible dangers.

The analogy serves as a reason in the argument.

What are the strengths and weaknesses of the analogy?

Strengths

- Both swimming pools and having photos of children on social networking sites involve possible risk, including possibly serious risk to children.

- Each has the same possible solution: that of giving children the skills to help to deal with the problem.

- Shutting down all swimming pools is completely unrealistic, in the same way as is not allowing photos of children to be placed on social networking sites.

Weaknesses

- Learning to swim involves a clear set of skills to use in specific situations, but teaching 'children to be careful' regarding strangers possibly looking for them as a result of their photos being on social networking sites involves skills that are much less specific. ('Be careful who you speak to.' 'When you think someone might be looking at you suspiciously…')

- The specific situation in which swimming skills are used cannot usefully be compared with the much more general situation requiring skills for dealing with undesirable attention from strangers.

- A child knows it needs to use swimming skills in a swimming pool, but a child does not necessarily know when to use the more general skills of being 'careful'.

- A child who cannot swim might well keep away from swimming pools, but a child without the skills of being 'careful' cannot avoid being in situations where there might be possible threats.

- Closing all swimming pools is almost impossible, given the number of them and their different owners (including private individuals). But getting restrictions placed on photos of children on social networking sites should be easier, given the limited number of such sites.

Judgement

The analogy is useful in highlighting that a problem of risk to children can be reduced by giving them skills to deal with it. But there are significant differences between giving children swimming skills and giving them much less specific skills in being 'careful' when out in the world. In this way, the role of the analogy as a reason is weakened. Just because there are more weaknesses than strengths in the assessment of this analogy does not in itself mean that it is a weak analogy. However, the quality of the weaknesses compared with the strengths does mean that the analogy is not very strong.

2 The analogy is that concluding there is no intelligent extraterrestrial life from the small search for it so far is like dipping a small glass into the ocean and, finding it empty, concluding that there are no fish in the sea.

(You might have wanted to amend the analogy to something like the following:

It's like dipping a small glass into the ocean and, on discovering it having nothing but water in it, concluding that there are no fish in the sea.

This is because, having dipped the glass into the ocean, it will have at least water in it — if nothing else.)

The analogy supports the reason 'The amount of evidence that has been collected so far is tiny compared with all that is out there to be analysed.'

What are the strengths and weaknesses of the analogy?

Strength

- The comparison between a small sample of the universe and a small sample of the oceans is effective in showing the scale of the task. Indeed, the sample from the ocean in a glass might be a bigger sample than has been possible at SETI, given the vastness of the universe.

We know that dipping a small glass in the ocean will tell us virtually nothing (from what we know of the oceans) and that we would need to carry out a bigger sample to get a more accurate picture. This emphasises the limited results that sampling on a very small scale produces.

Weaknesses

- Knowing when one has caught a fish in a glass is straightforward, but knowing when a meaningful signal has been detected is much less so.

- Dipping a small glass into the ocean at any one time is sampling only the top of the ocean; scanning the universe at any one time is sampling deep parts of it.

This last point can be emphasised by seeing the search so far as covering a sufficient sample of the sky to have found evidence of intelligent extraterrestrial life if it is there. This is because, if it exists, such life could well be evenly spread through the universe, so even a small sample should be sufficient. However, few, if any, fish will be found near the surface of the ocean.

Judgement

The analogy is very effective in strengthening the significance of the reason 'The amount of evidence that has been collected so far is tiny compared with all that is out there to be analysed' for the conclusion that 'not finding any evidence so far should not be seen as meaning that there is no such intelligent life "out there".' The analogy captures well the big problem of drawing a general conclusion from very limited evidence. However, there is the point that, as detailed above, perhaps the sampling in each case is sufficiently different in scope to weaken the relevance of the analogy. (This is, in turn, answered by the point that sampling the oceans with a glass provides a bigger sample than SETI has managed of the universe in 50 years.)

You will have seen that, numerically, the weaknesses outweigh the strengths but, in this example, the strengths outweigh the weaknesses in terms of their significance. As a result, it is a good analogy.

Past paper practice 35

(a) *What is being compared?* The madness of putting children in harm's way by parents allowing their children to have PCs with internet access in their bedrooms is being compared to the same madness of children put in harm's way if parents allowed their children to spend hours in a sweet shop with no control.

(b) *One point of evaluation ... how it effectively supports the author's reasoning.* There are controls that can be put on the internet to block harmful sites for children, which means that children may be less at risk in their bedroom with a PC than if left in a sweet shop with no control. So in this case the analogy is weak and the case against having PCs in children's bedrooms is not supported.

This is one possible answer. You can see that if your answer is focused, you can cover the assessment quite quickly. All you have to do is to look for one point of evaluation here and assess its impact on the reasoning.

Past paper practice 36

(a) Discussed in the answer to Past paper practice 23 on page 341.

(b) (i) A strength is that under-use leads to a decline in both muscles and parks and we can control the decline of both of these.

So this supports the view that if council parks are under-used, they should no longer be owned by councils so that they can function well again.

(b) (ii) A weakness is that it is vital that muscles are kept in good condition to function properly, whereas parks are not vital to society.

(c) If this is the case, it won't matter so much if they are under-used, so the case against council ownership is weakened.

Chapter 26

Past paper practice 37

The answer is **(b)**.

If it is wrong to take actions that could lead to loss of life, it is wrong to make hoax calls to emergency services. We punish wrong doing, so this principle would support the argument.

(a), **(c)** and **(d)** are not principles.

Past paper practice 38

The answer is **(b)**.

The principle that medicine should aim to prevent future harm implies that the health service should provide treatment to avoid repeated bone fractures.

(d) is not a principle.

(a) is a principle that weakens the argument.

(c) is a principle about a range of treatment choices rather than a particular form of treatment.

Chapter 27

Exercise 37

Given that the conclusion is drawn from only hypothetical reasons, we cannot have a conclusion that is not similarly hypothetical. The reason 'if you were to eat the granola, you'd eat 912 calories per serving' does not allow us to conclude that people *will* eat it (and so put on a lot of weight, as the conclusion claims). The reasoning is therefore weak.

Past paper practice 39

(a) The hypothetical reason is: 'If councils no longer had to look after parks, then the money would be spent on better things.'

(b) It is a hypothetical reason because it has a condition, 'If councils no longer had to look after parks,' and a consequence that it is argued would follow from this: 'then the money would be spent on better things'. This is a reason to support the conclusion, 'parks should no longer be owned by councils'.

(c) *Internal assessment.* The reasoning is weak because the consequence would not necessarily follow from councils no longer looking after parks. The money may not be spent or it might be spent on less worthy causes.

External assessment. It does not give strong support to the conclusion that parks should no longer be owned by councils. The money may not be used for other things. As the consequence might not occur, we cannot jump to a recommendation as if it were actually the case.

Chapter 28

Past paper practice 40

Here are some relevant reasons:

- It is more likely that students will get distracted while trying to do their homework on the internet.
- It could lead to students visiting unsafe internet sites.
- Students may not be able to pick out relevant information on the internet.
- Students unable to access the internet at home will be at a disadvantage.

Past paper practice 41

Both of the following answers have a condition and a consequence:

If there were free leisure facilities, *then* more people would be able to access them.

If there were free leisure facilities *then* the fitness levels of the country would probably be improved.

Past paper practice 42

For the answers to this question, you needed to have remembered not to take your example from the use of the internet.

- Not allowing children to cross the road on their own stops them from learning how to do this safely when they need to this later.
- If you don't allow children to try alcohol at an early age, then they may not appreciate how to drink sensibly.

Exercise 38

1 Principles that could be used to support the Greek Government's position:

- Permission to do something given a long time ago is not valid for all time.
- Important art and architecture should belong to the country where it was produced.
- Important buildings should not be dismantled.
- The historical origin of something/a work of art should take priority over the fact of possession.

2 Principles that could be used to support the BM's position:

- That which was obtained legally belongs to whoever obtained it.
- Legal possession overrides any other claims.

- If someone removes something to protect it from (certain/likely) damage, then it is acceptable/right for them to keep it.

Past paper practice 43

Here is a general principle that could be used in this situation and more generally in others:

Council money ought to be used to benefit a large number of people.

Chapter 29

Exercise 39

No specific answers are given here, because there is a variety of possible answers that could be given.

Past paper practice 44

Acceptable conclusions

Support:

- There should be a greater number of activities provided by the government for young people.

Challenge:

- There should NOT be a greater number of activities provided by the government for young people.

- The government should not provide activities for young people.

Examples of points that may be raised

Support:

- It will develop their social skills.

- The government has a duty of care.

- There are not enough private clubs.

- To deter young people from crime.

- To ensure that young people's talents are developed.

Challenge:

- Charities already do this.

- There is too much choice already.

- It will distract young people from their education.

- Most parents will already do this with their children.

- It is unfair to provide these activities for young people when we don't provide activities for older people.

Note: It is important in this question that answers respond effectively to the counter-argument.

Past paper practice 45

Acceptable conclusions

Support:

- Ball games should be banned in parks.

Challenge:

- Ball games should NOT be banned in parks.

- Ball games should be encouraged in parks.

Examples of points that may be raised

Support:

- The balls from the games may be a nuisance to others in the park.

- Ball games take up a lot of space in the park that other people could be using.

- The noise from ball games disturbs other people in the park.

Challenge:

- Ball games need the amount of space that parks can provide.

- Ball games develop community spirit in parks.

- Ball games in parks act as a focal point for young people.

Note: It is important in this question that answers have a fully supported IC.

Glossary

ability to perceive: a source's ability to see, hear, touch, taste or smell when assessing an experience relevant to a claim.

adequacy: the degree to which a reason provides support for a conclusion.

ad hominem: this translates as 'at (or to) the man (or person)'. This type of flawed reasoning attacks the arguer, not their argument.

ambiguity: the problem of a word or findings having two or more possible interpretations, and it is not clear which is intended.

analogy: an analogy takes one situation or scenario to be sufficiently similar to another one (using parallels), such that the first situation or scenario can be used in an argument about the other.

appeal to authority: this uses a recognised source to justify a conclusion that is drawn. It inevitably involves looking at the expertise of that source.

appeal to emotion: this uses reasoning designed to provoke an emotional response (such as pity, disgust or pleasure) in those reading the argument, to persuade them to accept the conclusion.

appeal to history: this uses evidence from a past event or events to persuade the reader to accept a conclusion about the future (and sometimes the present).

appeal to popularity: this uses the weight of numbers that demonstrate likes and dislikes or beliefs and attitudes amongst a particular group, in order to persuade the reader to accept a conclusion relevant to these.

appeal to tradition: this argues that because something (a ceremony, practice, belief, custom and so on) is very old and/or well established, it is a good reason for this to continue today.

arguing from one thing to another: here the author draws a conclusion that is not related to the reasoning. This is also known as *non sequitur* which literally means 'It does not follow'.

argument: a written or spoken attempt to convince or persuade, using reasons to support a conclusion.

argument indicators: words which show that reasoning is going on; they signpost argument elements such as reasons and conclusions.

assertion: where one claim, or several claims, are made and nothing further is drawn from them.

assumption: a missing reason in an argument, not stated by the author, but which is necessary to enable the conclusion to be drawn.

begging the question: the author either makes a claim, such that they are asserting what they are trying to prove, or they assume this step in the reasoning.

Glossary

bias: the tendency of a source (individual or organisation) to present or interpret claims selectively because of a position that they favour.

circular argument: in circular arguments, the conclusion is no more than a restatement of the reason(s) — that is, it says the same thing twice.

claim: a statement that is put forward.

coherence: where a set of claims fit together closely so that they form a rationally ordered argument.

conclusion: what the author wants to persuade you to accept based on their reasons.

conclusion indicators: words such as 'so', 'thus', 'therefore', 'in consequence', 'it follows that', that often show that a claim is being drawn from at least one other claim. Conclusion indicator words may also include words such as 'should', 'must', 'ought', and their negative forms.

conflation: this is where the author takes at least two different terms and treats them as if they are the same.

conflict: where sources make directly opposing claims, they are said to conflict.

confusing cause and effect: this where the actual effect is seen as the cause. It can be expressed simply as:

Where A has caused B, B is seen as having caused A.

confusing necessary and sufficient conditions: occurs when someone mistakes one for the other. A *necessary* condition is one that must be fulfilled alongside others for something to happen. A *sufficient* condition is one that is enough by itself to ensure that something will happen.

consistency: refers to claims that are relevant to each other and can both be held to be true at the same time.

contradiction: this is where two claims 'go against' each other. They conflict such that both cannot be held to be true at the same time.

corroboration: when a claim from one source directly agrees with another source's claim. It usually relates to data rather than opinion.

counter-argument: an argument that supports the opposite position to that argued for by the author. A counter-argument will contain at least one counter-reason and at least one counter-conclusion.

counter-assertion: a statement that supports the opposite position to that argued for by the author.

credibility: the degree to which a source or claim is believable.

credibility criterion: a standard that can be used to judge the believability of a source and their claims (plural *credibility criteria*).

disanalogy: a disanalogy takes one situation or scenario to be sufficiently different from another one, such that the first situation or scenario can be used in an argument about the other.

evaluate: to assess by identifying points of strength and weakness.

evidence: information that can be used to support a reason, or it may stand alone as an assertion or counter-assertion. Evidence may also be used to directly support a conclusion.

example: a specific instance, often used as an illustration to aid understanding.

expertise and experience: terms used to describe qualifications, knowledge, training and understanding that are relevant to the issue, subject or claim being made. These inform the source's ability to interpret the situation or data correctly. Expertise and experience make the claims more credible than if they had been made by someone without this knowledge. Expertise relates to special skills that have been attained whereas experience relates to participation in a particular field.

explanation: an explanation seeks to show why *something which is accepted* is/was/will be the case, i.e. it seeks to throw light on the case (unlike an argument which *requires reasons to establish/persuade* the reader that this is so.

false cause: this is when an author takes a correlation (connection) to indicate causation, without there being a very good reason to believe that causation has happened or is happening. It can be expressed as:

A and B have no causal relationship and are correlated coincidentally.

false dichotomy (also known as **false dilemma**)**:** this is a specific form of restricting the options, where only two options are presented when a number of other options are possible. Often one of the options is presented as a more favourable choice in comparison to an extreme option.

flaw: an error in the reasoning such that it weakens the support for the conclusion.

further argument: an argument in support of a given conclusion, that uses different reasons from those already used in an existing argument.

hasty generalisation: this flaw involves reasoning in which the author seeks to make a far-reaching or over-generalised claim from very limited evidence that is specific to a particular instance. It is known as 'hasty' because the author is rushing to apply this specific case more generally, without considering any wider evidence.

hypothetical reasoning (reason or conclusion): one in which a condition is given for a consequence to follow; for example: 'If this... then that... '

implication: it is what the author means you to draw from what they say, without them explicitly saying this. Literally it means what is intended but not actually stated.

inconsistency: refers to claims that cannot both be true at the same time.

infer: to draw a conclusion from the claims that are given.

inference: this is a conclusion drawn from the claims that are given or a conclusion that could be drawn from the claims given.

intermediate conclusion: a conclusion drawn on the way to the main conclusion. It is drawn from at least one reason and becomes itself a reason for the main conclusion. Arguments can have no intermediate conclusion, or any number of them.

main conclusion: the main conclusion of an argument is its final conclusion. An argument will therefore have only one main conclusion, with all the rest of the reasoning supporting it, including the intermediate conclusion if there is one.

motive: that which gives a reason for a course of action.

neutrality: being impartial, such that a neutral source has no reason to favour either side in a dispute.

overdrawn conclusion: one in which the reasons are insufficient for the conclusion to be drawn.

(over) simplifying causal relationships: this is a case of giving an oversimplified explanation, when in fact the situation is complex where a number of causes are interrelated. Put simply:

A is seen as causing B when in fact it is a case of A plus X, Y and Z.

plausibility: in OCR critical thinking this is used to answer the questions: is it likely? Is it reasonable?

post hoc: *post hoc* reasoning takes it that, because one thing *follows* another, the latter has caused the former, when in fact this is a coincidence and a third factor is involved. Put simply:

A is said to have caused B, when in fact it was C.

primary evidence: evidence from those with the ability to observe.

principle: a general rule that can act as guidance in a specific relevant situation.

rate: a rate is always expressed as per a given number. This number could be anything, but is often used as per 1,000 or 10,000, and so on. If it is per 100, it is called a percentage.

reason: a claim that is used to support a conclusion.

reason indicators: words such as 'because', 'since', 'given that', 'as a result of' that show that a claim is being used to support another.

refute: to refute an argument is to show it cannot be true because the claims cannot be accepted either because the reasons are untrue or because they do not support the conclusion — that is, to clearly demonstrate that the argument is unsound. This is much stronger than just evaluating an argument.

relevance: how closely things relate to the same topic.

representativeness: how far one thing is sufficiently similar to (or typical of) the wider category that the author is arguing about.

repudiation: this is where the opponent of an argument rejects it without giving reasons. They simply say that it isn't so.

reputation: the judgement made by others about the characteristics of a source. In some cases, the judgement of reputation (especially a good one) might be self-claimed, i.e. made by the individual or organisation itself, stressing their own reputation for such things as fairness, honesty or expert service.

restricting the options: this applies when an author has presented a number of options that do not exhaust the possibilities.

secondary evidence: a report based on another's primary evidence.

slippery slope argument: the flaw in slippery slope arguments is that the author wrongly argues that a particular claim must lead to another, which must lead to others, such that an extreme or even absurd conclusion is drawn.

source: this could be a document, person or organisation that provides information.

straw person (also known as **straw man**): a straw person/straw man flaw is found when an author deliberately misrepresents an opponent's position in order to attack it more easily. It should be clear why it's called a 'straw man' flaw: men made of straw are easy to knock down.

sweeping generalisation: this argues from one or a number of cases in a category to all cases in the category. It can be seen to create a stereotype where all instances within a category are seen as having the same characteristics.

tu quoque: this flaw is found when someone argues that something apparently unacceptable that they've done is actually acceptable on the basis that others have done this and it was accepted. The two Latin words translate straightforwardly as 'you too', indicating that the opposing arguer is guilty of the same wrong actions. The meaning is often extended to include others also doing this.

'two wrongs don't make a right': this is a familiar response to an argument in which someone tries to defend one wrong action on the basis that a different wrong action was accepted.

vested interest: *either* a motive to misrepresent the situation for personal gain or to prevent a loss, *or* a motive to represent the situation accurately, again for personal gain or to prevent a loss.

Index

Note: Bold page numbers indicate definitions of key terms.